VISUAL QUICKPRO GUIDE

Red Hat Linux 6

Harold Davis

Peachpit Press

Visual QuickPro Guide
Red Hat Linux 6
Harold Davis

Peachpit Press
1249 Eighth Street
Berkeley, CA 94710
510/524-2178
800/283-9444
510/524-2221 (fax)
Find us on the World Wide Web at: http://www.peachpit.com
Peachpit Press is a division of Addison Wesley Longman

Editor: Corbin Collins
Production Coordinator: Mimi Heft
Copyeditor: Judy Ziajka
Compositor: Maureen Forys, Happenstance Type-O-Rama
Technical Editor: Charles Seiter
Indexer: Emily Glossbrenner
Cover Design: The Visual Group

ISBN 0-201-35437-3

9 8 7 6 5 4 3 2 1

♻ Printed on recycled paper
Printed and bound in the United States of America

About the Author

Harold Davis is a software developer who specializes in the Web and e-commerce. Recently, he has worked as a Technical Director for Vignette Corporation, a company whose product is often used to enable Internet Relationship Management. He has also worked as a Principle Consultant for the Web and E-commerce division at Informix Software, where he specialized in developing enterprise-class Web solutions for Fortune 500 companies.

Harold is the author of many books on programming and software development, including the best-selling *Visual Basic Secrets* series, *Web Developer's Secrets*, and *Delphi Power Toolkit*. He is also the author of a number of books about photography, art, and publishing.

Harold holds a B.A. degree in Computer Science and Mathematics from New York University and a J.D. degree from Rutgers Law School.

He lives in Berkeley, California with his wife, Phyllis, and son, Julian. When not programming, writing or performing technical architecture reviews, he enjoys spending time in the garden.

Dedication

This book is dedicated to Linus and Julian, one for creating Linux and the other for being Julian.

Special thanks

Special thanks to Corbin Collins, a great project editor if ever there was one. I'd also like to thank Nancy Aldrich-Ruenzel, Mimi Heft, Maureen Forys, Charles Seiter, and the wonderful team at Peachpit. Nancy Davis, for suggesting me in connection with this book. Martin Davis, for help with Chapter 10. Norman Shapiro, for help with Chapter 12. And Matt Wagner. And, as always, Phyllis. And the Knights that say "Ni!"

CONTENTS AT A GLANCE

TABLE OF CONTENTS

TABLE OF CONTENTS

INTRODUCTION

I envy the fine, new adventure that you are about to embark on! Red Hat Linux 6 is not your father's Unix: the interface is visual, user-friendly, and completely customizable to the way you like to work.

Powerful personal productivity applications—such as Gnomecard, Gnotepad+, and the Gnumeric spreadsheet—ship with Red Hat Linux 6 and are ready to run. Familiar programs such as the Netscape Communicator suite and Corel WordPerfect can be used to browse the Web, send and receive email, and create word-processing documents. And there is so much more! To take just one example, the GNU Image Manipulation Program (affectionately called the "Gimp") ships with Red Hat Linux 6. The Gimp most certainly gives Adobe's expensive program Photoshop quite a run for the money.

But these applications are only the beginning. Red Hat Linux 6 is a powerful server operating system. It is capable of performing workhorse duties as a file and print sharer in a small home or office. It can be used to manage large, enterprise-class networks. Combined with Apache, the most widely used Web server software, it can be used to host world-class World Wide Web sites.

Even if money were no object, Red Hat Linux 6 would be a superb operating system choice for almost any application. Obviously, the price is right. No wonder so many people are deciding to run Linux as their operating system of choice, making it the world's fastest growing major operating system.

Red Hat Linux 6 is as good as it gets!

What is Linux?

Linux was originally created by Linus Torvalds, then a Finnish college student in his early twenties. It is a Unix-like operating system that runs on Intel's x86 microprocessor architecture (commonly called PCs, or Windows PCs).

The term *Linux* is actually used in two ways:

◆ To refer to the Linux kernel, the heart of the operating system.

◆ To more generally refer to a collection of applications that run on top of the Linux kernel. This is also called a *distribution*. Red Hat Linux 6 is one of the leading examples of a distribution.

While Linus Torvalds retains creative ownership over the Linux kernel, Linux as we know it today has been developed with the assistance of programmers from around the world.

Unlike any other desktop operating system—and like other versions of Unix—Linux is a true multi-tasking and multi-user operating system.

Understanding the General Public License

The Linux kernel is freely distributable under the General Public License (GPL) developed by the Free Software Foundation. (For the full text of the GPL, see Appendix B. This license is also called *The GNU General Public License*.)

It is the intention of the GPL to promote free distribution and open development of software. The Free Software Foundation is at pains to point out that free under the GPL does not mean the same thing as "no cost." In fact, you are allowed to sell software

licensed under the GPL, but you cannot place restrictions on others reselling what you have sold to them. As the Linux evangelists say, think free speech, not free beer.

Hence, the word "free" is really being used in a political, or visionary, sense. It means liberated from licensing restrictions, and intellectually free. This is in keeping with the vision of the Free Software Foundation: its goal is to create a complete operating system with all necessary applications and utilities that can be distributed without restriction.

What is Gnome?

Gnome is short for GNU Network Object Model Environment.

The Gnome project has built a complete, user-friendly visual desktop made up of large applications and smaller utilities. The visual desktop is referred to as the *Gnome Desktop Environment*. Applications that were written as part of the Gnome project generally start with a 'G' for example, the Gimp and Gnotepad+. Gnome and GNU applications are pronounced with a hard "G"—for example, "guh-notepad."

Gnome applications and the Gnome Desktop Environment share a common look and feel. The Gnome Desktop Environment and related applications are free software, available under the GPL.

What is Red Hat Linux 6?

Red Hat Software's distributions of Linux are the most popular and best-known Linux distributions available.

In addition to the Linux kernel, Red Hat Linux 6 includes installation programs written by Red Hat, the Gnome Desktop Environment, and many, many applications and utilities.

What makes Red Hat Linux 6 revolutionary compared to previous Linux distributions—including those from Red Hat—is the seamless inclusion of Gnome, a world-class visual desktop. The transition from previous versions of Linux could well be compared with the transition from DOS to Microsoft Windows.

Who should read this book?

If you have purchased *Red Hat Linux 6 Visual QuickPro Guide*, it is a safe assumption that you own a copy of Red Hat Linux 6 (Publisher's Edition)—because you'll find it in the back of this book.

If you are simply curious about Linux, and how it compares to Microsoft Windows, this book will help satisfy your curiosity.

You should read this book if you are installing Linux, or Red Hat Linux 6, for the first time. This book will help you get up and running quickly with Gnome applications, Netscape Communicator, and programs such as Corel WordPerfect for Linux.

If you are already up and running with Linux, there is also plentiful information about more advanced topics. Perhaps you'd like to know how to work with the SQL database server that ships with Red Hat Linux 6. Or how to work with the Bash shell, and the Linux command line. Or get quickly up and running with a Linux network or Web server.

It's all here!

How this book is organized

Red Hat Linux 6: Visual QuickPro Guide is organized in four parts:

◆ Part I, *Installing Red Hat Linux 6*, takes you through installing Red Hat Linux 6, configuring the Gnome Desktop, getting up and running with email and the Web, and finding documentation.

◆ Part II, *Doing Windows in Red Hat Linux 6*, explains how to use Gnome personal productivity applications and programs such as Corel WordPerfect for Linux and PostgreSQL.

◆ Part III, *Working with Linux on the Command Line*, explains the Bash shell, covers many Linux commands and shows you how to get started with shell scripting.

◆ Part IV, *Networking and the Web*, covers configuring Red Hat Linux 6 as a server. It also explains how to work with Apache, the world's most widely used Web server.

How to use this book

Red Hat Linux 6 Visual QuickPro Guide presents easy, step-by step directions and illustrations to help you install, configure, and enjoy Red Hat Linux 6.

If you are a first time Linux user, I'd suggest browsing Parts I and II to begin with. Then, follow the step-by-step directions to help you quickly get up and running.

More experienced users should regard *Red Hat Linux 6: Visual QuickPro Guide* as a reference guide that will help you achieve specific tasks.

You may notice that in some places in the text—mostly examples involving Linux commands that you are supposed to enter—I've used a special character, _, to indicate line continuation. When you see the line continuation character, it means that the text should be entered (or read) all on the same line.

Contacting the author

I have made every effort to be as accurate as possible. However, it is inevitable in life that some errors may have crept in. I'd greatly appreciate any corrections. Drop me a line at

`harold@bearhome.com`

A Web page for the book will be available on the publisher's Web site:

`http://www.peachpit.com/vqp/linux/`

Onward and upward

Red Hat Linux 6, with its user-friendly, fully-integrated Gnome desktop, opens up a whole new world to novice and experienced users alike. Red Hat Linux 6 lets you control and customize the operating system any way you prefer. Why wait? Why not get started now...and welcome to the amazing world of Red Hat Linux 6!

Part 1 Installing Red Hat Linux 6

Part I covers installing Red Hat Linux 6 and the Gnome Desktop Environment. You'll find enough information in this part to quickly get up and running and to find your way around the desktop! You'll also learn how to install software, surf the Web, and much more. In fact, all the information you *really* need to use Red Hat Linux 6 is here.

Chapter 1: Quick Start explains how to get Red Hat Linux 6 running on a machine of its own. You may be amazed at how easy this is.

Chapter 2: Detailed Installation Instructions shows you how to install Red Hat Linux 6 on a machine that is also running Microsoft Windows. In addition, some advanced configuration and installation troubleshooting information is provided.

Chapter 3: Configuring Gnome shows you how to customize the Gnome desktop to your personal taste, and make the most of this powerful environment.

Chapter 4: Email and the Web tells you how to quickly connect to the Internet—and get up and running with the Netscape Communicator suite.

Chapter 5: Linux Documentation explains how to find more of the information you need.

Enough! It's time to get started with Red Hat Linux 6!

Part 1
Installing
RedHat Linux 6

QUICK START INSTALLATION

Linux is an extremely powerful operating system. It can be installed in a number of different configurations: for example, as a single desktop, as a file and print server, or with a custom combination of components. Linux can be installed to occupy the entire file system of your computer or to co-exist with another operating system (such as Microsoft Windows). This "Quick Start" chapter assumes that you will be turning your computer over to Linux in its entirety.

As you are quite possibly all too aware, Windows computers running on the Intel platform come with a mind-boggling array of hardware peripherals, components, and configurations. Although it is becoming somewhat more mainstream to purchase an Intel-compatible machine with Linux preinstalled, most likely you will be installing Linux on a machine running Windows.

The combination of a flexible and powerful operating system and the possibility of installation on a huge variety of hardware leads to complex installation issues.

As explained in the introduction, Linux itself is freely distributable software. A large part of the value added by Red Hat—and some other Linux vendors—is the software these vendors have added to make installation of the Linux operating system (and the software running on Linux) easier.

This "Quick Start" chapter is intended to show you how to install Linux using the CD that accompanies this book. It covers a typical installation and does not attempt to troubleshoot all possible problems. (You'll find lots of information on customizing Linux in the other chapters in Part I of the *Red Hat Linux 6: Visual QuickPro Guide*.)

In other words, the goal of this chapter is to get you up and running on Linux with no pain and in no time at all.

Gathering Information

Before you start installing Linux, you should gather information about your current hardware. Assuming that you are currently running Windows, one of the best sources of information is Windows itself. (I'll show you how to obtain this information in a moment.)

Other sources of information include

◆ Printed documentation—manuals—for your hardware

◆ The hardware itself (you may have to open your computer to find this)

◆ The system vendor: for example, Dell

◆ The manufacturer of a specific piece of hardware: for example, 3Com

To obtain information about your current hardware from Windows:

1. Right-click the My Computer icon on your desktop.

A pop-up menu will appear.

2. Choose Properties from the pop-up menu.

The System Properties dialog box will open (**Figure 1. 1**).

3. Select the Device Manager tab (**Figure 1. 2**).

The Device Manager tab displays a list of the hardware in your computer by category. A plus sign on the left of the category indicates that an item can be expanded to show more information.

4. Highlight an individual hardware component and click the Properties button to display more information about that specific piece of hardware (**Figure 1. 3**).

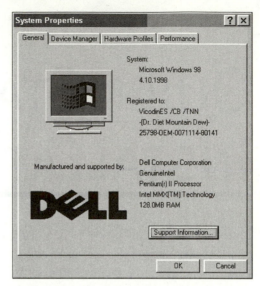

Figure 1.1 You can use the System Properties dialog box to learn about your hardware.

Figure 1.2 Windows Device Manager provides a list of hardware categories that can be expanded to display individual hardware components.

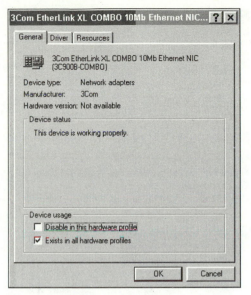

Figure 1.3 Clicking the Properties button displays detailed information about a specific hardware item.

What you need to know

You should be prepared to supply the following hardware information. It's a good idea to write this down before you proceed:

◆ Your **mouse** type and, if it is a serial mouse, the port it is connected to

◆ **Disk controller** type(s) and, for SCSI devices, the make and model

◆ **CD-ROM** type

◆ The make and model of your **monitor** and, possibly, its horizontal and vertical refresh rates

◆ The make and model of your **video card**, its chip set, and the amount of RAM it uses

◆ The make and model of your **network interface card** (NIC)

✔ Tips

■ Red Hat Linux 6 with the graphical Gnome desktop environment requires a minimum of 8MB of RAM and a minimum total of about 120MB of hard drive space. Clearly, your system will run better with more RAM (what else is new?). In addition, if you are going to install many of the components and applications that come with Red Hat Linux 6 and Gnome—such as those included in the default installations—you'll find the program taking up a great deal more space, perhaps as much as 450MB.

■ **Warning!** The procedure outlined in this chapter replaces the Windows file system with the Linux file system. All the current data and applications on your hard drive will be lost, and unless you have made backups, there will be no way to retrieve them.

■ **Warning!** Install at your own risk! The version of Red Hat Linux 6 on the CD-ROM bundled with this book does not come with free technical support from either Red Hat or Peachpit Press. That means if you install it, and something goes wrong, you have to figure out how to fix it using this book and the documentation on the CD-ROM and the Red Hat Web site (`www.redhat.com`). You can purchase technical support from Red Hat by calling 1-888-REDHAT1.

GATHERING INFORMATION

Securing Your Retreat

Besides gathering information, another crucial piece of preparation is to secure your retreat by making (and testing) a Windows boot floppy. Typically, Windows is installed from a CD. To start the installation program, you'll need a floppy disk that can be booted and that can access the CD-ROM drive with the Windows installation disk.

Of course, it is likely that you will be so happy with Linux that you'll never want to go back to Windows. But on the off chance that you change your mind, you'll need the Windows boot disk.

To create a Windows boot floppy:

1. Place a floppy disk in your boot drive.

2. Right-click My Computer on your desktop and select Explorer from the pop-up menu.

   Windows Explorer will open (**Figure 1. 4**).

3. Select your boot floppy drive (usually drive A) in Explorer. Right-click it and select Format from the pop-up menu.

   The Format dialog will appear (**Figure 1. 5**).

4. Make sure that Copy System Files is checked (the system files are what make the floppy bootable). Click Start.

Figure 1.4 To create a Windows boot disk, open Windows Explorer, select your floppy drive, and choose Format from the pop-up menu.

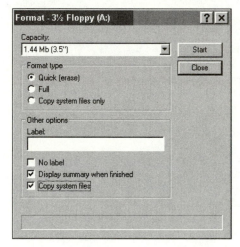

Figure 1.5 By checking Copy System Files, you are telling Windows to create a bootable floppy disk.

✔ Tip

■ Creating a bootable floppy disk may not be sufficient, depending on your system. To reinstall Windows, you'll need to be able to access the CD-ROM drive. Depending on your system, this may require drivers that are not copied with the system files as part of the process of creating a bootable disk. If this is the case for your system, you should determine from documentation which files are needed. Then, copy the appropriate files to your boot floppy. Make sure to add any required Windows configuration files such as autoexec.bat and config.sys. Finally, test your new boot floppy to make sure that you can access the CD-ROM drive, as detailed in the following sections.

To test your Windows boot floppy:

1. Make a note of the letter designation for your CD-ROM drive: for example, drive D.

2. Place the boot floppy in the drive.

3. Shut down Windows.

4. Turn your computer off and then on again.

   If the boot floppy is working, the computer will boot up to a DOS prompt with the designation for the floppy drive, usually A:.

5. Test that you can access the CD-ROM drive by typing at the A:> prompt the letter of the CD-ROM drive: for example, **D :**.

   If the prompt now says D:>, and no error messages have appeared, you can access your CD-ROM drive from the boot floppy.

SECURING YOUR RETREAT

Creating a Linux Boot Disk

Before you can install Red Hat Linux from the CD bundled into the back of this book, you will need to create a Linux boot disk.

You can create a Linux boot disk using your Windows computer or using a computer already running Linux. (You may need the boot disk to upgrade an existing Linux installation or to install Linux on an additional computer.)

To create a Linux boot disk with Windows:

1. Place the Linux CD in the drive on your Windows machine.

2. Place a blank floppy disk in your boot drive.

3. Choose MS-DOS Prompt from the Programs menu found on the Start menu. A DOS Window will open (**Figure 1.6**).

4. Change to your CD-ROM drive. For example, if your CD-ROM drive is drive E, at the prompt enter **E**.

5. Change to the dosutils directory, by entering the following at the prompt: **cd\dosutils**.

6. Run the rawrite program by typing the following at the prompt: **rawrite**.

7. You will be prompted to enter the disk image source file name. Type **e:\images\boot.img**.

8. Press Enter on the keyboard.

9. You will be prompted for a target diskette. Type the name of the boot drive: for example, type **a:**.

10. Press Enter on the keyboard.

11. You will be prompted to place a floppy disk in the drive. Once you have done so, press Enter again, and the Linux boot disk will be created.

Figure 1.6 You can use the rawrite program from within a DOS command prompt window to create a Linux boot disk.

Figure 1.7 Under Linux, you can create a boot disk by copying the boot image to your floppy disk.

✔ Tip

- If you have a recent computer, it may feature a bootable CD-ROM drive. (You should check your system documentation to find out if this is the case.) If you can boot directly from your CD-ROM drive, you do not need to create a Linux boot disk and can start the installation process simply by placing the CD-ROM from the back of this book in your drive and restarting the computer.

To create a Linux boot disk with Linux:

1. Open a Linux telnet window (**Figure 1.7**) or access the Linux command-line prompt.

2. If you don't have root (or superuser) privileges, type **su root** at the prompt and supply the root password.

3. Place the CD in its drive and *mount* it—that is, connect it to the rest of the Linux file system—by entering the following at the prompt: **mount /dev/cdrom /mnt**.

4. Change to the images directory on the CD by typing **cd /mnt/images**.

5. Place a blank disk in the floppy drive.

6. Copy the boot image to the floppy disk by typing

   dd if=boot.img of=/dev/fd0

7. If you want, unmount the CD by typing the following:

   cd /

   umount /mnt

✔ Tip

- The images directory on the CD-ROM distributed with *Red Hat Linux 6: Visual QuickPro Guide* contains disk images, not pictures.

Installing Linux

Enough with preliminaries! It is time to install Linux.

To boot the installation program:

1. Power down your computer.

2. With the CD-ROM in its drive and the Linux boot disk that you created in the floppy drive, turn the power back on. After a brief delay, a text-based boot screen will appear.

3. Press Enter to accept the default options. The installation program will begin.

✔ Tip

■ If you don't press Enter, after one minute the installation program will start running with the default options.

To run the installation program:

1. The first dialog box you'll see once the installation starts asks you to select a language to be used during the installation process (**Figure 1.8**). Use the arrow keys to highlight the language of your choice.

2. Press the spacebar to select the language.

Figure 1.8 The first step in the installation process is to select a language that the program will use.

Figure 1.9 You must specify the installation media, most likely a CD.

Navigating the installation windows

Once the Red Hat Linux installation program begins, you will need to use your keyboard for navigation because the program does not respond to mouse commands.

The following keystrokes are used in the installation dialog boxes:

◆ Left, right, up, and down arrow keys move the cursor in the direction of the arrow.

◆ Tab, Alt+Tab cycle forward or backward through the options on the screen.

◆ Spacebar, Enter select options.

◆ F12 accepts the current values and moves to the next dialog box (equivalent to clicking OK).

Figure 1.10 You can use the installation program to upgrade, which preserves your current data and configuration, or to perform a completely new installation.

Figure 1.11 There are three classes of installation: Workstation, Server, and Custom.

Figure 1.12 A Server-class installation deletes all the partitions on your hard drive.

3. Tab to the OK box and press Enter to select it.

4. In the next dialog box, select a keyboard type. If your keyboard is not on the list, the best choice is US.

5. You will be asked to choose an installation method (**Figure 1.9**). Choose Local CDROM and select OK.

6. The installation program will prompt you to make sure the CD is in place. Press Enter on the keyboard to verify that it is. If the installation program doesn't find your CD-ROM, reboot your computer with the CD-ROM in place and restart the installation program.

7. The program will probe your system to find and identify your CD-ROM drive. If your CD-ROM drive is controlled by a SCSI controller, you will be asked if there are additional SCSI controllers in your system. Select No (unless you have other SCSI controllers).

8. Choose whether you want to upgrade or perform a new installation (**Figure 1.10**). Upgrading will preserve applications and data files and existing configuration files (which will be renamed with a .rpmsave extension). You should choose Upgrade only if your system is already running Red Hat Linux version 2.2 or greater.

9. In the next dialog box, you will be asked to choose the installation class (**Figure 1.11**). There are three choices: Workstation, Server, and Custom. A Workstation-class installation erases all current Linux partitions from your system. A Server-class installation erases *all* partitions from your system. A Custom-class installation gives you complete control over partitioning, and over which components are

(Continued...)

CREATING A LINUX BOOT DISK

installed. See Chapter 2 for more information on Custom-class installations. Tab to the Server check box and press the spacebar to select it.

10. Press the F12 key to continue to the next dialog box.

11. You will be warned that you are about to delete all the partitions on your hard drive, meaning that all your data will be lost (**Figure 1.12**). Tab to the OK box and press Enter to continue.

12. Select your mouse type and connection using the Tab key, arrow keys, and spacebar.

13. If the installation program detected a network card, you will be asked to configure networking (**Figure 1.13**). See Chapters 3 and 4 for more information.

14. Enter a password for root (**Figure 1.14**), also called the superuser. The root password must be at least six characters long. It gives access to the entire system—you should take care not to lose it and not to share it with any high-security-risk individuals.

15. You are given the opportunity to create a custom boot disk for the new system (**Figure 1.15**). Select Yes.

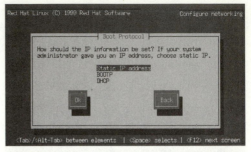

Figure 1.13 You can configure networking during the installation process.

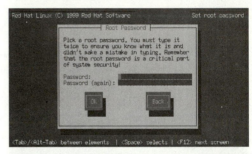

Figure 1.14 You must supply a root password, which should be protected and not forgotten.

Figure 1.15 You are given the opportunity to create a custom boot disk.

Figure 1.16 If you decide to create a boot disk, you must insert a floppy disk in your drive (drive A in Windows is /dev/fdo in Linux).

Figure 1.17 The installation program will attempt to identify your video subsystem.

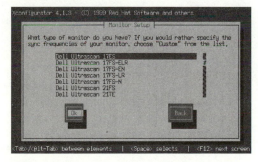

Figure 1.18 For the display to work properly, you'll need to identify your monitor.

16. At the prompt, insert a blank floppy disk (**Figure 1.16**).

17. You will be asked if you want X-Windows to start automatically at bootup. Select Yes.

The installation program will attempt to identify your video adapter (**Figure 1.17**).

18. Select your video monitor from the list (**Figure 1.18**) using the Tab key, the arrow keys, and the spacebar. If your monitor is not listed, you can specify horizontal and vertical refresh rates directly. This procedure is covered in more detail in Chapter 2.

19. Remove the floppy drive from the disk so the system can reboot.

✔ Tip

- If your monitor isn't listed and you don't have refresh rate information, try choosing a Dell monitor in the right size.

CREATING A LINUX BOOT DISK

For the Very First Time...

Provided you selected automatic start of X-Windows, when the installation program reboots after a startup process, you will see the Red Hat logon screen (**Figure 1.19**). Log on as root with the password you supplied during installation. Congratulations! You've successfully installed Red Hat Linux.

Figure 1.19 After the installation completes, your system will reboot; you will then be ready to log on for the first time.

It's a bad idea to run your system as root. Once you've booted up, your first step should be to add yourself as a new user.

You'll also need to know how to reboot and shut down your new system.

To add yourself as a user:

1. Open a terminal window, either by clicking the terminal icon on the Gnome panel or by choosing Gnome Terminal from the Gnome Utilities menu.

2. Click the Terminal window so that it has the focus of keyboard entries.

3. At the prompt, type **useradd** *jpublic*, where *jpublic* is your name.

To add your password:

1. You must specify a password for your new user. You can use the passwd command to give *jpublic* a password. At the prompt, enter:

   `[root@linuxbear /root]# passwd jpublic`

2. You'll be prompted to enter a password:

   `New UNIX password:`

3. You will be prompted to re-enter the password:

   `Retype New UNIX password:`

   `passwd: all authentication _`
   `    tokens updated successfully`

   `[root@linuxbear /root]#`

   Note that when you enter the new password, it will not be echoed to the screen.

To reboot:

With the Terminal window still open, type

`shutdown -r now`

To shut down the system:

In the Terminal window, type

`shutdown -h now`

The system will proceed to shut down. When a message saying "Power Down" appears on the screen, it is safe to turn off the computer.

Summary

In this chapter, you learned how to:

◆ Gather information about your Windows hardware.

◆ Create and test a Windows boot disk.

◆ Create a Linux boot disk using a Windows machine.

◆ Create a Linux boot disk using a Linux machine.

◆ Install Linux.

◆ Add a user.

◆ Add a user password.

◆ Reboot the system.

◆ Shut down the system.

SUMMARY

DETAILED INSTALLATION INSTRUCTIONS 2

In Chapter 1, "Quick Start," I showed you how to install Red Hat Linux 6 in the best of all possible worlds. However, the best of all possible worlds is not the real world. In the real world, what can go wrong likely will go wrong. Also, to paraphrase Leo Tolstoy, easy installations are all alike, but difficult installations are each different. This chapter concentrates on making "different" installations if not easy, at least easier.

To take one very important point, the "Quick Start" installation in Chapter 1 assumed you were willing to turn your computer over to Linux (and delete everything currently on your hard drive). If this is not, in fact, the case, you will have to *partition* your hard drive so that Linux and DOS/Windows can happily coexist. In this chapter, I'll show you how to do this.

I'll also explain Custom installations and how to select individual components for your system.

The truth of the matter is that many Windows users installing Linux for the first time view the process as an experiment. Typically, this means trotting out that old "junker" PC, relieving it of its duties as a door stop, and installing Linux.

There is no problem with this once Linux is running, as Linux and Gnome do perform better on less powerful hardware than do DOS and Windows 98. However, it does mean that it is likely that Linux will be installed on older systems with archaic hardware. This leads to problems during installation, particularly with the video subsystem. I'll provide some pointers for configuring your video card and monitor.

Finally, this chapter will explain how to add and configure a printer.

Linux and Windows on the Same System

Many people want to run Linux and Windows on the same system. Why? Well, you might want to do this if you have only one computer and are not ready to give up running your Windows applications until you have tried those available under Linux. Or you might just want to be able to run both Linux and Windows on the same machine.

It is perfectly reasonable to *want* to do this. However, you should understand before you start that this "double OS" kind of installation involves many variables, some degree of difficulty, and some danger to all the data on your system.

This "double OS" kind of installation involves many variables, some degree of difficulty, and some danger to all the data on your system.

Before you start, it is *essential* to back up any data you care about.

You should also have a clear conceptual understanding of the process before you start the repartitioning process. That process is outlined next.

Note: the following roadmap is provided as a conceptual overview. The steps for completing it are described in detail later in this chapter.

To install Linux and keep Windows:

1. Make sure you have enough space on your hard drive for Linux as well as your current Windows files.

   If you have less than 750MB free, you probably will not be able to perform an optimal Red Hat Linux 6 installation.

2. Defragment your Windows hard drive to move all the data on it to the beginning of the drive so that there will be space for Linux partitions.

3. Before leaving Windows, jot down your hardware settings (a page is provided in the back of this book, just after the index, for you to jot down this information).

4. Repartition your Windows hard drive to add Linux partitions.

5. Complete the installation program to install Linux on the appropriate partitions.

6. Copy the LILO bootstrap loader to one of the partitions on your hard drive.

   If, for some reason, LILO will not work to multi-boot with your system, then you will need to organize another way to start Linux: for example, from a boot floppy.

✔ Tips

■ If you have an extra machine, strongly consider giving Linux a "room of its own" by installing it by itself on that machine.

■ It's easier to install Linux on a system with Windows if each operating system has its own physical hard drive.

■ You may have only have one *physical* hard drive but more than one *logical* hard drive under Windows. If so, you may want to consider reformatting one of the logical Windows drives as a Linux drive, rather than carving a partition out of a logical Windows drive for Linux.

■ Using a boot floppy means that a Linux floppy disk is placed in your A drive when you want to start the computer in Linux. When you want to start it in Windows, the disk is left out of the drive. This is actually a sane way to do things, and quite bullet-proof (more on this later).

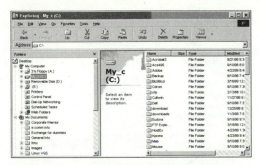

Figure 2.1 To defragment a drive—which moves all the data on the drive to the beginning of the drive—first select it in Windows Explorer.

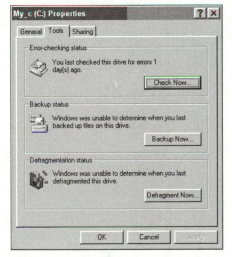

Figure 2.2 Choose Defragment Now from the Tools tab of the drive's Properties dialog box to open the defragmentation utility.

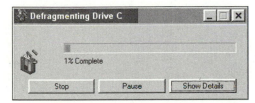

Figure 2.3 Choose Show Details to view a display of disk data being moved.

To defragment a Windows drive:

1. Right-click the My Computer icon on your Windows desktop and select Explore from the pop-up menu.

   Windows Explorer will open (**Figure 2.1**).

2. Find and select the drive you want to defragment.

3. Right-click the drive and select Properties from the pop-up menu.

   The drive's Properties dialog box will open.

4. Choose the Tools tab of the Properties dialog box (**Figure 2.2**).

5. Click Defragment Now.

   A dialog box containing a slider bar that shows defragmentation progress will open (**Figure 2.3**).

✔ Tips

■ If you'd like to see a real-time graphic representation of the disk data that the defragmentation utility is moving, click Show Details.

■ The defragmentation utility may uncover errors on your hard drive that must be fixed before it can proceed (see the next section).

LINUX AND WINDOWS ON THE SAME SYSTEM

To fix errors on a hard drive:

1. With Windows Explorer open, select the drive you want to defragment.

2. Right-click the drive and select Properties from the pop up menu.

   The drive's Properties dialog box will open.

3. Choose the Tools tab of the Properties dialog box.

4. In the Error-Checking Status frame, choose Check Now.

   The ScanDisk dialog box will open (**Figure 2.4**).

5. Check the Automatically Fix Errors box.

6. Click Start.

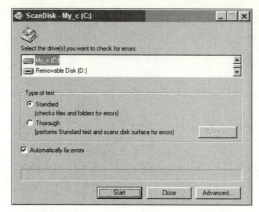

Figure 2.4 Run ScanDisk to fix any errors on your drive that the defragmentation utility finds.

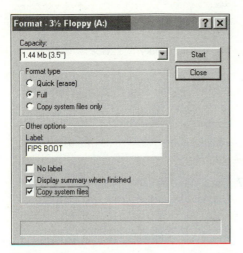

Figure 2.5 Check Copy System Files to make a floppy disk bootable.

■ **Warning!** As mentioned elsewhere, the version of Linux on the CD in this book is *not* supported by Red Hat or Peachpit Press. We've made every effort to make these instructions as accurate and complete as possible, but there are simply too many installation possibilities and configurations to fully cover them here. See the documentation on the Red Hat Web site (`http://www.redhat.com`) and on the CD-ROM itself. You may *purchase* techical support for the software by calling 1-888-REDHAT1.

Using FIPS

The FIPS program is a DOS utility that is used to carve a Linux partition out of your existing hard drive. It is easy to use and should be your first choice for proceeding if you want to keep Windows on your Linux box-to-be.

To repartition using FIPS:

1. Place a blank floppy disk in your drive.

2. Using Windows Explorer, select the floppy drive (usually drive A).

3. Right-click the drive and select Format from the pop-up menu.

   The Format dialog box will open (**Figure 2.5**).

4. Check Copy System Files to make the floppy disk bootable.

5. Click Start.

6. After the disk has been formatted, use Windows Explorer to copy the files fips.exe and restorrb.exe from the \dosutils\fips20 directory on the Red Hat Linux 6 CD to the floppy disk.

7. Shut down Windows and reboot your computer.

   It will power up to an A:> prompt.

8. At the prompt, type **fips** and press Enter.

   You'll see a copyright notice screen along with some warnings and the notation that FIPS comes with "Absolutely no warranty."

9. Press any key to continue.

(Continued...)

10. You will see a number of screens containing information and warnings. Keep on pressing any key to move to the next screen until you reach the screen asking whether you want to make a backup copy of sectors.

11. Press **y** for yes. You will be prompted to place a floppy disk in drive A (you can just use the one running FIPS).

Once a backup of your sectors has been made, the business of FIPS begins. A screen appears with three columns: Old Partition, Cylinder, and New Partition. The old partition is the DOS/Windows partition of your drive, and the new partition is the new Linux partition that you will be creating.

To perform a full installation of Red Hat Linux 6, you should have 750MB available on the new partition.

12. Use the left and right arrow keys to change the size of the Old Partition and New Partition fields.

To perform a full installation of Red Hat Linux 6, you should have 750MB available on the new partition.

13. When you are satisfied with your selections, press Enter.

FIPS will display the size of the new partition that has been created.

14. If you are *not* satisfied with the size of the new and old partitions, type **r** to re-edit them. If you are satisfied, type **c** to continue.

15. If you typed **c**, you will see some informative messages about your disk. Then a message will appear telling you that FIPS is ready to save the new partition scheme.

If you have cold feet by now, type **n** to exit FIPS without making any changes; otherwise, type **y** to save the new partition changes.

16. If you typed **y**, once FIPS has completed, remove the floppy disk and reboot your computer.

This is what is known as *the moment of truth!*

17. Once Windows has restarted, run ScanDisk as explained earlier in "To fix errors on a hard drive" to make sure that your disk and file system are still in good repair.

✔ Tips

■ FIPS should not be run from a DOS box within Windows.

■ You'll find a great deal of helpful documentation about the FIPS utility on the Red Hat Linux 6 CD, in the back of this book, in the \dosutils\fipsdocs directory.

DOS fdisk

If FIPS could not repartition your hard drive, then you cannot add another drive to your system; but if you are intent on running Windows as well as Linux, you can proceed with *destructive* repartitioning using either the DOS or Linux version of fdisk.

Before you destructively repartition using DOS fdisk, say to yourself, "I am about to wipe everything off my hard drive. I can restore it from back-ups." If this does not ring entirely comfortable, then do not proceed. Once you have wiped a partition using DOS fdisk, there is no going back.

Warning! My recommendation is *firmly* against using DOS fdisk unless you *have* to.

To destructively repartition using DOS fdisk:

1. Make a backup of your Windows system, following the instructions provided in your backup software's documentation.

2. Create a boot floppy disk following the instructions in steps 1 through 5 of "To repartition using FIPS."

3. Copy the files Fdisk.exe and Format.com to the floppy disk. These files are located in the \Windows\Command folder.

4. Copy any files required to initiate a backup onto the floppy disk. (Check your backup software documentation for further information.)

5. With the disk you just created in your A drive, reboot your computer.

6. At the A:> prompt type `fdisk` and press Enter.

7. Use the fdisk menu options to delete partitions to create space for new Linux and DOS partitions (option 3). You will probably want to delete all existing partitions. Do not choose Large Disk Support.

8. Use the fdisk menu options to create a DOS partition (option 1).

9. Enter the DOS partition size in megabytes.

10. Press Esc to continue.
    The fdisk menu screen will reopen.

11. Set the active partition to your new DOS partition (option 2).
    This is the same as making the partition bootable.

12. Press Esc to return to the fdisk menu screen.

13. Press Esc to exit fdisk.

14. Type `format /s C:` to format the new DOS partition and then copy the system files to it.

15. Restore the backup you made of your Windows system following directions supplied with the backup software.

✔ Tip

- As the term *destructive* implies, DOS fdisk destroys all the data on your hard drive.

DOS FDISK

Linux fdisk

You may want to delete a partition if your plan is to turn a logical (or physical) DOS drive over to Linux. After the partition is deleted, you can add new Linux partitions.

Linux fdisk is a powerful program that can be used to destructivly repartition as well as to create new Linux partitions.

To delete a partition using Linux fdisk:

1. Start the Linux installation program using a boot floppy and the CD from the back of this book, as described in Chapter 1.

2. When you are prompted, select the Install option rather than the Upgrade option.

3. When you are prompted, select Custom installation rather than Workstation or Server.

   For more information on these options, see "Workstation, Server, and Custom Installations" later in this chapter.

4. When you are prompted to select a disk partitioning tool (**Figure 2.6**), select fdisk.

   A command prompt and a list of possible actions will appear (**Figure 2.7**).

5. Enter **p** to list current partitions and devices (**Figure 2.8**).

6. Make a note of the number of the partition you want to delete, counting from the top.

   Most likely, the device name for the first partition is hda1 (if it is an IDE drive) or sda1 (if it is a SCSI drive). See the sidebar "Linux device names and partitions" for more information.)

7. Enter **d** to delete a partition.

8. Enter the number of the partition you want to delete.

Figure 2.6 You can use Disk Druid or Linux fdisk as a partitioning tool.

Figure 2.7 The fdisk program presents a prompt with a list of possible command actions.

Figure 2.8 Use the p option to verify changes before writing them to disk.

9. Enter **p** to display the new partition table to verify your change.

10. Enter **w** to save the changes and exit Linux fdisk.

11. If you are prompted to reboot your system, do so.

✔ Tips

■ Entering **m** displays the list of fdisk command actions.

■ You may need to use both Linux fdisk and Disk Druid (explained later in this chapter) to get your partitioning right. If so, you can use the Back option to navigate between the two utilities.

To add a Linux partition using fdisk:

1. Start Linux fdisk as described in the preceding section.

2. Type **p** to view the partition table, and make a note of the last cylinder of the partition preceding the one you want to create.

3. Type **n** for new partition.

4. Type **p** for primary partition.
   You could also enter **e** for extended partition; see the sidebar "Linux device names and partitions" for more information.

5. Enter the partition number you want to create. For your first Linux partition, this will probably be **2**.

6. Enter the number of the first cylinder of the partition.
   Normally, you'll want to accept the default. If you are creating partition number 2, the default offered will be one cylinder greater than the ending cylinder for partition 1.

7. Enter the size, or ending cylinder, of the partition.
   The partition size can be specified in bytes, kilobytes, or megabytes—or you can name the ending cylinder.

8. Enter **p** to display the partition table.

9. You can add more partitions, or modify existing ones. To modify a partition, enter **t**. To change the boot partition, enter **a**.

10. When you have completed your changes, enter **w** to save them and exit fdisk.

11. If you are prompted to reboot your system, do so.

Linux device names and partitions

Linux, like other flavors of Unix, references everything as a file. This means that the name for a hard drive is the file identifier of its driver. For example, /dev/hda is the name of the first IDE drive on a system, and /dev/sdc is the name of the third SCSI drive on a system. You can easily crack this code: hd stands for hard drive and sd is short for SCSI drive.

Unlike drives, partitions are denoted with numbers rather than letters. For example, /dev/sda2 is the second primary partition located on the first SCSI drive.

Linux is limited to four primary partitions: numbers 1 through 4. In addition, one primary partition can be an *extended* partition, which itself contains logical partitions. Logical partitions are designated by numbers that are 5 or greater.

LINUX FDISK

Disk Druid

Disk Druid is part of the Red Hat installation program. It features a user-friendly interface, so if it does all that you need, by all means use it in place of Linux fdisk.

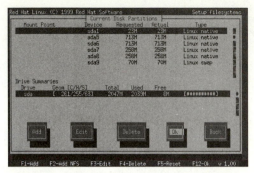

Figure 2.9 You can use Disk Druid to add, edit, or delete partitions.

To add or edit Linux partitions using Disk Druid:

1. Start the Linux installation program as described previously.

2. When you are prompted to choose a disk partitioning tool, select Disk Druid.

   The Disk Druid screen will appear (**Figure 2.9**).

3. Use the Tab key to select Add, Edit, or Delete to add, modify, or delete partitions.

4. When you are through, use the Tab key to select OK. Then press Enter.

At a minimum, you need a root partition to install your Linux kernel. A root partition is indicated by a / (slash). When the program asks you for a mount point, type the name of the the the partition you're creating (see bulleted examples below).

In addition, if your system has less than 128MB of RAM, you should create a swap partition. (Swap partitions are used as virtual memory.) This may be sufficient for a simple system. But most users create separate partitions for various functions, including:

◆ A root, or /, partition

◆ A /home partition, to store users' home directories

◆ A /tmp partition for storing temporary files in large server installations

◆ A /usr partition, where Linux packages are installed

◆ A /usr/src partition for Linux source code

Partitioning Strategies

Partitioning a disk, is more of an art than an exact science. There are many possible approaches. See the documentation on the Red Hat Linux 6 CD-ROM and also on the Red Hat Web site (`www.redhat.com`), particularly:

```
http://www.redhat.com/corp/
support/manuals/RHL-6.0-
Manual/install-guide/manual/
doc037.html
```

and

```
http://www.redhat.com/corp/
support/manuals/RHL-6.0-
Manual/install-guide/manual/
doc021.html
```

DISK DRUID

Booting to Windows and Linux

The final step is to set your computer up so that you can boot to Linux or Windows. There are a number of different possible approaches to accomplish this. If it works, the easiest thing to is to configure LILO, the Linux *bootstrap loader* that actually starts the Linux kernel.

Once LILO has been configured, when you reboot your system, the LILO prompt will appear:

`LILO boot:`

If you press the Tab key, the names for booting the different operating systems will be displayed: for example, DOS and Linux. Type the name of the operating system you want to boot the computer to.

Another very good approach is to use a boot floppy to load Linux. Otherwise, if you are booting from DOS, you may want to write a DOS batch file to load the Linux kernel.

To configure LILO:

1. When you reach the LILO installation dialog box, you will first be asked whether to place LILO on the master boot record (MBR) or on the first sector of your root partition. Choose the MBR unless you are using another bootstrap loader such as that supplied with OS\2.

2. Use the Tab key to highlight OK; then press Enter.

3. Next, you will be asked to supply special options to identify your hardware to Linux. Leave this field empty.

(Continued...)

If LILO won't...

Suppose you've followed these instructions and then you get to the moment of truth and reboot your computer, and it won't reboot. Perhaps it hangs when the LILO prompt appears. This can happen! The most likely cause is a conflict between LILO and your computer's BIOS. Fear not. There are always alternatives in life.

First, don't panic. You should be able to boot to Linux using the Linux boot disk you prepared during installation, and you should be able to start Windows using the boot disk you made when preparing to run the FIPS utility.

As a second step, you will probably want to reinstall Linux on the Linux partitions. Make sure to bypass LILO installation by clicking the Skip button when you get to the LILO installation screen. (I know this is a lot of work, but at least you have done it once before, so you'll know the routine.)

Once Linux has been reinstalled without LILO, you have several viable alternatives. One is to have your system boot by default to Windows. When you want to boot to Linux, simply insert the Linux boot disk in your boot floppy drive.

Another possibility is to use the Loadlin utility to boot Linux directly from the DOS prompt in your Windows partition (see the nearby section "To boot Linux from DOS using Loadlin").

4. Also leave LBA mode empty, unless you are using LBA to access your SCSI drive (you know who your are!).

5. Use the Tab key to highlight OK; then press Enter.

6. A dialog box appears that lists the different partitions on your system, the type of file system present on the partition, whether the partition is the default boot partition, and the label for the partition that LILO will use. Use the Tab and arrow keys to select a partition for editing.

7. If you want, you can change the default boot partition and also the LILO label for a partition (this is the text you type to select a particular partition when LILO boots).

8. After you are through editing, use the Tab key to select OK; then press Enter.

✔ Tip

■ Once you have Linux running, you can manually edit the file lilo.conf, located in the /etc/ directory, to make changes to the way LILO is configured. After saving changes to this file, you must run the program /sbin/lilo to make them effective.

To boot Linux from DOS using Loadlin:

1. From your Windows desktop, select Shut Down on the Windows Start menu.

2. Choose Restart in MS-DOS Mode from the Shut Down Windows dialog box (**Figure 2.10**).

3. Choose OK. Your computer will exit to a full-screen DOS window, and your prompt will probably say C:\WINDOWS. Note that DOS mode is different from running a DOS box in Windows.

4. To move to the C root directory, type **c d ** and then press Enter.

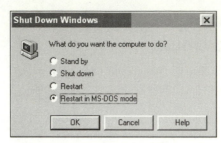

Figure 2.10 Select Restart in MS-DOS Mode from the Shutdown dialog box.

5. Create a directory for the Loadlin utility by typing `md loadlin` and then pressing Enter.

6. Create a directory for the Linux kernel image by typing `md vmlinuz` and then pressing Enter.

7. Place the Red Hat Linux VQS 6 CD in your CD-ROM drive.

8. Change to the loadlin subdirectory by typing `cd loadlin` and then pressing Enter.

9. Copy Loadlin.exe to the loadlin subdirectory by typing

   `copy d:\dosutils\loadlin.exe`

   where *d* is the drive letter that designates your CD-ROM drive. Then press Enter.

   A message will appear stating that one file has been copied.

10. Move to the vmlinuz directory that you created earlier by typing `cd \` and then pressing Enter. Then type `cd vmlinuz` and press Enter once again.

11. Copy the Linux kernel to the vmlinuz subdirectory by typing

    `copy d:\dosutils\autoboot\ _`
    `vmlinuz`

    where *d* is the drive letter that designates your CD-ROM drive. Then press Enter.

    A message will appear stating that one file has been copied.

12. Return to the loadlin directory by typing `cd \loadlin` and then pressing Enter.

13. Type

    `loadlin c:\vmlinuz\vmlinuz _`
    `root=/dev/hda2 ro`

    and then press Enter.

    In this example, the Linux root partition established in Disk Druid is /dev/hda2. The computer will start to boot to Linux.

(Continued...)

BOOTING TO WINDOWS AND LINUX

✔ Tips

- If you didn't make a note of the designation of your Linux root partition when you ran Disk Druid, you can rerun the installation program as far as Disk Druid to obtain this information. Once you've obtained the information you need, simply reboot the computer and remove the CD.

- If you are planning to use Loadlin to regularly boot to Linux from DOS, you should probably do a few things to make this process easier. You can set Windows to boot to the DOS prompt rather than to the Windows GUI. You can also write a batch file to automate invoking Linux. Once you have done these things, when you turn on your computer, it will boot to a DOS C:> prompt. To start Windows, type **win** and press Enter. To start Linux, type **linux** and press Enter.

To set Windows to boot to the DOS prompt:

1. Open Windows Explorer and locate the C: folder.

2. Highlight the file named Msdos.sys and right-click with your mouse.

3. Select Properties from the pop-up menu. The Properties dialog for Msdos.sys will open (**Figure 2.11**).

4. In the Attributes box at the bottom of the Properties dialog box, uncheck the Read-Only attribute.

5. Choose OK to accept the change and close the Properties dialog box.

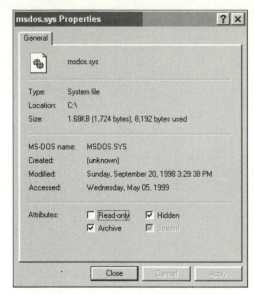

Figure 2.11 To be able to save changes to a file, you should clear the Read-Only box in the Properties dialog box.

6. Open Windows Notepad, which can be started from the Accessories fly-out on the Windows Program menu.

7. Select Open from the File menu.

8. In the File Name box of the Open dialog box, type `c:\msdos.sys` and press Enter.

9. Edit the [Options] section of Msdos.sys so that it contains this line:

`BootGUI=0`

(For help, see **Figure 2.12**.)

10. Select Save from the File menu.

The next time you restart your computer, it will boot directly to the DOS prompt.

Figure 2.12 Set BootGUI=0 to boot to the DOS prompt.

To create a batch file that invokes Linux:

1. Open a new document in Notepad. Enter the following two lines in the document:

`cd\loadlin`

`loadlin c:\vmlinuz\vmlinuz _`
`  root=/dev/hda2 ro`

(For help, see **Figure 2.13**.)

2. Select Save As from the File menu.

3. Select All Files from the Save As Type drop-down list.

4. Enter `c:\linux.bat` in the File Name box.

5. Choose Save.

The next time you boot up to the C: prompt, you can start Linux by typing `linux` at the prompt followed by Enter.

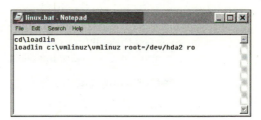

Figure 2.13 You can write a DOS batch file to automate the loading of the Linux kernel from DOS.

Different Types of Installations

As you may have noticed in Chapter 1, Linux can be installed in three basic ways:

◆ Workstation, which is a default installation suitable for a desktop user

◆ Server, which is a default Internet server and network file and print server installation

◆ Custom, which lets you pretty much decide what to install and where to install it

The important point is that Workstation and Server installations do not let you specify the partitions on which Linux is installed. In other words, they wipe out all existing data on the drive.

The only way to install Linux on your drive without wiping out Windows is to perform a Custom installation. In addition, a Custom installation gives you the ability to decide which Linux components you want installed.

To install selected components:

1. After you have completed formatting and configuring partitions, the installation program will open the Components to Install dialog box. Use the arrow keys and the spacebar to choose the components you want to install.

2. When you have finished selecting components, use the Tab key to highlight the OK button; then press Enter.

✔ Tip

■ To select all components, use the down arrow key to scroll to the bottom of the Components list. Highlight Select Everything and then press the spacebar.

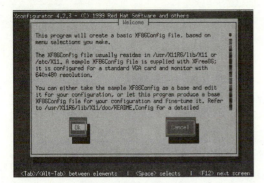

Figure 2.14 Use Xconfigurator to configure Linux to work with your video card and monitor.

Figure 2.15 You should select your monitor if it is on the list; otherwise, you can manually enter monitor settings by choosing Custom.

Configuring Your Video Card and Monitor

One of the biggest problems with Linux installations can be correctly configuring Linux for your video card and monitor. This is an issue because there are so many different video systems in use, and also because Linux is often installed on older hardware.

You will be asked to configure your video system as part of the Linux installation process. However, the same video configuration process can be performed at your convenience from the Linux command prompt without rerunning the installation program. (For information on using the Linux command prompt, see Chapters 3 and 6.)

To use Xconfigurator:

1. At the Linux prompt, in either full-screen or terminal mode, type **Xconfigurator**. The video configuration program will start with an information screen (**Figure 2.14**).

2. Use the Tab key to highlight OK; then press Enter. The Choose a Card dialog box will open.

3. Use the arrow keys and spacebar to select your video card. If you cannot find your video card, Generic VGA is a reasonable choice.

   See the information on SuperProbe in the next section. You may also find it helpful to review the information in Chapter 1 on obtaining information from Windows about your current hardware.

4. When you are satisfied with your choice, highlight OK and press Enter.

5. You will next be asked to enter your monitor type (**Figure 2.15**). If your monitor is not listed, choose Custom to manually select refresh rates (described later) or choose a generic monitor type.

6. Depending on your type of video card, and whether it can respond to automated probes, you may be asked to specify the amount of RAM it has and the RAMDAC chipset used.

7. If you chose a custom monitor, you will be asked to enter its horizontal sync range (**Figure 2.16**).

8. Next, you will need to specify your monitor's vertical sync range (**Figure 2.17**).

9. Finally, you will be asked to accept a color depth resolution setting (**Figure 2.18**). If you do not like the default settings, select Let Me Choose to enter your preferred resolution and color depth.

10. When you are satisfied with your choices, click OK. Xconfigurator will turn your monitor off and on several times, and you will be asked to verify that video is still working by clicking Yes.

11. You will be asked whether you want Linux to automatically boot to X-Windows. If you have reasonable confidence in your choices of video card and monitor, choose Yes.

✔ Tips

■ Note that the sequence of screens and options is the same whether this program is run from the command line or as part of the installation process.

■ Before running Xconfigurator, you can find some information about your video card by running SuperProbe (described later in this chapter).

■ If X-Windows (Gnome) is not set to start automatically, you can start it from the command prompt by typing **startx** and pressing Enter.

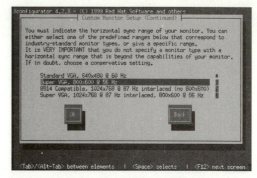

Figure 2.16 If you are entering custom monitor settings, you must select a horizontal sync rate.

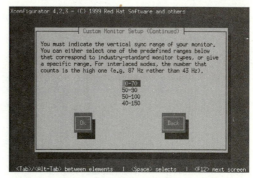

Figure 2.17 If you are entering custom monitor settings, you must select a vertical sync rate.

Figure 2.18 If you do not like the default color depth and resolution settings selected by Xconfigurator, you can enter your own choices.

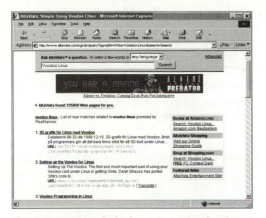

Figure 2.19 You can find information on configuring specific graphics hardware for Linux by using a Web search engine.

Figure 2.20 SuperProbe provides information about your graphics card.

■ If all else fails, go to a Web search engine and type the name of your video card and the word **Linux** in the search box. You are likely to get good tips for dealing with your specific problems. (**Figure 2.19** shows the results of a lookup for the Voodoo video card and Linux on Alta Vista.)

SuperProbe is used to find information about your video card. However, it is not perfect. Not only does it not always provide helpful information, but it also has been known to crash systems. However, if you can't find out about your video chipset in any other way, it is certainly worth a shot.

To run SuperProbe:

1. Log on as root or su to root.

2. At the command prompt, type
   `cd /usr/bin/X11`

3. Type `./SuperProbe`.

   SuperProbe will—hopefully—display information about your system (**Figure 2.20**).

CONFIGURING YOUR VIDEO CARD AND MONITOR

Configuring a Printer

You can configure your printer during the installation process or you can configure it at your convenience using the Printer Configuration applet in the Linux control panel. In either case, the process is the same.

To add a printer with the Printer Configuration applet:

1. Open a terminal window, either by clicking the terminal icon on the Gnome panel or by choosing Gnome Terminal from the Gnome Utilities menu.

2. Click the terminal window, so that it has the focus of keyboard entries.

3. With the terminal window open, at the prompt type **su root**.

4. Enter the root password at the prompt.

   You'll see at the next prompt that you are effectively logged on as root.

5. In the terminal window, type

   control-panel

   The Linux control panel will open (**Figure 2.21**).

6. Select the Printer applet by clicking its icon (the third from the left in **Figure 2.21**).

   The Red Hat Print System Manager will open (**Figure 2.22**).

Figure 2.21 Select the Printer Configuration applet from the Linux control panel.

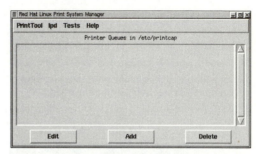

Figure 2.22 The Print System Manager is used to add, edit, and monitor printers.

CONFIGURING A PRINTER

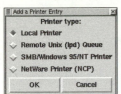

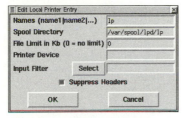

Figure 2.23 If your printer is connected directly to your Linux system, you should choose Local Printer.

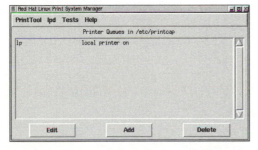

Figure 2.24 It is likely that you will not need to edit the default printer entries.

7. To add a printer, choose Add.

The Add a Printer Entry dialog box will appear (**Figure 2.23**).

8. Choose your printer type. Choose Local Printer if you have a printer directly connected to your Linux system.

For information on configuring a Windows printer using Samba, see Chapter 8.

9. Choose OK.

The Edit Local Printer Entry dialog box will open (**Figure 2.24**).

10. If the default settings are correct, choose OK.

You should now see your new printer listed in the Print System Manager (**Figure 2.25**).

Figure 2.25 When your printer has been added, you will see it listed in the Print System Manager.

Summary

In this chapter, you learned how to:

◆ Run Linux and Windows on the same system.

◆ Defragment a Windows drive.

◆ Fix errors on a Windows drive.

◆ Repartition using FIPS.

◆ Repartition using DOS fdisk.

◆ Delete a partition using Linux fdisk.

◆ Add a partition using Linux fdisk.

◆ Add and edit partitions using Disk Druid.

◆ Configure the LILO boot loader.

◆ Boot Linux from DOS using Loadlin.

◆ Install individual components.

◆ Configure Linux for your video card and monitor.

◆ Configure a printer.

CONFIGURING GNOME 3

Red Hat Linux Version 6.0 is the first version of the Red Hat Linux product that is integrated "out of the box" with a visual shell—called a *desktop environment*. In fact, it actually comes with several desktop environments that you can switch among. The default—and most complete—desktop environment is Gnome (pronounced with a hard G: "Guh-nome").

Gnome is not the only desktop environment available to you: For information on the K and Another Level desktop environments, see Chapter 6. But if you accepted the suggestions made by the Red Hat installation program, your computer will start up with Gnome.

Gnome is a very complete and powerful graphic desktop. In look and feel, it is probably closer to the Mac OS than to Windows 98, but it incorporates suggestions of both. It is probably more user-configurable than either of those commercial OSes.

With the advent of Red Hat Linux 6 and Gnome, it is perfectly possible to use Linux visually — that is, to never access the Linux command line. (In truth, even Windows users find a few tasks that are easier to perform at the old DOS prompt. This is probably true of Gnome and Linux as well.) Gnome is a visual desktop environment equal to any other available. This chapter discusses how to configure your Gnome environment so that you can make the most of it.

Using the Gnome Control Center

The Gnome Control Center allows you to configure most aspects of your Gnome desktop. The Gnome Control Center works in configuring Gnome just as the Display Properties dialog box in Windows is used to configure the Windows display.

The choices you can make regarding your desktop range from the trivial to the sublime. In other words, some things you can configure have merely cosmetic implications, while others will affect the way you work.

To open the Gnome Control Center:

Select GNOME Control Center from the Settings menu on the Gnome main menu.

✔ Tips

■ The Gnome main menu is activated by clicking the leftmost applet button on the Gnome panel, which by default sports an icon of a footprint.

■ You can also open the Gnome Control Center by clicking the third applet button from the left on the Gnome panel (its iconic representation looks something like a digital calculator).

To set a desktop background:

1. With the Gnome Control Center open, select Background (**Figure 3.1**).

2. Click the Color button on the left side of the Background panel.

   The Pick a Color dialog box will open (**Figure3.2**).

3. Select a color by clicking within the color wheel or by using the sliders.

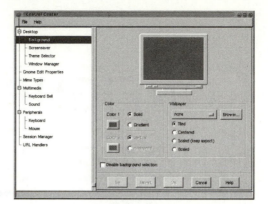

Figure 3.1 You can set your desktop background or wallpaper using the Gnome Control Center.

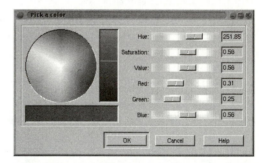

Figure 3.2 You can choose a color by clicking the color wheel.

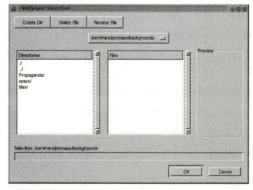

Figure 3.3 The Wallpaper Selection dialog box allows you to browse to find a graphic file to use for wallpaper.

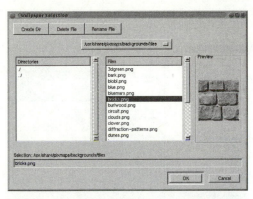

Figure 3.4 The graphics files are organized by likely functionality; for example, all the images appropriate for tiling are in one directory.

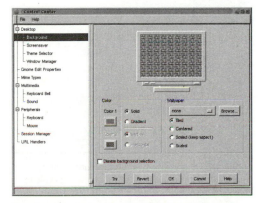

Figure 3.5 The image you select will be displayed in the preview window.

Figure 3.6 Once you click OK, your choice will be used as desktop wallpaper.

4. Click OK in the Pick a Color dialog box.

   The new color will now be previewed in the window on the Background panel.

5. To save your new desktop color, click OK in the Background panel.

Wallpaper

You may prefer to set your background as wallpaper. Gnome comes with many graphics files that can either be used by themselves as a desktop background or patterned to give an interesting textural effect.

To set wallpaper as the background:

1. On the right side of the Background panel (**Figure 3.1**), select a wallpaper mode.

   Choose Tiled to create a pattern of a small image repeated on your desktop, Centered to place an image in its natural size in the center of the desktop, Scaled (Keep Aspect) to enlarge the image vertically to the height of the desktop while keeping its horizontal proportion, or Scaled to use a single image enlarged to fill the desktop.

2. Click the Browse button to find an image file.

   The Wallpaper Selection dialog box will open (**Figure 3.3**). The location opened in the Wallpaper Selection dialog box will be /usr/share/pixmaps/backgrounds.

3. Use the mouse to navigate the directories on the left side to find an appropriate graphic. For example, the tiles subdirectory contains many images suitable for tiling (**Figure 3.4**).

4. Select an image and click OK.

   The new pattern will be displayed in the preview window (**Figure 3.5**).

5. Click OK to use the new tiled image as wallpaper on your desktop (**Figure 3.6**).

USING THE GNOME CONTROL CENTER

To select a screen saver:

1. With the Gnome Control Center open, select Screensaver from the hierarchical list in the left panel (**Figure 3.7**).

2. Choose a screen saver from the Screen Saver list in the middle of the panel.

   The screen saver you select will be displayed in the preview box in the Control Center. (Deco is shown selected in **Figure 3.7**.)

3. To configure the screen saver, click the Settings button.

   A configuration dialog box that is specific to the screen saver you have chosen will appear (**Figure 3.8**).

4. Make changes that you would like to the screen saver's configuration and click OK.

5. In the Control Center, make any global changes to the way screen savers operate. For example, enter the number of minutes of inactivity before the screen saver starts, or whether a password is required (**Figure 3.7**).

6. Click OK to save your changes and activate the screen saver.

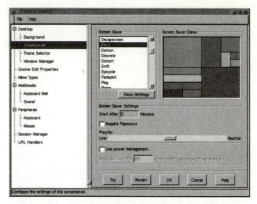

Figure 3.7 You can choose from many screen savers that ship with Gnome.

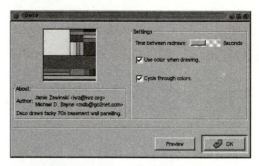

Figure 3.8 Each screen saver has a configuration dialog box that you use to set properties specific to that screen saver.

USING THE GNOME CONTROL CENTER

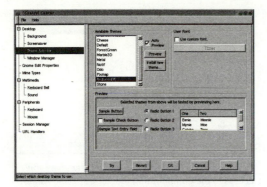

Figure 3.9 Desktop themes control the appearance of windows components such as check boxes and buttons.

Desktop themes

Desktop themes are coordinated schemes that determine the appearance of standard window elements such as check boxes and scroll bars.

To select a desktop theme:

1. With the Gnome Control Center open, select Theme Selector from the hierarchical list in the left panel (**Figure 3.9**).

2. Choose a theme from the Available Themes list in the middle of the panel.

   Provided that the Auto Preview box is selected, the results of your choice will be previewed in the lower right of the Control Center panel. (Redmond95 is shown selected in **Figure 3.9**.)

3. Click OK to enable the desktop theme.

✔ Tip

■ Admittedly, this may not be your goal, but if you want to make your Linux desktop look and behave as much like Windows as possible, select Redmond95 as your desktop theme.

Using the Window Manager

Under Gnome, you are not necessarily locked into one way of controlling the behavior of windows. It's possible to write programs that control most aspects of the way the Gnome desktop windows behave. You can have more than one of these types of program—called a Window Manager—loaded. Each Window Manager comes with a Configuration tool that lets you control important aspects of window behavior.

The Configuration tool for your Window Manager should be used in conjunction with a desktop theme selection so that you will have Linux and Gnome the way you prefer.

To run the Configuration tool:

1. With the Gnome Control Center open, select Window Manager from the hierarchical list in the left panel (**Figure 3.10**).

2. Highlight the current Window Manager and click the Run Configuration Tool button.

   A *Configuration Editor* will open (**Figure 3.11**).

3. Make the changes you want in the Configuration Editor and click OK when you are done.

Figure 3.10 The Gnome Window Manager gives you access to the Configuration tool for a specific Window Manager.

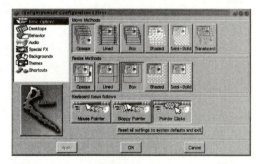

Figure 3.11 The Configuration Editor allows you to control many aspects of the way windows behave.

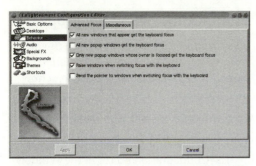

Figure 3.12 The Advanced Focus tab allows you to control the way windows receive the focus.

Figure 3.13 You can turn tooltips off and on to suit your own style.

Giving a Window focus

A window is said to receive the *focus* if keyboard commands and mouse clicks are received and processed by that window (as opposed to other windows on the desktop).

By default, a new Gnome window will not receive the focus until you've clicked in it. This is not the behavior that Microsoft Windows users are used to and can be slightly annoying.

To automatically give a new window the focus:

1. With the Configuration Editor open, select Behavior from the list at the upper left (**Figure 3.12**).

2. On the Advanced Focus tab, put a check in the box next to All New Windows that Appear Get the Keyboard Focus (**Figure 3.12**).

3. Click OK.

Tooltips

Tooltips are the helpful hints that appear on your screen when you pass your mouse over an object.

To turn tooltips on (or off):

1. With the Configuration Editor open, select Behavior from the list at the upper left.

2. On the Miscellaneous tab, check (or uncheck) Tooltips On/Off (**Figure 3.13**).

3. Click OK.

To restore the window defaults:

1. With the Configuration Editor open, select Basic Options from the list at the upper left.

2. Click the Reset All Settings to System Defaults and Exit button.

Working with Virtual Desktops

Gnome incorporates the concept of *virtual desktops*. Virtual desktops provide a cheap way to extend the available screen real estate. Each virtual desktop can have many open windows—more than would fit on one desktop.

To navigate among virtual desktops:

1. On the Gnome panel, locate the Virtual desktop console (**Figure 3.14**).

   The console displays a small representation of each desktop with its open windows.

2. Click the representation of a desktop to open that virtual desktop *or* use the mouse to move off the current screen to the next virtual desktop.

Eliminating virtual desktops

If virtual desktops disturb you, you might want to eliminate all but one of them. **Note:** There's a small but noticeable performance drop when you run multiple desktops.

To eliminate all but one desktop:

1. Use the Gnome Control panel to open the Configuration Editor in the Window Manager pane.

2. With the Configuration Editor open, select Desktops from the list at the upper left.

3. Use the thumbs of the slider to indicate that you want a 1×1×1 desktop (**Figure 3.15**).

4. Click OK.

To enable multiple desktops:

1. With the Configuration Editor open, select Desktops from the list at the upper left.

2. Use the thumbs of the slider to indicate the number and positioning of the multiple desktops you want (**Figure 3.16**).

3. Click OK.

Virtual desktop console

Figure 3.14 You can navigate between virtual desktops using the Virtual desktop console on the Gnome panel.

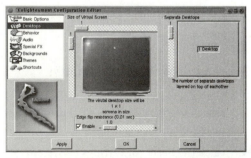

Figure 3.15 Use the sliders to eliminate multiple desktops.

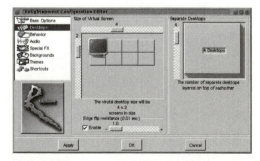

Figure 3.16 You can use the sliders to determine the number and positioning of virtual desktops.

Figure 3.17 Check GNOME Sound Support to enable sound.

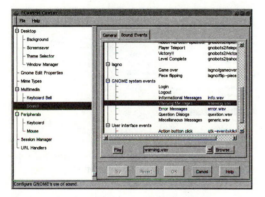

Figure 3.18 Using the Gnome Control Center, you can associate sounds with events.

Using Multimedia

You can use the Gnome Control Center to enable and configure multimedia support.

To enable sound support:

1. In the Gnome Control Center, double-click Multimedia in the list at the left. This expands the category.

2. Choose Sound, beneath Multimedia. The Sound panel will appear (**Figure 3.17**).

3. Select GNOME Sound Support to enable sound.

4. Click OK.

To associate sounds with events:

1. In the Gnome Control Center, double-click Multimedia in the list at the left. This expands the category.

2. Choose Sound, beneath Multimedia. The Sound panel will appear (**Figure 3.17**).

3. Select Sound for Events.

4. Choose the Sound Events tab. A window listing events and the associated sounds will open (**Figure 3.18**).

5. To associate an event with a sound, highlight the event.

6. Click the Browse button to find the sound file.

7. To play the sound, click the Play button.

8. When you are satisfied with your choices, click OK.

USING MULTIMEDIA

Using Peripherals

It's easy to change your keyboard and mouse settings with the Gnome Control Center.

To change your keyboard settings:

1. In the Gnome Control Center, double-click Peripherals in the list at the left. This expands the category.

2. Choose Keyboard, beneath Peripherals. The Keyboard panel will appear (**Figure 3.19**).

3. Make the changes you'd like to your keyboard settings.

4. Click OK to save the configuration.

To change your mouse settings:

1. In the Gnome Control Center, double-click Peripherals in the list at the left. This expands the category.

2. Choose Mouse, beneath Peripherals. The Mouse panel will appear (**Figure 3.20**).

3. Make the changes you'd like to your mouse settings.

4. Click OK to save the configuration.

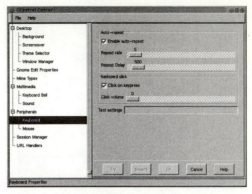

Figure 3.19 Using the Gnome Control Center, you can easily change your keyboard configuration.

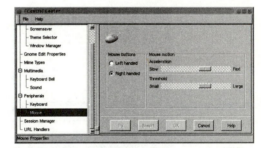

Figure 3.20 Using the Gnome Control Center, you can easily change your mouse configuration.

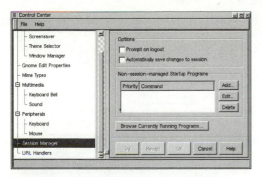

Figure 3.21 The Session Manager panel can be used to change your session settings.

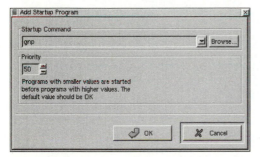

Figure 3.22 You can have a program start automatically by typing its command-line invocation in the Add Startup Program dialog box.

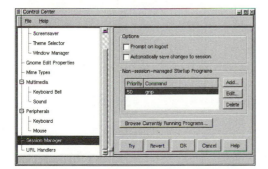

Figure 3.23 Programs that you add to the startup list will appear in the Session Manager panel as Non-Session Managed—meaning that you, rather than Gnome, have told them to start automatically.

Using Session Manager

Using Session Manager, you can control some aspects of the way Gnome handles logon and logoff. In particular, you can tell Gnome to automatically launch particular programs when you start your session.

To open Session Manager:

In the Gnome Control Center, select Session Manager from the list on the left. The Session Manager panel will appear on the right (**Figure 3.21**).

To set a program to run automatically and launch when Gnome starts:

1. On the Session Manager panel, click the Add button.

   The Add Startup Program will appear (**Figure 3.22**).

2. Type an executable command in the Startup Command box *or c*lick the Browse button to select an executable program file by browsing.

   For example, you can enter the command **gnp** in the Startup Command box, as shown in **Figure 3.22**, to start the gnotepad+ application.

3. Assign a priority to the program by using the up and down arrows beside the Priority box.

   The lower the priority number, the earlier the program will launch in the startup process.

4. Click OK to close the Add Startup Program dialog box.

   When it closes, the program you added will appear in the Session Manager panel (**Figure 3.23**).

5. Click OK to set the program to automatically launch at startup

To view the priorities of currently running programs:

With the Session Manager panel open, click the Browse Currently Running Programs button. The Session Manager Properties dialog box will open (**Figure 3.24**).

✔ Tip

■ You can use the Session Manager Properties dialog box to change the priority or to close currently running programs.

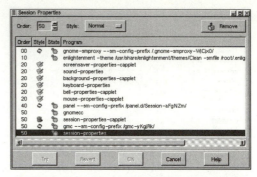

Figure 3.24 You can use the Session Properties dialog box to review and edit program launch priorities.

Figure 3.25 The Desktop Switcher tool can be used to change to a new desktop environment.

Switching Desktop Environments

Red Hat Linux 6 ships with several desktop environments—also called X-Window *shells*—besides Gnome. These desktop environments are actually programs written to run on top of the older, command-line Linux. They launch automatically when Linux starts. By and large, you won't know that Linux is running under the shell, any more than Microsoft Windows users know that DOS is running. In addition, with the release of Red Hat Linux 6, so many features are built into the Gnome desktop environment that you may not ever need to leave the graphical environment.

Gnome is the default desktop environment and the one that Red Hat Linux 6 automatically activates. It is also clearly an extremely rich and robust visual environment. However, you may want to explore the offerings of the other desktop environments that are installed with Red Hat Linux 6: the K Desktop Environment (KDE) and Another Level. You may also switch to another environment by mistake and then want to get back to Gnome. This section explains how to switch among desktop environments.

To switch desktops:

1. Select the Desktop Switching tool from the System menu on the Gnome Main menu.

   The Desktop Switcher will open (**Figure 3.25**).

2. Select the desktop you want to switch to: for example, KDE.

(Continued...)

3. If you want the change to become permanent—for example, if you want this desktop to appear each time you start Red Hat Linux 6—uncheck the Change Only Applies to Current Display check box. If you want to change the desktop for only the current session, put a check in the check box.

4. Click OK.

   Your desktop environment will change to reflect your choice.

To switch back to Gnome:

1. Log off of the current shell *or* reboot the computer.

2. At the main Red Hat logon screen (**Figure 3.26**), click the Options button.

3. From the Session menu, select Gnome.

4. Log on normally.

✔ Tip

■ You can use the Desktop Switcher tool to make Gnome your default desktop environment, if this setting has been changed.

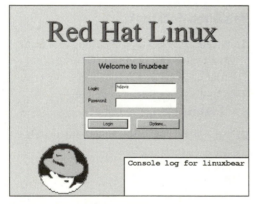

Figure 3.26 You can start up a desktop environment by clicking Options on the Red Hat logon screen and selecting the desktop environment from the Sessions menu.

Booting to the command line

Of course, there are those among us who do not like visual desktops. With Red Hat Linux 6, you can configure your system to simply boot to the command prompt.

To boot to the command prompt directly:

1. Log on as root by typing `root` for the logon ID and the root password at the Red Hat Linux 6 log on screen; *or* open a terminal window, type `su root` at the command prompt, and enter the root password.

2. If you are logged on as root, select Control Panel from the System menu on the Gnome Main menu; *or* in the open terminal window, type `control-panel`.

   The control panel will open (**Figure 3.27**).

3. Open the System Configuration applet by clicking the button that displays an orchestra conductor (fourth button from the left in **Figure 3.27**).

   The Gnome Linux Configuration applet will open (**Figure 3.28**).

4. Scroll down the list on the left side to Miscellaneous services.

5. Double-click Miscellaneous Services to expand the category.

6. Select Initial System Services.

Figure 3.27 The System Configuration applet can be launched from the control panel by clicking the button with the icon of a conductor.

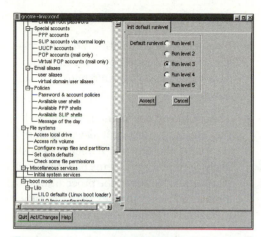

Figure 3.28 To set your system to boot to the command line only, set the initial default run level to run level 3.

7. On the right side, change the initial default run level from run level 5 to run level 3.

8. Click the Accept button.

9. Click Save Changes.

10. Click Quit.

11. Reboot your computer.

    It will boot to the Linux command prompt.

To start Gnome from the command prompt:

At the command prompt, type `startx`.

To restore booting to a visual environment:

Once you have started Gnome, follow the procedure outlined in "To boot to the command prompt directly." Set the initial default run level to run level 6.

Linux run levels

Linux run levels are used to determine what activities can or should be taking place. Here are some more specifics:

Run level 0   When the system enters this run level, the system shutdown sequence is initiated. This sequence includes killing all processes, turning off virtual memory, cleaning up swap files, and unmounting file systems.

Run level 1   A single-user administrative state used for performing low-level maintenance. No one besides the administrator can log on or off.

Run level 2   Simple multiuser state, with networking enabled but with the file system disabled.

Run level 3   The default command-line run state, with all services, including remote file sharing, enabled.

Run level 4   A user-configurable run level that, in theory, you can set up to selectively stop or start processes.

Run level 5   The default run state in Red Hat Linux 6. All run level 3 services are enabled, with the addition of the X-window server.

SWITCHING DESKTOP ENVIRONMENTS

Rebooting and Shutting Down

You can shut down or reboot your system in many different ways. Everyone should know more than one way to turn off (or reboot) the computer.

To reboot or shut down using Log Out:

1. Select Log Out from the Gnome main menu.
   The Red Hat Linux logon screen will open.

2. Click the Options button.

3. Choose Reboot or Halt from the System menu.

✔ Tip

- Whatever method you use to shut down your system, make sure the powering-down sequence has completed before you turn off the power. You will know the sequence is complete when the message "Power down" appears on the screen.

To reboot using a terminal window:

1. Open a terminal window.

2. At the Linux prompt, enter **shutdown -r now** or enter **reboot**.

To shut down using a terminal window:

1. Open a terminal window.

2. At the Linux prompt, enter **shutdown -h now** or enter **halt**.

✔ Tips

- If you are logged on without root permission, you will be prompted for the root password before you can reboot or shut down.

- The shutdown command is considered the safest and most genteel way to initiate a Unix shutdown or reboot. It is least likely to produce problems next time you start Linux. However, the procedure is longer and more complex than the rather quick and dirty halt or reboot.

- For more information on shutdown command options, see Appendix A.

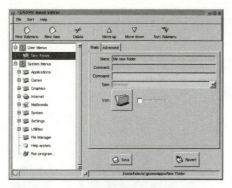

Figure 3.29 The Gnome Menu Editor is used to add folders and items to the main menu.

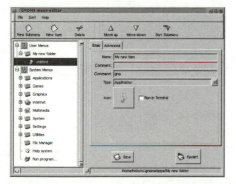

Figure 3.30 Once you have created a folder, you can add a new item to it by clicking the New Item button.

Figure 3.31 The folders and items you have added will appear on the Gnome main menu.

Using the Menu Editor

The Gnome Menu Editor enables you to add folders and menu items to the Gnome main menu.

To add a folder to the main menu:

1. Select Menu Editor from the Settings menu on the Gnome main menu.
   The Menu Editor will open (**Figure 3.29**).

2. In the left pane, highlight User Menus.

3. Click the New Submenu button on the toolbar.

4. Enter a name for the new folder in the Name box.

5. Click Save.

✔ Tip

■ Unless you are logged on as root, you will only be able to edit the user menus that apply to your session. These are located beneath User Menus in the left pane. In addition to these menus, the root user can add or modify system menus—those located below System Menus in the tree.

To add an item to a menu:

1. With the menu folder selected in the left pane of the Menu Editor, click the New Item button on the toolbar (**Figure 3.30**).

2. Enter a name for the item in the Name box.

3. Click Save.
   The new menu item will appear on your Gnome main menu (**Figure 3.31**).

Configuring File Manager

The Gnome File Manager—also known as Midnight Commander—can be used to inspect folders and files and to perform operations on them.

To open File Manager:

Select File Manager from the Gnome main menu. The Midnight Commander File Manager will open.

To edit File Manager preferences:

1. With File Manager open, select Preferences from the Edit menu.

    The File Display tab will open (**Figure 3.32**).

2. Make the changes you want and then click Apply or OK.

To change the columns displayed in File Manager:

1. With the Preferences dialog box open, choose the Custom View tab.

    The Custom View tab displays available columns on the left and displayed columns on the right. (**Figure 3.33**).

2. Make changes to the columns displayed by selecting a column and clicking the Add or Remove button.

3. Click Apply or OK to save your changes.

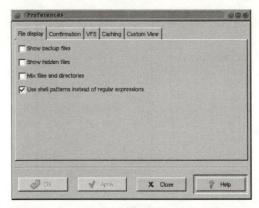

Figure 3.32 Use the File Manager Preferences dialog box to set the way you view files.

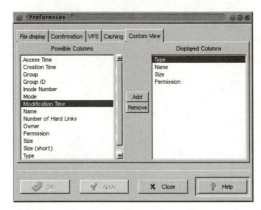

Figure 3.33 The Custom View tab is used to control the columns that are displayed in File Manager.

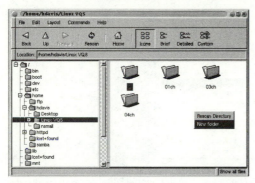

Figure 3.34 To create a new folder, right-click and choose New Folder.

To add a new folder:

1. With File Manager open, select the folder to which you want to add a new folder (**Figure 3.34**).

2. Right-click the right pane and select New Folder from the pop-up menu.

3. Enter a name for the new folder when you are prompted.

4. Click OK.

5. To set the folder's properties, right-click the new folder and select Properties from the pop-up menu.

✔ Tip

■ Folders and directories are the same thing.

Choosing an Editor

Gnome gives you a great many options for your default editor. The out-of-the-box setting is Emacs, but other popular choices include:

◆ xEmacs, an X-Windows version of Emacs

◆ vi, which is often used because it is available on almost every variant of Unix

To set the Gnome editor:

1. Select Gnome Edit Properties from the Settings menu on the Gnome main menu.

   The Gnome Editor panel will open (**Figure 3.35**).

2. Select the editor you want to use from the drop-down list.

3. Click OK.

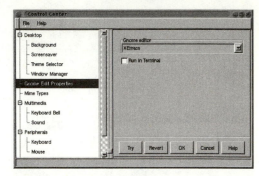

Figure 3.35 Use the Gnome Editor panel to choose the default editor you want to use.

Figure 3.36 The Gnome Panel (in corner mode).

Figure 3.37 The Panel Properties dialog box.

Setting the Panel Properties

The Gnome Panel (**Figure 3.36**) is in many ways command central for the Ret Hat Linux Gnome desktop environment. The Gnome Panel is used to launch the Gnome main menu, control virtual desktops, launch Netscape, and much more.

As you'd expect, it is very configurable. For one thing, there is no telling where this panel will show up. It can be positioned along the top or bottom or on either side of the screen. In addition, it can be set to run the entire length of the screen (an *edge* panel), or it can be made to sit in the corner (a *corner* panel).

Some panel properties change only a particular panel, while others change all of a user's panels.

To set this panel's properties:

1. Right-click the panel.

2. Select This Panel Properties from the pop-up menu.

   The Panel Properties dialog box will open (**Figure 3.37**).

3. Make the changes you'd like.

4. Click OK.

To set properties for all panels:

1. Right-click the panel.

2. Select Global Properties from the pop-up menu.

   The Panel Properties dialog box will open (**Figure 3.38**).

3. Make the changes you'd like.

4. Click OK.

✔ Tip

■ Changing global properties will change the panel in all sessions, not just the current user's session. Of course, this requires appropriate permissions.

To change a corner panel to an edge panel:

1. Right-click the panel.

2. Select Convert to Edge Panel from the pop-up menu.

To change an edge panel to a corner panel:

1. Right-click the panel.

2. Select Convert to Corner Panel from the pop-up menu.

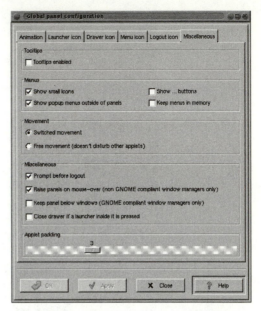

Figure 3.38 The Global Panel Properties dialog box.

SETTING THE PANEL PROPERTIES

Figure 3.39 GnoRPM displays the available packages.

Using GnoRPM

One of the main features that distinguishes Red Hat Linux 6 from other versions of Linux that incorporate the Linux 2.2 kernel is the inclusion of Red Hat Package Manager (RPM).

Red Hat has developed RPM as a standardized way to distribute, install, and upgrade Linux software, or *packages*.

GnoRPM is the version of RPM that runs under the Gnome desktop environment. If you plan to install any programs that were not installed with the original CD, or to upgrade any programs, you will be using GnoRPM.

✔ Tip

■ An available package is a package that is ready to be installed. Availability of a package does not mean that the package has been installed. Also, the package file is different from the binary it contains, which may have its own installation script once it has been unpackaged.

To list available packages:

1. Select GnoRPM from the System menu on the Gnome main menu.

2. Select a folder in the left pane.

   The packages in that folder are listed in the right pane (**Figure 3.39**).

Querying a package

The way to discover what is in a package is to query the package.

To query a package:

1. Select a package in the right pane of GnoRPM.

2. Click the Query button on the GnoRPM toolbar.

   The Package Info window will open, displaying information about the contents of the package (**Figure 3.40**).

Verifying a package

You may want to check that the files in a package have not been corrupted and that the package contains all necessary dependencies. To check this, you will need to verify the package.

To verify a package:

With a package selected in GnoRPM, click the Verify button; or with the Package Info window open, click the Verify button.

The Verify Packages window will scan the package and then open (**Figure 3.41**). If there are no error messages or warnings in the window, then the package has been verified.

To install a package from a CD:

1. Open a Linux telnet window or access the Linux command-line prompt. If you don't have root (or superuser) privileges, su to root by typing `su root`.

2. Supply the root password when it is requested.

3. Place the CD in its drive and mount it by entering `mount /dev/cdrom /mnt` at the prompt.

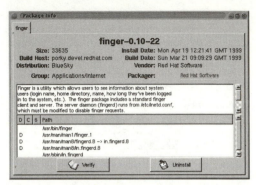

Figure 3.40 Package Info usually includes a description and other useful information about a package.

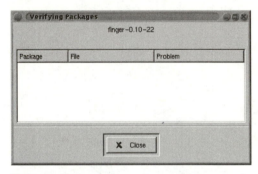

Figure 3.41 If no error messages or warnings appear in the Verifying Packages dialog box, then the packages have been verified.

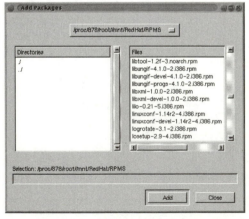

Figure 3.42 To add a package to the install list, select it and click the Add button.

Figure 3.43 Packages that have been added and are ready to install will appear in the Install dialog.

Figure 3.44 RPMfind allows you to install packages over the Web.

Figure 3.45 When you select an available package over the Web, the package information will be displayed.

4. With GnoRPM open, click the Install button.

The Install dialog box will open.

5. Click the Add button.

The Add Packages dialog box will open (**Figure 3.42**).

6. Find and select the package you want to install (**Figure 3.43**).

7. Click the Add button.

The package will be added to the Add Packages dialog box.

✔ Tip

■ The default location for packages on CDs distributed by Red Hat is //mnt/Redhat/ RPMS.

To install a package from the Web:

1. With GnoRPM open, click the Web Find button.

The RPMfind dialog box will open with no contents listed (**Figure 3.44**).

2. Pass the mouse over the area to the right of the URL label until a button appears.

3. Click the button.

The list of packages available over the Web from Red Hat will appear.

4. Select a package to obtain information about it (**Figure 3.45**).

5. To install the package, click the Install button.

✔ Tip

■ Don't try this without a broadband (read: very fast) connection to the Web. Otherwise, this process may take a while!

Summary

In this chapter, you learned how to:

◆ Use the Gnome Control Center.

◆ Work with virtual desktops.

◆ Add sound to your window events.

◆ Set a program to start automatically.

◆ Switch desktop environments.

◆ Switch to a command-line boot.

◆ Reboot and shut down Linux and Gnome.

◆ Use the Menu Editor to add folders and items to your Gnome main menu.

◆ Configure the File Manager.

◆ Set a default editor.

◆ Set your Gnome Panel properties.

◆ Use GnoRPM to query and install packages.

EMAIL AND THE WEB

If you are like me, the first thing you'll want to do when you get your new Linux system up and running is to surf the Web. The next thing will be to send and receive email.

Under the Gnome desktop environment, you can run Netscape Messenger to send and receive email. Netscape Communicator or Navigator 4.51 for Linux can be used to browse the Web. These products work the same way—and have the same look and feel—as their counterparts in other visual operating systems, such as Windows. They are automatically installed as part of the standard Red Hat installation.

But before you can use these programs to do these things, you must first configure your system so you are connected to the Internet. In this chapter, I'll show you how to configure a dial-up connection.

If you have a direct LAN connection to the Web (or—the functional equivalent—are connected via a cable modem), you may have already configured the appropriate network settings during the Red Hat installation. However, if you skipped this step during the Red Hat installation, or if you need to make changes to the settings you did enter, I'll show you how to configure your network settings for direct Internet access.

Then you'll launch the Netscape product suite and configure Messenger for incoming mail (by specifying a POP server) and outgoing mail (by specifying a SMTP server).

Becoming Root

Changing system settings, such as the modem or network configurations, generally requires *root* access. Root is the term used for the all-powerful Linux superuser. (For more information on Linux users and privileges, see Chapter 12.)

If you are not logged on as root, you can log off and log back on as root. Or, you can *su*—change your effective user identity—to root.

To su to root:

1. Open a terminal window, either by clicking the terminal icon on the Gnome panel or by choosing Gnome Terminal from the Gnome Utilities menu (**Figure 4.1**).

2. Click in the Terminal window, so that it has the focus of keyboard entries.

3. With the terminal window open, type **s u root** at the prompt.

4. Enter the root password at the prompt. You'll see at the next prompt that you are effectively logged on as root (**Figure 4.1**).

✔ Tip

■ It's better practice to log on with your own identity and su to root, rather than logging on as root, even if you are the only user of your Linux machine. (For instructions on creating your own identity as part of your initial installation, see Chapter 1.) The main reason for getting in the habit of logging on with your identity and using su to change to root access, if necessary, is to save you from yourself—you are less likely to inadvertently make changes to the system that you will regret later. In addition, this approach is preferable for security reasons, particularly if you are logging on remotely.

Figure 4.1 Use a terminal window to su to root, giving yourself the privileges of a system administrator.

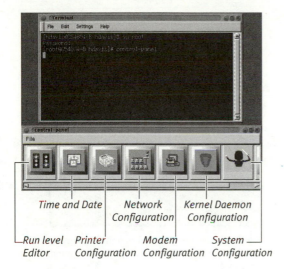

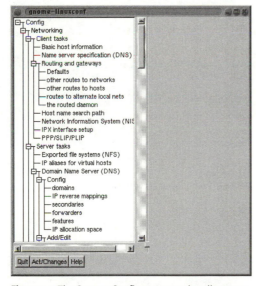

Time and Date   Network   Kernel Daemon
Configuration   Configuration

Run level   Printer   Modem   System
Editor   Configuration Configuration Configuration

Figure 4.2 The Gnome control panel allows you to configure most system settings.

Figure 4.3 The System Configurator applet allows you to edit most settings, but it is more complicated to use than individual applets.

Configuring Your System with Control Panel

The Gnome control panel is used to configure most aspects of your system. Each button on the control panel opens a different configuration applet (**Figure 4.2**). This control panel functions in much the same way as the Windows control panel.

The configuration applets include the following:

◆ Printer Configurator

◆ Network Configurator

◆ Modem Configurator

◆ System Configurator

To open the control panel:

With the terminal window still open, and while you are still logged on as root (**Figure 4.2**), enter `control-panel` at the terminal prompt.

✔ Tip

■ The System Configurator applet (**Figure 4.3**) presents a hierarchical window that allows you to change many settings, including those that can be changed by the Network and Modem Configurator applets. However, the separate applets are easier to work with.

Configuring a Modem

If you are going to connect to the Internet using a modem that works over phone lines, sometimes called a *dial-up adapter*, you have to tell Linux what serial port your modem is connected to. You also have to set various network configuration settings. Your Internet service provider (ISP) should supply these. It's a good idea to make sure you have all the configuration information supplied by your ISP before you try to enter your settings in Linux.

To choose a serial port:

1. Open the Modem Configurator applet (**Figure 4.4**).

2. Select the serial port your modem is connected to.

3. Click OK to close the dialog box.

✔ Tips

■ For information on using Windows to determine your hardware settings before you install Linux, see Chapter 1.

■ The default—and most usual—serial port for a modem is com 2. The Linux device name for com 2 is ttyS1.

■ If all else fails, use trial and error. After all, there are only four possible settings.

■ You'll know you have the right serial port—after you have entered the other network settings—if you hear a dial tone and the modem starts to dial when you turn on networking. I'll explain this and show you how to test your connection to the Internet later in this chapter.

To enter DNS information:

1. Open the Network Configurator applet.

2. Select the Names tab (**Figure 4.5**).

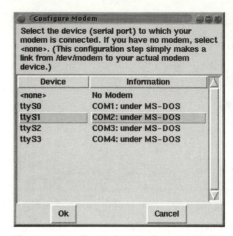

Figure 4.4 Use the Modem Configurator Applet to tell your system what serial port your modem is connected to.

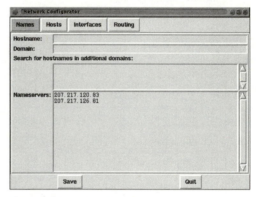

Figure 4.5 Enter the DNS information provided by your ISP in the Nameservers box.

CONFIGURING A MODEM

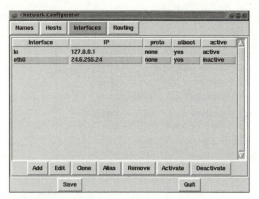

Figure 4.6 The Interfaces tab of the Network Configurator dialog box is used to add and modify network connections.

Figure 4.7 Use the Interface Type dialog box to select the type of network interface.

3. Type the tuplets (series of numbers) provided by your ISP in the Nameservers box.

4. Click Save to close the dialog box.

✔ Tips

■ Domain name servers (DNSs) are used to look up locations on the Internet based on text the URL supplied. Locations on the Internet are indicated by a series of four numbers, called a *tuplet*. For example, **www.bearhome.com** translates (or *resolves*) to 204.0.134.135.

■ The tuplets entered on the Names tab of the Network Configurator applet are used to tell your system where to look for DNS *resolution*—in other words, the translation of text URLs to physical tuplets.

■ Generally, your ISP will supply a primary and a secondary DNS tuplet. Enter the primary DNS tuplet in the Nameservers box above the secondary tuplet.

■ To find this information if it has been entered on a Windows computer, right-click on the Network Neighborhood icon and select Properties. On the Configuration tab, select the TCP/IP component that you use to access the Internet. Choose Properties. To read the information, select the DNS Configuration tab of the TCP/IP Properties dialog.

To add a PPP interface:

1. Click the tab to open the Interfaces page of the Network Configurator dialog box (**Figure 4.6**).

2. Click the Add button at the lower left of the Interfaces page.

The Interface Type dialog will open (**Figure 4.7**).

(Continued...)

CONFIGURING A MODEM

3. Select PPP and click OK.

The Create PPP Interface dialog will open (**Figure 4.8**).

4. Enter your ISP's phone number, your user name, and your password in this dialog box.

5. Click Done.

The new PPP Interface will now appear on the Interfaces page (**Figure 4.9**).

6. Use your mouse to highlight the interface (labeled PPP0) and click the Edit button.

7. Enable the Allow Any User to De(Activate) Interface setting (**Figure 4.10**).

This allows any user—not just root—to dial and hang up.

8. Click Done.

9. Click Save on the Interfaces page (**Figure 4.9**).

To dial your ISP:

1. Open a Terminal window (**Figure 4.11**).

2. Enter the following at the prompt:
`/sbin/ifup ppp0`

If all is well, you should hear your modem dialing, following by the connection tones.

To check the connection:

With the terminal window still open (**Figure 4.11**), enter the following command to attempt to communicate with an important domain at Compaq computers:

`ping gatekeeper.dec.com`

You should receive a series of reply messages with the time of a round-trip journey to the computer you are pinging (**Figure 4.11**). If you receive a message back, it verifies that the two computers can communicate.

Figure 4.8 Your ISP phone number and identification information should be entered in the Create PPP Interface dialog box.

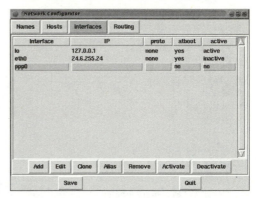

Figure 4.9 Once a new interface has been added, you can edit its properties using the Interfaces tab.

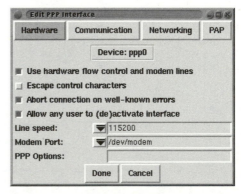

Figure 4.10 It's a good idea to allow any user—not just root—to activate and deactivate the network connection.

Figure 4.11 Use a terminal window to enter the commands to dial up your ISP, test the connection, and disconnect.

✔ Tip

- You can ping any computer you want to test your connectivity. For example, enter

  `ping informix.com`

To close the connection:

1. In the terminal window (**Figure 4.11**), type

   `/sbin/ifdown ppp0`

2. Enter the following at the prompt:

   `/sbin/ifup ppp0`

   If all is well, you should hear your modem dialing, following by the connection tones.

To check the connection:

With the terminal window still open (**Figure 4.11**), enter the following command to attempt to communicate with an important domain at Compaq computers:

`ping gatekeeper.dec.com`

You should receive a series of reply messages with the time of a round-trip journey to the computer you are pinging (**Figure 4.11**). If you receive a message back, it verifies that the two computers can communicate.

To close the connection:

In the terminal window (**Figure 4.11**), type
`/sbin/ifdown ppp0`

CONFIGURING A MODEM

Configuring a Direct Connection

If you have a direct—or *broadband*—connection to the Internet, there are a few things you have to configure differently than when you use a dial-up connection.

A broadband connection typically means that you are interfaced with the Internet via a LAN or a cable modem.

There is no reason that you can't have multiple connections: for example, one dial-up connection and one via a LAN.

To add an Ethernet interface:

1. Open the Interfaces page of the Network Configurator applet (**Figure 4.12**).

2. Click Add to add a new interface.

3. Select Ethernet from the Interface Type dialog box (**Figure 4.13**).

4. Click OK.
   The Edit Ethernet/Bus Interface dialog will open (**Figure 4.14**).

5. Enter the IP for your machine and the netmask that should be used. Enable the Activate Interface at Boot Time option if you want Internet access to automatically be available when you boot up your computer.

6. Click Done.

7. Click Save on the Interfaces page of the Network Configurator applet.

8. Select the Names tab to open the Names page of the Network Configurator (**Figure 4.15**).

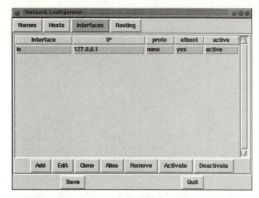

Figure 4.12 Open the Interfaces page of the Configurator to add a direct connection.

Figure 4.13 Select Ethernet as the interface type for a direct connection.

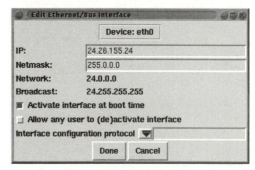

Figure 4.14 You'll need to enter a unique IP for your machine in the Edit Ethernet/Bus Interface dialog box.

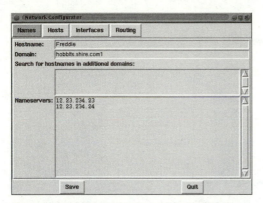

Figure 4.15 Enter your host name, domain, and IP addresses for you name servers on the Names page of the Configurator.

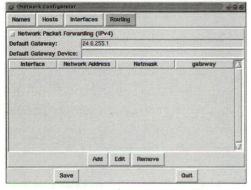

Figure 4.16 Enter your default gateway on the Router page of the Configurator.

9. Enter your host name, domain, and name servers.

10. Click Save.

11. Select the Routing page of the Interface Configurator. Enter the default gateway. (**Figure 4.16**).

12. Click Save.

13. Close the Interface Configurator and reboot your system by entering the following at the command prompt in the terminal window: `shutdown -r now`.

✔ Tips

■ Even though you might think that a cable modem is a modem-style connection, actually the cable modem functions as a gateway between your computer and a network that is connected to the Internet. The cable modem connects to a network card in your computer. Thus, a cable modem connection should be set up as an Ethernet interface.

■ You'll need to enter an Internet protocol (IP) and netmask for your machine, since in a direct connection your computer functions as a node on a TCP/IP network. Your system administrator or cable modem provider should supply this information.

■ Your system administrator or cable modem provider should also supply IP addresses for your name servers, host name, domain, and default gateway.

■ If you need to specify different gateways for different interfaces—as opposed to one default gateway—you can use the Routers page of the Network Configurator to do so.

CONFIGURING A DIRECT CONNECTION

Configuring and Using Netscape Communicator

From here, the process of configuring and launching the Netscape product suite to browse the Web and to send and receive email is the same as in any environment.

To launch the Netscape browser:

1. Select the Netscape icon on the Gnome panel *or* select Netscape Communicator from the Internet folder on the Gnome Start menu.

2. Now you can open any site you'd like. For example, enter `www.peachpit.com` to go to that site (**Figure 4.17**).

To configure the Netscape products:

1. With the Netscape browser open, select Preferences from the Edit menu.

You'll see a hierarchy of options that can be configured (**Figure 4.18**).

2. For example, to configure Navigator's home page, select Navigator from the list on the left and enter the home page on the right (**Figure 4.18**).

To configure Messenger to send and receive mail:

1. With the Netscape Preferences dialog still open, expand Mail and Newsgroups.

2. Scroll down and select Identity on the left-hand menu (**Figure 4.19**).

3. Enter your name and your email address on the right.

4. Select Mail Servers on the left (**Figure 4.20**).

5. Enter the name of your incoming mail server (this is usually a POP server) and the name of your outgoing (SMTP) mail server.

6. Click OK.

Figure 4.17 You can browse any site you like by opening it in Linux Navigator.

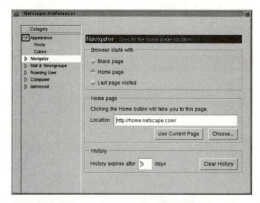

Figure 4.18 The Netscape Preference dialog box is used to configure the Netscape product suite.

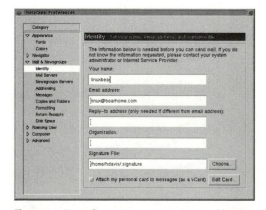

Figure 4.19 To configure Messenger, enter your identity.

To receive email:

1. Select Messenger from the Communicator menu on the browser.

   Netscape Messenger will open (**Figure 4.21**).

2. Click the Get Msg button (**Figure 4.21**).

3. Enter your email password when prompted (**Figure 4.22**).

To send email:

1. With the main Messenger window open, select New Msg (**Figure 4.21**).

   The Compose dialog box will open (**Figure 4.23**).

2. Address and compose your email.

3. Click the Send button.

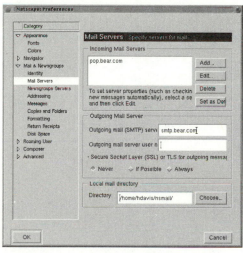

Figure 4.20 You'll need to identify your incoming (POP) mail server and outgoing (SMTP) mail server.

Figure 4.22 When you get your messages, you will be prompted for your email password.

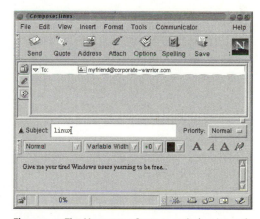

Figure 4.23 The Messenger Compose window is used to create and send email.

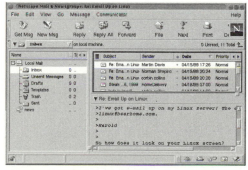

Figure 4.21 The main Netscape Messenger window is used to organize your email.

Summary

In this chapter, you learned how to:

◆ Change your effective identity to root (using su).

◆ Use the Gnome control panel.

◆ Configure a modem.

◆ Add a PPP interface.

◆ Configure a direct connection.

◆ Add an Ethernet interface.

◆ Configure Netscape Communicator

◆ Use Netscape Messenger to send and receive email.

LINUX DOCUMENTATION

5

Red Hat Linux 6 and the Gnome desktop combine to make an immensely rich, powerful, and complex operating environment. Although many of its features are intuitively easy to use, undoubtedly at some point you will need to find documentation.

There is good news and bad news regarding Gnome and Linux documentation. The goods news is that vast archives of information are available, covering almost any topic on which you are likely to want help.

The bad news is that this documentation is disorganized. It was written by many people all over the world, most of whom volunteered. It is not standard in form or content. There is no central mechanism for accessing all of it.

This chapter provides an overview of the various kinds of documentation that are available to you. I'll also show you some techniques for quickly uncovering the specific information that you need.

Applications and Help

Often, you will need help with a specific application. Your need for help may range from wanting to understand the concepts behind an application to wanting to know how to use a particular feature.

Most applications that run on the Gnome desktop provide an HTML help file that runs in a Netscape browser window.

To access Help in an application:

1. Open the application: for example, GnoRPM.

2. Choose an item—other than About— from the Help menu.

   The application's Help file will open in a Netscape window (**Figure 5.1**).

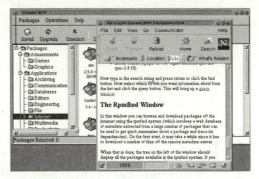

Figure 5.1 To open an application's Help system, choose an item from the Help menu.

Figure 5.2 The Index page is used to navigate the Gnome Help Browser.

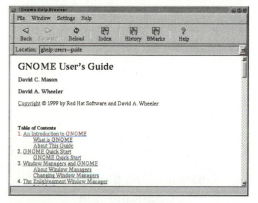

Figure 5.3 The Gnome User's Guide provides detailed instructions on configuring Gnome.

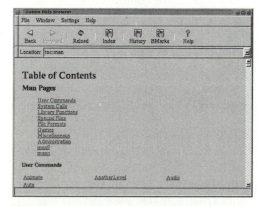

Figure 5.4 As an alternative to using the command line, you can find the Man pages for commands using the Gnome Help Browser.

The Gnome Help Browser

The Gnome Help Browser is distinct from the individual Help files supplied with applications. It contains a great deal of information about Gnome.

The Gnome Help Browser is an application itself; it can be thought of as an interface to the various kinds of documentation on your computer and on the Web.

To open the Gnome User's Guide:

1. Click the Gnome Help Browser button on the Gnome Panel (it is the second button from the left; its icon is a question mark).

   The Gnome Help Browser will open with its Index page loaded (**Figure 5.2**).

2. With the mouse, choose the Gnome User's Guide link.

   The table of contents for the Gnome User's Guide will open (**Figure 5.3**).

Man pages

Man pages are manual pages that describe specific Linux commands.

To open Man pages:

1. Click the Gnome Help Browser button on the panel.

   The Gnome Help Browser will open with its Index page loaded.

2. Select the Man Pages link.

   The Man pages table of contents will open (**Figure 5.4**).

THE GNOME HELP BROWSER

Info pages

Info pages contain more general, conceptual information than Man pages.

To open Info pages:

1. Click the Gnome Help Browser button on the panel.

   The Gnome Help Browser will open with its Index page loaded.

2. Select the Info Pages link.

   The Info pages table of contents will open.

3. Choose a specific item: for example, bash.

   The Info Page for that item will open (**Figure 5.5**).

Gnome Documents

Gnome Documents are usually fairly comprehensive discussions of entire applications. Sometimes they are the text used in an application's Help system.

To open Gnome Documents:

1. Click the Gnome Help Browser button on the panel.

   The Gnome Help Browser will open with its Index page loaded.

2. Select the Gnome Documents link.

   The Gnome Documents table of contents will open.

Figure 5.5 Info pages contain conceptual information about specific topics.

Opening Man pages at the command line

You may find it more convenient to view Man pages at the command line, rather than in the Gnome Help Browser. At the command line, you can get the information you need directly without having to drill down through a table of contents.

To open a Man page, at the Linux prompt enter **man** followed by the name of the command. For example, to view the syntax for the shutdown command, enter **man shutdown**. Of course you could also use the man command to find out more about working with man: **man man**. To quit a man command-line documentation screen and return to your prompt, type **q**.

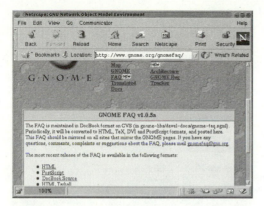

Figure 5.6 To view the FAQ in your browser, select the HTML format.

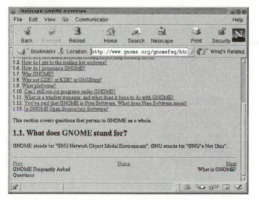

Figure 5.7 The Gnome FAQ contains a great deal of useful and interesting information.

Finding Information on the Web

Many good sources of information about Linux and Gnome are available on the Web. Red Hat and the Gnome Project sponsor some of these.

The trick, of course, is finding the information that *you* need.

To open Gnome frequently asked questions (FAQ):

1. Open your Netscape browser.

2. In the location box, type

   `http://www.gnome.org/`

3. Press Enter.

   If you are connected, the Gnome Web site will open.

4. Select the FAQ link.

   A menu of choices regarding the FAQ format will open (**Figure 5.6**).

5. Select the HTML link to view the FAQ in your browser.

   The FAQ page will open in your browser (**Figure 5.7**).

✔ Tip

■ The default Gnome installation places an icon linked to the Gnome Web site on your desktop. Clicking the icon opens your browser with the Gnome site loaded.

To open the Red Hat Knowledge Base:

1. Open your Netscape browser.

2. In the location box, type
   `http://www.redhat.com`

3. Press Enter.

4. If you are connected, the Red Hat Web site will open.

5. Select the Knowledge Base link at the left of the Web page (**Figure 5.8**).

✔ Tip

■ The default Gnome installation places an icon linked to the Red Hat Web site on your desktop. Clicking the icon opens your browser with the Red Hat site loaded.

To search for a specific topic:

1. With the Red Hat Web site open, enter a topic in the search box at the lower left of the site (**Figure 5.9**)

2. Select an option to search just the Red Hat site or all Linux sites.

3. Click the Go button.

   Items that relate your topic will be served back to your browser (**Figure 5.10**).

To access the Red Hat support site:

1. Open your Netscape browser.

2. In the location box, type
   `http://support.redhat.com`

3 Press Enter.

   If you are connected, the Red Hat Web site will open.

✔ Tip

■ The default Gnome installation places an icon linked to the Red Hat support Web site on your desktop. Clicking the icon opens your browser with the Red Hat support site loaded.

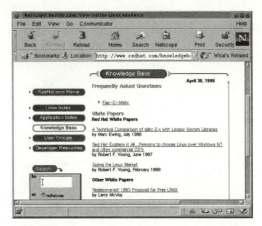

Figure 5.8 The Red Hat Knowledge Base is a useful resource.

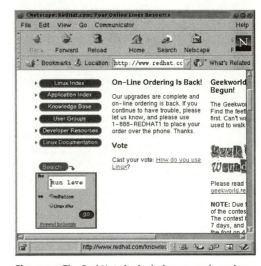

Figure 5.9 The Red Hat site includes a search engine.

Figure 5.10 The search engine returns topics on the Red Hat site, or on Linux sites in general.

Figure 5.11 The Red Hat Errata page explains problems and fixes that became known after a product's release.

Red Hat errata

Errata is information about known errors in programs or its documentation that come to light after the program is released.

To view Red Hat errata:

With the main Red Hat support page open, select the Product Updates, Fixes and Errata link. The Errata page will open (Figure **5.11**).

The Linux Document Project

The Linux Document Project is an attempt to provide comprehensive Linux documentation. It is hosted on mirrored sites throughout the world.

To open the Linux Document Project site:

1. Open your Netscape browser.

2. In the location box, type

   ```
   http://www.redhat.com/
   mirrors/LDP/
   ```

3. Press Enter.

   If you are connected, the Red Hat Web site will open.

✔ Tip

■ The default Gnome installation places an icon linked to the Linux Document Project on your desktop.

To open the Linux HOWTO Index:

1. With the main Linux Document Project window open, click the HOWTO link.

   The next page will list the possible formats for the HOWTO information.

2. Select the HTML link.

   The HOWTO Index page will open (**Figure 5.12**).

Figure 5.12 The Linux HOWTO Index page provides a convenient way to get practical answers to many questions.

Summary

In this chapter, you learned how to:

- Get help in an application.

- Open the Gnome User's Guide.

- Open Man pages.

- Open Info pages.

- Open Gnome Documents.

- Access the Gnome FAQ.

- Open the Red Hat Knowledge Base.

- Search the Red Hat and other Linux sites for information.

- Access the Red Hat support site.

- Access the Red Hat Errata page.

- Access the Linux Document Project site.

- Open the Linux HOWTO Index.

SUMMARY

Part 2
Doing Windows
in Red Hat Linux 6

Red Hat Linux 6 does windows—with a small 'w'. The Gnome desktop environment is a world-class windowing environment. Using Gnome, you can have your windows any way you'd like them—even mimicking the look and feel of Windows 98 if that is your pleasure. And Gnome is not the only desktop environment available with Red Hat Linux 6.

Now that top-of-the-line applications such as Corel's WordPerfect for Linux are available, there's no reason not to make Red Hat Linux your personal platform of choice.

Chapter 6: Desktop Environments explains the concept of multiple windowing environments, and how to switch between them. You'll also learn how to use the initial log on screen options.

Chapter 7: Gnome Applications provides a guided tour of the powerful suite of applications that ship with the Gnome desktop.

Chapter 8: WordPerfect for Linux tells you how to obtain and install WordPerfect, and how to use some of its sophisticated features.

Chapter 9: Doing the Database Thing provides an introduction to working with the PostgreSQL database server that ships with Red Hat Linux 6.

Part 2
Doing Windows in
Red Hat Linux 6

DESKTOP ENVIRONMENTS

Chapter 3, "Configuring Gnome," explained how to configure the Gnome desktop environment to suit your personal preferences. In this chapter, you'll learn about the two alternative desktop environments that also ship with Red Hat Linux 6:

◆ Another Level

◆ K Desktop Environment (KDE)

This chapter begins with a discussion of the Red Hat Linux logon screen options. Next, you'll learn how to configure the alternative desktop environments to suit your desires. I'll then show you how to use come of the applications that ship with these environments, and how to access alternative environments using menus within the default environment, Gnome.

Finally, I'll show you how to handle some important administration tasks—configuring users, groups, and permissions—from within a visual environment using the Gnome control panel.

Alternative Desktop Environments

Why do these alternative desktop environments exist? Why would you want to use them? And what does the "K" in KDE stand for?

The answer to the first question is that the world of Linux—unlike the world of Microsoft Windows—is a free and open environment. Alternative desktop environments exist because a person, or group of people, decided to create them. And they are maintained in a similar fashion.

For more information about KDE, you can visit the K Desktop Environment home page at **http://www.kde.org**.

You can decide for yourself after reading this chapter whether you are interested in using either KDE or Another Level. I think you'll find compelling reasons to try these alternatives, particularly after you learn about the KOffice suite.

Another reason for using KDE is that it is the shell that shipped with older versions of Linux, so some users may be used to it.

Of course, many things in life come down to the adage: "Because it's there."

As for the "K" in KDE, it stands for absolutely nothing. It would seem to have this in common with the stripped-down automobile made for a while by Chrysler Motors, the K-Car. So think of the KDE as a stripped-down—but very functional—desktop environment.

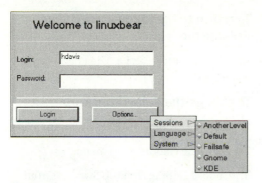

Figure 6.1 You can click Options on the logon screen to select the Session, Language, or System option.

Logon Screen Options

In Red Hat Linux's default configuration, the system boots to a graphical desktop environment. (For more information on how this is configured, see Chapters 1 through 3.) If you've left your system configured this way, when you turn it on, after various processing steps, the Red Hat Linux 6 logon screen will appear.

As its name implies, you use this screen to enter your logon identification and password. In addition, using the fly-out menus that appear when you click the Options button, you can:

◆ Choose a *session*, meaning either a desktop environment or a terminal-like Failsafe command-line mode.

◆ Use the *System menu* to reboot or shut down.

◆ Select the *language* that many of the desktop environment menus and objects—such as buttons—will use.

You should also know that when you log off from a desktop environment, the Red Hat Linux 6 logon screen will appear.

Sessions options

Sessions options determine which shell Red Hat Linux 6 will start with.

To choose a session:

1. When the Red Hat Linux 6 logon screen appears, click the Options button.

   A fly-out menu with the choices Sessions, Languages, and System will appear (**Figure 6.1**).

2. To access the Sessions menu items, pass your mouse over the word Sessions.

   A new fly-out menu with five choices will appear (**Figure 6.1**).

(Continued...)

3. Click the session of your choice.

4. Enter your logon ID.

5. Press the Tab key to move to the Password field.

6. Enter your password.

7. Click OK.

✔ Tips

■ You can enter your logon ID and password either before or after you make selections from the Options menus.

■ Your password will not appear on the screen as you type it.

■ If you choose Failsafe, a command-line interface will open (see the following paragraphs).

■ The default environment is the Gnome desktop environment. (For instructions on changing the default logon session, see "To change the default desktop" later in this chapter.)

Failsafe mode

Failsafe mode is a text-based interface that appears at the bottom right of the logon screen (without the logon box). It allows you to directly enter Linux commands at the prompt.

Because X-Windows servers do not need to operate for Failsafe mode to work, if your system gets as far as the logon screen, it is almost certain that Failsafe mode will start. Thus, if your computer won't boot into a windows environment, but you can get your computer as far as the logon screen, Failsafe mode can be used to debug the problem.

Of course, you may never need Failsafe mode. But, if you do, for information on working directly with Linux commands, see Chapters 9 through 12 and Appendix A.

To return to the logon screen from Failsafe mode:

At the prompt type `exit`. The Logon screen will reappear.

To change the default desktop:

1. Start the Gnome desktop environment.

2. Open the Gnome main menu.

3. Choose Gnome Desktop Switcher from the System fly-out menu.

   The Desktop Switcher dialog box will open (**Figure 6.2**).

4. Using the radio buttons, select the desktop you want from the Available Desktops list.

5. Make sure the Change Only Applies to Current Display option is not selected.

6. Click OK.

✔ Tip

■ For more information on using the Desktop Switcher, see Chapter 3.

Adding the Desktop Switcher

If you can't find the Desktop Switcher on the System menu, that doesn't mean that the utility hasn't been installed on your system.

If it is present on your system, you can add it to your System menu by following these steps:

◆ Locate the Desktop Switcher's command line invocation.

◆ Use the Menu Editor to add the Desktop Switcher's command-line invocation as an item on the System menu.

Figure 6.2 You can use the Desktop Switcher to set the default desktop by making sure that Change Only Applies to Current Display is not selected.

Figure 6.3 You can use Gnome RPM to see if a particular package was installed.

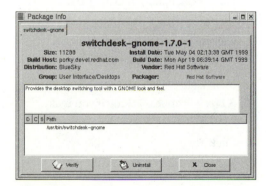

Figure 6.4 The Package Info window will tell you an application's command path.

To verify that Desktop Switcher has been installed if there is no menu item for it:

1. Open the Gnome main menu.

2. Choose GnoRPM from the System fly-out menu.

   The Gnome RPM window will open.

3. Expand the Package hierarchy pane on the left of Gnome RPM so that Desktops (under User Interface) is selected (**Figure 6.3**).

   You will see the installed desktop packages listed in the right pane.

4. Highlight the package labeled switchdesk-gnome.

5. Click the Query button on the Gnome RPM toolbar.

   The Package Info window will open (**Figure 6.4**). Provided that the Desktop Switcher has been installed, the Package Info window will provide a description of the application and the path for the command-line invocation of the application.

6. Make a note of the Desktop Switcher's path: **/usr/bin/switchdesk-gnome**.

7. Click Close to close the Package Info window.

8. Choose Quit from the Gnome RPM Packages menu to close Gnome RPM.

✔ Tips

- Using the command-line invocation for the Desktop Switcher, you can start the Desktop Switcher in a terminal window or in Gnome File Manager, or by adding it to the Gnome main menu as described in the next section.

- For more information on using Gnome RPM, see Chapter 3.

Language options

You can choose a language from the extensive list on the Languages fly-out menu. The language you select is then used to build the text of menu items, dialog boxes, and windows bars. But no matter the language, some desktop environment elements are still displayed in English.

To display the desktop in French:

1. When the Red Hat Linux 6 logon screen appears, click the Options button.

   A fly-out menu with the choices Sessions, Languages, and System will appear.

2. To access the Languages menu items, pass your mouse over the word Languages.

   A new fly-out menu with a long list of languages will appear.

3. Click French.

4. Enter your logon ID.

5. Press the Tab key to move to the Password field.

6. Enter your password.

7. Click OK.

   The desktop environment will appear using French instead of English in many places (**Figure 6.6**).

✔ Tip

■ Once you select a language, it becomes the default language until you select another language.

Figure 6.6 The language you select is used to build your desktop environment.

Using Another Level (Fvwm)

Another Level—also called *Fvwm*—is the simplest and cleanest of the desktop environments that ship with Red Hat Linux 6. It is probably most useful on an older, under-powered machine. On this kind of hardware, you can expect it to perform better than the more fully loaded X-Windows shells (Gnome and KDE — of course, even Gnome goes like the blazes compared to Windows 98 on a 486 box).

A helpful feature of Fvwm is direct menu access to many configuration utilities.

To start Fvwm:

1. Make sure that your system is set to automatically start X-Windows, as explained in Chapters 1 and 2.

2. At the Red Hat Linux logon screen, click Options. From the Sessions fly-out menu, choose Another Level.

3. Enter your ID and password.

4. Click OK.

   The Fvwm desktop environment will start (**Figure 6.7**).

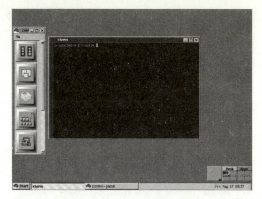

Figure 6.7 Another Level—also known as Fvwm—is the most basic of the desktop environments that ship with Red Hat Linux 6.

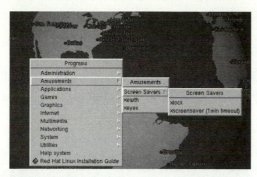

Figure 6.8 The Fvwm Programs menu is opened by right-clicking the desktop.

To access the Fvwm Programs menu:

Right-click with your mouse anywhere on the Fvwm desktop *or* left-click anywhere on the Fvwm desktop and then select Programs from the Fvwm Start menu. The Fvwm Programs menu will appear (**Figure 6.8**).

✔ Tips

■ To access configuration and administration applets, select Administration from the Fvwm Programs menu.

■ The background shown in **Figure 6.8**— which displays Red Hat Software offices at the center of the earth—is started by selecting xearth from the Fvwm Amusements menu.

To exit Fvwm:

1. Click Start at the lower-left of the Fvwm window *or* left-click the Fvwm desktop.

2. From the Fvwm Start menu, select Exit Fvwm.

   The Really Quit Fvwm? fly-out menu will open.

3. Select Yes, Really Quit.

Using the K Desktop Environment

The K Desktop Environment, also called KDE, is somewhere between Fvwm and Gnome. It is not as stripped down as the former, but not as full featured as the latter.

KDE should be familiar to users of earlier versions of Red Hat Linux, because prior to version 6 it was the default X-Windows shell.

If you explore KDE, you'll find quite a few interesting and useful applications and utilities that are not available in the other desktop environments.

To start KDE:

1. Make sure that your system is set to automatically start X-Windows, as explained in Chapters 1 and 2.

2. At the Red Hat Linux logon screen, click Options. On the Sessions fly-out menu, choose KDE.

3. Enter your ID and password.

4. Click OK.

   The K Desktop Environment will start (**Figure 6.9**).

The KDE Control Center

Many aspects of KDE can be configured using the KDE Control Center.

To open the KDE Control Center:

1. Click K at the lower left of the KDE window.

   The K Start menu will open.

2. Select KDE Control Center.

   The KDE Control Center will open (**Figure 6.10**).

3. Choose the feature you want to configure from the expandable list in the left pane.

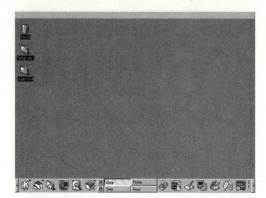

Figure 6.9 KDE is a full-featured windowing environment.

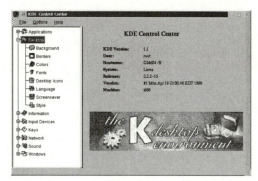

Figure 6.10 Many aspects of KDE can be configured using the KDE Control Center.

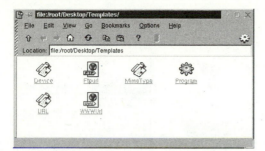

Figure 6.11 KDE file windows serve a dual purpose as Web browsers.

The KOffice suite

The KOffice suite is a full-fledged suite of office software applications created as free software under GNU open licensing arrangements. KOffice is under continual development, meaning that some features and components may not be completely finished. The applications that are part of the KOffice include:

♦ KSpread, a spreadsheet program similar to Excel

♦ KPresenter, a slide presentation program along the lines of Powerpoint

♦ KIllustrator, a drawing program along the lines of CorelDraw

♦ KWord, a word processing program

♦ KDiagramm, a charting and diagramming program

♦ KFormula, a scientific formula editor

To install KOffice:

1. Open a KDE file window.

    KDE file windows function both as file managers and Web browsers. An easy way to open a file window is to double-click the Templates folder which is placed by default on the KDE desktop. If you double-click this folder, a file window will open showing the contents of the folder (**Figure 6.11**).

2. Make sure your computer is connected to the Internet.

3. In the Location text box, type
    `http://koffice.kde.org`

(Continued...)

4. Press Enter.

The KOffice home page will open (**Figure 6.12**).

5. Follow the links at the KOffice site to download via FTP the packages containing the source code for the KOffice applications.

6. Compile the source packages following the instructions located at

`http://koffice.kde.org/`
`install-source.html`

To quit KDE:

1. Click K at the lower left of the KDE window.

The K Start menu will open.

2. Choose Logout.

The Logout window will open.

3. Click Logout.

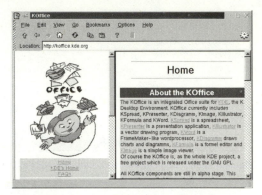

Figure 6.12 You can download the KOffice suite from the KOffice site.

Using Another Level and KDE menus from Gnome

Much of the KDE and Another Level menu system can be accessed from the Gnome desktop environment.

◆ To open Another Level menus, select Another Level menus from the Gnome main menu.

◆ To open KDE menus, select KDE menus from the Gnome main menu.

Setting Up Users and Groups

In Unix systems—including Linux—each file and process (a *process* is an activity started by a program) is *owned*. The owner of a file or process has the primary right to control it. These rights can be overridden only by the superuser, called root.

Each file has both an owner and a *group* owner. These owners can set the *permissions* on a file so that no one else can access it.

You may find it interesting to discover that there are users (and groups of users) on your Linux system who are not human. These include:

◆ *daemon*, which is both an owner and a group of owners of system software processes

◆ *bin*, who often owns the directories that contain system commands and executables

◆ *sys*, whose group members own such things as swap files and memory images

◆ *nobody*, who is the owner of software that doesn't need—or shouldn't have—special permissions

It's standard practice to set up these nonhuman users so that their accounts cannot be logged onto by placing an asterisk in the password field for the account.

Organizing human users in groups helps with the process of ensuring that people have an organized place to store their data, have their own initialization files, and have the right level of access privileges. Users and groups can be configured manually by editing the appropriate configuration files, as I'll show you in Chapter 11.

Fortunately, under Gnome you can add and edit user and group information using the Linux Desktop Configuration tool.

To add a user:

1. Log on as root, *or* su to root following the instructions in Chapter 1.

2. Open the control panel by selecting Control Panel from the System menu fly-out on the Gnome main menu.

3. Click the System Configuration button to open the Linux Configuration tool.

4. Scroll down the hierarchical list in the left pane until you see User Accounts.

5. Click Users to expand the left pane.

6. Select User Accounts under Normal. The Users Accounts tab will open on the right (**Figure 6.13**).

7. Click Add. The User Account Creation tab will open (**Figure 6.14**).

8. At a minimum, you must enter a logon ID and a full name.

9. Right-click the down arrow next to the group box to select a group for the new user from a list of available groups.

10. Click the Privileges tab to display the list of privileges that will be granted to the new user (**Figure 6.15**).

11. Make your selection of privileges.

12. Click OK to accept the new user.

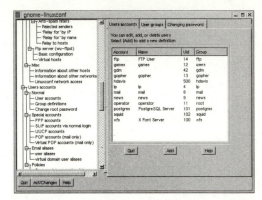

Figure 6.13 The Users Accounts tab is used to add or edit users.

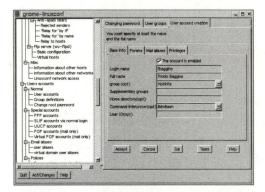

Figure 6.14 The User Account Creation tab is used to specify information for a new user.

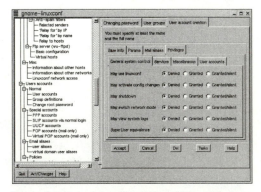

Figure 6.15 You can set the privileges that will be available to a new user on the Privileges tab.

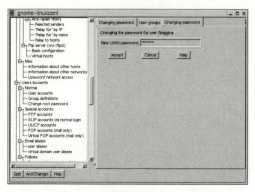

Figure 6.16 You must specify a password for each new user.

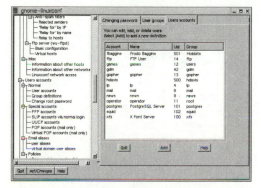

Figure 6.17 Successfully added new users will appear in the list of user accounts.

Figure 6.18 The location of home directories for new users can be established on a per-user or group basis.

13. Click OK.

The Changing Password tab will open (**Figure 6.16**).

14. Enter a password for the new user in the New UNIX Password box.

15. Click OK.

Your new user will now appear in the list of user accounts (**Figure 6.17**).

16. Open File Manager to verify that a home directory has been added for the new user (**Figure 6.18**).

✔ Tips

■ Be very careful about granting root-equivalence privileges on a multiuser system.

■ You can edit user information by clicking the user ID in the User Accounts list.

■ You can specify the location of the home directories for new users, or these can be established on the basis of the group to which a user belongs (see the next section).

SETTING UP USERS AND GROUPS

To add a group:

1. With the Linux Desktop Configuration tool open to User Accounts, select the User Groups tab (**Figure 6.19**).

2. Click Add.

   The Group Specification tab will open (**Figure 6.20**).

3. Enter a name for the group in the Group Name box.

4. Click Directories.

   The Directories tab will open (**Figure 6.21**).

5. To establish a home directory based on each user's name, check Different Directory for Each Member.

6. Enter a home directory for the group of users.

7. Click Accept.

   If the home directory you specified does not exist, you will be asked if you want to create it.

✔ Tips

■ You can edit group information by clicking the user ID in the User Groups list.

■ Be *very* cautious when editing or deleting nonhuman users or groups. These may be an important part of your system configuration.

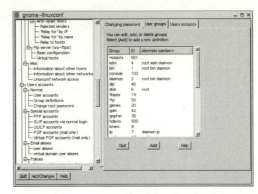

Figure 6.19 The Users Group tab is used to add or edit groups.

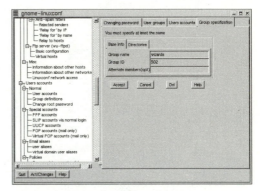

Figure 6.20 The Group Specification tab is used to provide information about new groups.

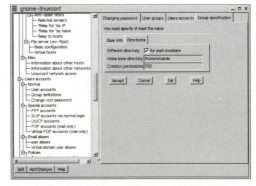

Figure 6.21 If Different Directory for Each Members is checked, then a home directory for each group member—based on the group member's name—will be created off the home base directory.

SETTING UP USERS AND GROUPS

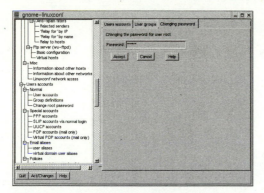

Figure 6.22 Select Change Root Password to change your root password.

To change the root password:

1. With the Linux Desktop Configuration tool open to User Accounts, select Change Root Password (**Figure 6.22**).

2. Enter the new password in the Password box.

3. Passwords must be a minimum of six characters. If your password contains a dictionary word, a message will appear stating that it is not a good Unix password. It's your choice to use it anyway. Enter the password again to confirm it.

Summary

In this chapter, you learned how to:

◆ Log on and off Another Level and KDE.

◆ Use the Desktop Switcher to set the default desktop environment.

◆ Install the Desktop Switcher.

◆ Use the Red Hat Linux Sessions menu.

◆ Use the Red Hat Linux System menu.

◆ Use the Red Hat Linux Languages menu.

◆ Install KOffice.

◆ Using Gnome, add and edit users and assign them to a group.

◆ Using Gnome, add and edit groups.

◆ Change the root password.

GNOME APPLICATIONS

The Gnome desktop that ships with Red Hat Linux 6 comes with a suite of preinstalled personal productivity applications. These include:

- ◆ Calendar, a personal appointment organizer
- ◆ GnomeCard, a contact manager
- ◆ Gnotepad+, a text editor
- ◆ Gnumeric, a spreadsheet program
- ◆ GTimeTracker, a project management tool

In this chapter, I'll show you how to use these applications.

You might want to bear in mind that although these applications are both very powerful and free—good things, indeed!—they are not commercially produced or supported. As a consequence, although these applications are stable, not all of their components are fully functional.

Red Hat Linux 6 ships with many desktop applications. This chapter discusses the following important utilities:

- ◆ The Gimp, an image manipulation tool
- ◆ xPDF, an Acrobat file viewer

I also show you how to use Lynx, a text-based Web browser, and provide an overview of the Netscape Communicator Suite for Linux.

All the applications covered in this chapter are installed as part of both the Workstation and Server default installations. However, if you performed a Custom installation, they may not be present on your system. In that case, use GnoRPM to install the applications you want from the Red Hat Linux 6 VQS CD in the back of this book. (See Chapters 1 and 2 for installation instructions.)

Working with Gnome Calendar

Gnome Calendar—written by Miguel de Icaza, Federico Mena, and Arturo Espinosa—enables you to set up appointments, automate repeated items, and set alarms. You can view your calendar items on a daily, weekly, or monthly page—or you can review a year in a single screen.

Linux is intended as a multiuser system. The expectation is that each user on the system will have his or her own files, configuration, and applications. In keeping with this philosophy, each user has a calendar. By default, the calendar is named using the full name supplied when the user was added to the system: for example, Harold Davis's calendar. (For information on adding users with the Red Hat Linux control panel, see Chapter 6.) In addition to your default calendar, you can save multiple calendars of your own.

To open Gnome Calendar:

With the Gnome desktop running, select Calendar from the Applications menu fly-out on the Gnome main menu. The Calendar will open (**Figure 7.1**).

To change Gnome Calendar to a 12-hour format:

1. With Gnome Calendar open, choose Preferences from the Settings menu. The Preferences dialog box will open (**Figure 7.2**).

2. Click OK or Apply. Then close the dialog box.

Figure 7.1 Gnome Calendar can be used to keep track of appointments and tasks.

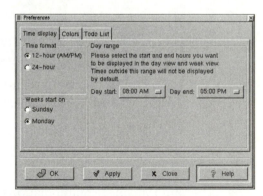

Figure 7.2 You can use the Gnome Calendar Preferences dialog box to configure the display of calendar pages.

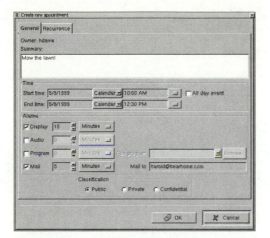

Figure 7.3 The Create New Appointment dialog box is used to enter a calendar item.

Figure 7.4 You can configure calendar events to trigger alarms, such as the display shown (other alarms play a sound, run a program, or automatically send email).

To create a new appointment:

1. Click New on the Calendar toolbar.

   The Create new appointment dialog box will open (**Figure 7.3**).

2. In the Summary box, enter a description of the item as you want it to appear in your calendar.

3. In the Time frame, enter a start date and time and an end date and time.

   You can enter dates and times using the keyboard or by clicking the Calendar and Time buttons.

4. If you want an event to be scheduled for an entire day, select the All Day Event box.

5. If you want an event to trigger an alarm, check the box for the alarm type you want. Select Display to display a message, Audio to play a sound, Program to run a program, or Mail to send email to the address you designate.

6. Click OK.

   If you configured an alarm, it will be triggered at the time you specified. **Figure 7.4** shows a display alarm in action.

To delete an appointment:

1. With Gnome Calendar open to a page displaying the appointment, right-click the appointment you want to delete.

2. Select Delete This Appointment from the fly-out menu.

✔ Tip

■ If the appointment is one that recurs, you will be asked if you want to delete all instances of the appointment or just this appointment.

Recurring appointments

A *recurring* appointment is one that is automatically entered at the designated time in your calendar. For example, you might want to change backup tapes every day.

To enter a recurring appointment:

1. Open the Create New Appointment dialog box and enter the information for the appointment item on the General tab (**Figure 7.5**).

2. Click Recurrence.
   The Recurrence tab will open (**Figure 7.6**).

3. Use the controls on the Recurrence tab to set how often you want the item to be added, when you want the item to stop being added, and whether there are any exceptions to your rules.
   An example of an exception would be adding a task every day *except* February 14.

4. Click OK.

To go to a particular date:

1. Click the Go To button on the Calendar toolbar.
   The Go To Date dialog box will open (**Figure 7.7**).

2. Select a year, month, and day.
   When you click a date, you will be taken to the calendar page for that date.

✔ Tip

■ To go to the current day, click the Go To Today button.

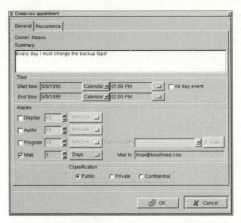

Figure 7.5 To create a recurring appointment, first create a one-time instance of the appointment item.

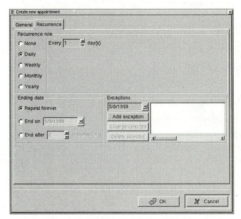

Figure 7.6 Use the Recurrence tab to set when and for how long an item appears in your calendar.

Figure 7.7 You can use the Go To Date dialog box to open a specific date in your calendar.

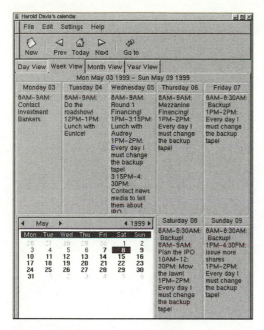

Figure 7.8 You can use the View tabs to select Daily, Weekly, Monthly, or Yearly views.

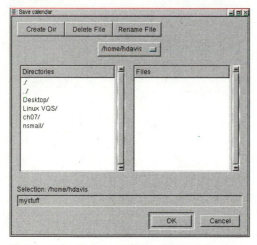

Figure 7.9 You can save multiple calendars, but the calendar created for your user ID will open by default.

To view all your appointments for a week:

Choose the Week View tab in the Gnome Calendar main window. The Week View display will open (**Figure 7.8**).

✔ Tip

- You can also select Month View or Year View to open the corresponding views.

To save your calendar:

Choose Save from the Gnome Calendar main menu.

✔ Tip

- To save a calendar that is different from the one created for you by default, select Save As from the File menu and give the calendar a name (**Figure 7.9**).

To start a new calendar:

Select New from the Gnome Calendar File menu (**Figure 7.10**).

Figure 7.10 To open a new calendar, select New from the File menu.

Working with GnomeCard

GnomeCard combines the functionality of an address book or contact management program with an electronic business card manager.

GnomeCard information is saved in the vCard format, which is a standard format used for automating the exchange of information in applications including email, personal information managers (PIMs), personal digital assistants (PDAs), digital wireless phones, and more. The Internet Mail Consortium is responsible for developing and promoting the vCard standard.

Essentially, the vCard format is a text-based standard that can easily be read and saved by many applications. For more information, open the Internet Mail Consortium's Web site, at **http://www.imc.org/pdi/**.

To open GnomeCard:

With the Gnome desktop running, select GnomeCard from the Applications menu fly-out on the Gnome main menu. GnomeCard will open (**Figure 7.11**).

✔ Tips

- GnomeCard always displays the full information for the active card on the right. A summary List view is displayed on the left. You can decide which columns will be displayed in the List view (described later in this chapter).

- The first time you open GnomeCard, there will be no entries.

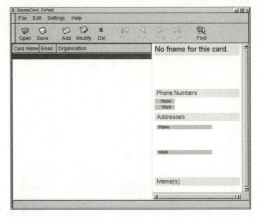

Figure 7.11 GnomeCard display the active card on the right and lists all cards on the left.

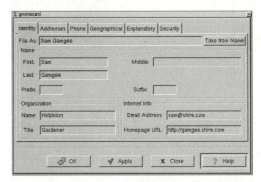

Figure 7.12 A tabbed dialog box is used to add or edit card information.

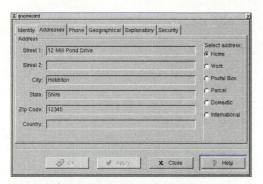

Figure 7.13 The Addresses tab is used to enter information for multiple addresses.

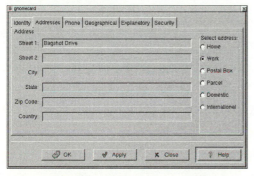

Figure 7.14 You can enter many addresses on one card by using the choices in the Select Address frame.

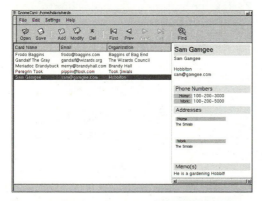

Figure 7.15 The complete card information that you entered appears on the right, with a summary in a list on the left.

To add a card:

1. With GnomeCard open, click Add on the GnomeCard toolbar.

   The Identity tab will open (**Figure 7.12**).

2. For the time being, leave the File As box empty.

   (The File As field becomes the Card Name field in GnomeCard List view.)

3. Enter first name, last name, organization, email, and any other information you'd like. You can click the Take from Name button to use the first and last name you entered in the File As field.

4. Click Apply to save the information.

5. Click Addresses to open the Addresses tab (**Figure 7.13**).

6. Enter home address information.

7. Select Work in the Address Selection frame on the right.

   The home address information that you entered will no longer be visible, and you will have a chance to enter work address information (**Figure 7.14**).

8. When you are through entering addresses, click Apply.

9. Enter other information on the remaining tabs. After you finish with each tab, click Apply to save the information.

10. When you are through, click Close.

    Your complete card information will be displayed on the right, with a summary on the left (**Figure 7.15**).

WORKING WITH GNOMECARD

✔ Tips

■ If you enter text in the Comment field on the Explanatory tab, it will appear in the active card display as a memo.

■ If you leave the default column headings in List view, Card Name—obtained from File As—is the primary sort field. (To change the default, see the sections that follow.) This means that if you left File As empty when you created a card, the card will appear to have no name in the alphabetic Card Name list.

To search for a card:

1. Click Find on the GnomeCard toolbar. The Find Card dialog box will open (**Figure 7.16**).

2. Enter the name you want to find.

3. Click Find.

To delete a card:

1. Right-click a card in List view.

2. Choose Delete This Item from the fly-out menu.

✔ Tip

■ You will not receive a confirmation message before the card is deleted. Once it is deleted, it is gone.

To edit a card:

1. Right-click a card in List view.

2. Choose Edit This Item from the fly-out menu.

   The Identity tab will open, with current information for the card in place.

3. Change the information on the various tabs.

4. Save your changes by clicking Apply or OK.

To change the primary sort field in List view:

Click the column header that you want to use as the new primary sort field. The items in List view will be rearranged so that they are alphabetically sorted using the entries in the new column.

To change the columns displayed in List view:

1. Choose Preferences from the Settings menu.

   The Layout dialog box will open (**Figure 7.17**).

2. Use the buttons in the dialog box to select and arrange the columns you want displayed in List view.

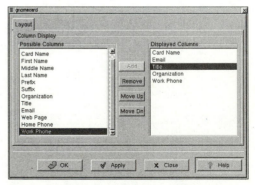

Figure 7.17 The Layout dialog box is used to choose the columns you want displayed in List view.

Figure 7.16 You can search for a card by opening the Find Card dialog box.

Working with Gnotepad+

Gnotepad+ is intended to be an easy-to-use, yet fairly feature-rich, simple text editor. It admirably meets these goals. This application is far closer to "word processing lite" than to a basic tool such as Windows Notepad.

Gnotepad+ features a jaunty multiple-document interface. You can easily control most aspects of fonts and formatting. In addition, Gnotepad+ can be used to edit text files—although it is certainly not a full-fledged programmer's editor. Last but not least, Gnotepad+ is a fairly versatile—though not WYSIWYG—HTML editor that provides several ways to view files written in HTML.

Although Gnotepad+ is a great lightweight application, if you need a full-fledged word processing program, you should consider using Corel WordPerfect for Linux. (See Chapter 8 for more information on obtaining, installing, and using Corel WordPerfect for Linux.)

You can find more information about Gnotepad+, which was primarily written by Andy Kahn, at

`http://ack.netpedia.net/gnp/`

Because most of Gnotepad+'s features, such as opening and saving documents and setting fonts, are intuitive and easy to use, I won't explain them here.

To open Gnotepad+

With the Gnome desktop running, select Gnotepad+ from the Applications menu fly-out on the Gnome main menu. Gnotepad+ will open.

To create an HTML document:

1. With Gnotepad+ open, choose the Toolbar fly-out from the Options menu (**Figure 7.18**).

2. Use buttons on the HTML toolbar to create well-formed HTML tags in your document.

   The HTML toolbar is the second toolbar from the top in **Figure 7.19**.

2. To view the document as it will appear as HTML, select View HTML from the File menu.

4. You can choose to view the document in a special HTML viewer (**Figure 7.20**), as a Gnotepad+ document, or in the Netscape browser.

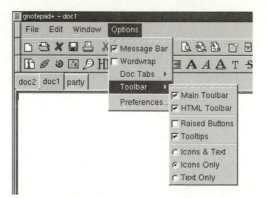

Figure 7.18 If you enable the HTML toolbar, you can easily create HTML files.

Figure 7.19 You can click the buttons on the HTML toolbar to add beginning and ending HTML tags to the document.

Figure 7.20 You can view HTML documents created in Gnotepad+ in a special viewer (shown here) or in Netscape.

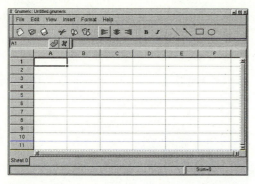

Figure 7.21 The Gnumeric spreadsheet opens with a blank worksheet ready to go.

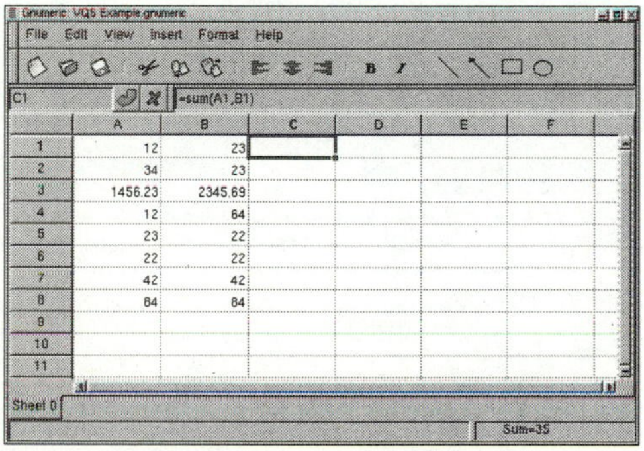

Figure 7.22 To use a function in a cell, select the cell and enter the function in the Input box.

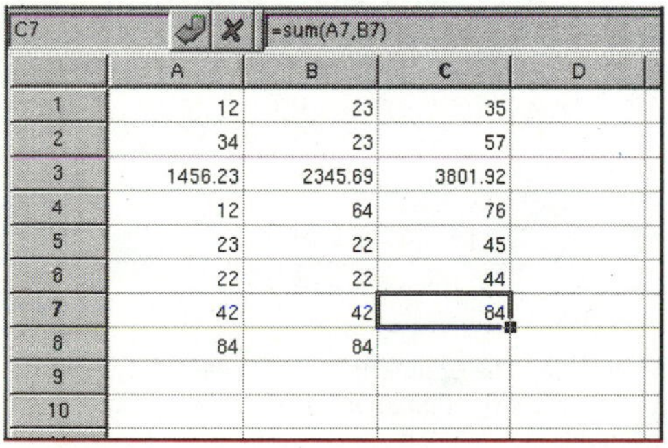

Figure 7.23 To autofill a column, drag a cell down the column using the handle box at the cell's lower right.

Working with the Gnumeric Spreadsheet

The Gnumeric spreadsheet is a world-class spreadsheet program, and it's also a work in progress. In other words, it is very, very good right now—but not complete.

Highlights include an extensive and powerful library of functions, an extensible architecture that accepts plug-ins, and a native XML format. An Excel import and export module is in the works.

Documentation for the Gnumeric spreadsheet is excellent.

This program is primarily the work of Miguel de Icaza. You can learn more about it at

`http://ack.netpedia.net/gnp/`

To open the Gnumeric spreadsheet:

With the Gnome desktop running, select Gnumeric Spreadsheet from the Applications menu fly-out on the Gnome main menu. The Gnumeric spreadsheet will open with a new blank worksheet (**Figure 7.21**).

To use a function in a cell:

1. With a worksheet open, select the cell in which you want to use a function (**Figure 7.22**).

2. In the Input box, type an equal sign, followed by the function and its arguments. For example, to make the contents of cell C1 equal to the sum of the contents of cells A1 and B1, you would type `=sum(A1,B1)`.

3. Click the Acceptance button (to the left of the Input box, with a curved arrow).

   The calculated total will appear in the cell.

Autofilling

Autofill is achieved by dragging a cell using the handle box at the lower-right of the cell. The Gnumeric spreadsheet does its best to figure out what the new cells should be filled with. For instance, if the original cell was filled with a function, as in the preceding example, the new cells will be filled using the same function.

To autofill a column:

1. Using the handle box at the lower right of the starting cell, drag down the column you want to autofill (**Figure 7.23**).

2. Release the mouse.

   The column will be filled based on the formula in the original cell (**Figure 7.24**).

✔ Tip

■ Note that the content of the Input box for cell C8 has been automatically set to =sum(A8,B8) (**Figure 7.24**). This is the formula from the original cell, C1, extrapolated with the row number replaced appropriately. Other rows will have an appropriate formula: for example, the Input box for cell C5 will read =sum(A5,B5).

To get more information on Gnumeric spreadsheet functions:

1. Choose Gnumeric Function Reference from the Gnumeric Help menu.

   The Gnumeric Function Reference will open in a Netscape window (**Figure 7.25**).

2. To find out more about a specific function, click the link for that function.

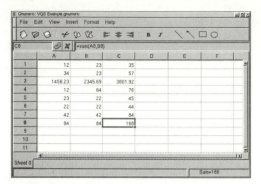

Figure 7.24 All the cells in the column are filled appropriately when you release the mouse.

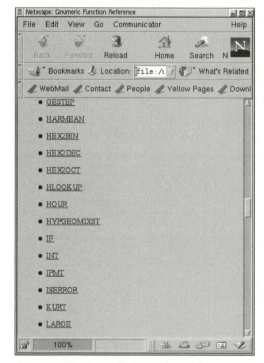

Figure 7.25 The Gnumeric Function Reference provides information about the functions that are available.

✔ Tip

- The descriptions of the functions can be less than elucidating. For example, if you click the KURT function, you will learn that it is the *kurtosis* function, and that using it in some circumstances will cause a divide-by-zero error. There is no explanation of kurtosis. Fortunately, you can usually get information about anything using your favorite Web search engine.

  (By the way, the kurtosis function is, essentially, a measure of how many outliers there are off a statistical random distribution—in other words, a measure of statistical "skewedness.")

WORKING WITH GNUMERIC SPREADSHEET

Working with GTimeTracker

GTimeTracker, the Gnu time-tracking tool, should not be confused with a full-fledged project management system, such as Microsoft Project. Instead, it is a handy-dandy utility that can be used to track elapsed time and how it is spent.

You could use GTimeTracker simply to better understand how you are using your time. You could also use it to track billable time spent doing specific work. Or you could configure GTimeTracker to open each time you begin a Gnome session (see the following paragraphs). Your computer use could be allocated between work and play, with the results used to report deductibility to the IRS.

GTimeTracker—which was written by Eckehard Berns—groups related projects in *configurations*. You can have as many configurations as you like.

When a configuration is open and the timer is started, time is allocated to the selected project. This time is tracked with a running total. In addition, total time spent on all projects in the configuration is tracked.

To open GTimeTracker:

With the Gnome desktop running, select Time Tracking Tool from the Applications menu fly-out on the Gnome main menu. GTimeTracker will open (**Figure 7.26**).

✔ Tip

■ Total elapsed time is displayed in the title bar at the lower left (**Figure 7.26**).

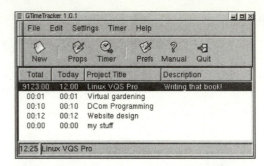

Figure 7.26 The Gnome time-tracker utility tracks related items—called *projects*—that are grouped in a *configuration*.

WORKING WITH GTIMETRACKER

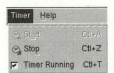

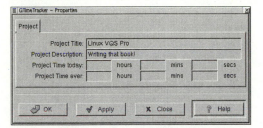

Figure 7.27 The Timer Running item on the Timer menu shows whether or not the timer is on.

Figure 7.28 The Project Properties page is used to start a new project.

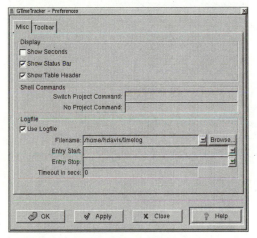

Figure 7.29 You can use the Preferences dialog box to set a log file to track time spent on projects.

To toggle the timer:

Click the Timer button on the toolbar to start the timer if it is off or to stop the timer if it is on.

✔ Tip

■ The best way to determine whether the timer is on—besides watching for elapsed time to be displayed—is to select the Timer menu. If the timer is on, the Timer Running box will be checked (**Figure 7.27**). The Timer menu items can also be used to stop and start the timer.

To add a new project to a configuration:

1. With a configuration open in the time tracker, click the New button on the toolbar *or* select New Project from the File menu.

   The Project Properties page will open (**Figure 7.28**).

2. Enter a project title and description.

3. If the project has consumed time previously, you can enter this time in the Project Time Today and Project Time Forever fields.

4. Click OK.

✔ Tip

■ If you edit an existing project using its Properties page, the Project Time Today and Project Time Forever fields will contain the elapsed time that applies to the project.

To change the selected project:

With a configuration open in the time tracker, select the project you want to make active.

WORKING WITH GTIMETRACKER

To record the time-tracking information in a log file:

1. Choose Preferences from the Settings menu.

   The Misc tab of the GTimeTracker Preferences dialog box will open (**Figure 7.29**).

2. Check Use Logfile.

3. Enter a file name and path.

4. Click OK.

✔ Tip

■ You can use the Browse button to locate the file you want to use to log elapsed time.

To automatically start GTimeTracker with Gnome Desktop sessions:

1. Choose Session Manager from the Settings fly-out of the Gnome main menu.

   The Session Manager dialog box will open (**Figure 7.30**).

2. Click Add.

   The Add Startup Program dialog box will open (**Figure 7.31**).

3. Enter g t t in the Startup Command box.

4. Click OK.

   GTimeTracker will be added to the Non-Session-Managed Startup Programs list (**Figure 7.32**).

5. Click OK.

   The next time you log on, the time-tracking tool will be started automatically.

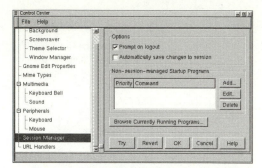

Figure 7.30 The Gnome Session Manager can be used to start programs automatically when Gnome starts.

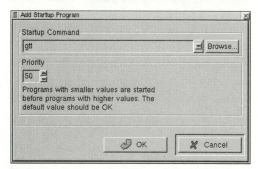

Figure 7.31 You can add start up commands directly, or you can browse for the program you want to activate.

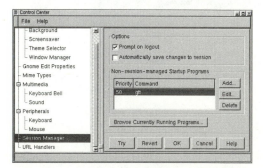

Figure 7.32 Programs that you choose to activate will appear in the Non-Session-Managed Startup Programs list.

Working with the Gimp

The Red Hat Linux 6 CD in the back of this book contains a terrific graphics tool called the Gimp. The Gimp—*Gnu Image Manipulation Program*—is a full-featured application along the lines of Adobe Photoshop. You can use to it create images, retouch photos, and much more.

Written by Peter Mattis and Spencer Kimball, the Gimp is as powerful as any comparable program available on any platform. Like Photoshop, it is a visual artist's delight. You can find some of the images that artists have created using it—as well as downloads and useful information—at the Gimp's Web site, `http://www.gimp.org`

When you set out to explore the Gimp on your own, you'll realize that it has many more features than could ever be covered in *Red Hat Linux 6: Visual QuickPro Guide.* (Indeed, the Gimp deserves a book of its own!) These features include:

♦ A complete set of painting tools, including Brush, Pencil, Airbrush, and Clone tools

♦ Tile-based memory management so image size is limited only by available disk space

♦ Anti-aliasing support for the highest quality rendering

♦ Implementation of full alpha channel support

♦ Layers and channels

♦ The ability to write scripts that can be invoked in the Gimp, and the ability to call Gimp objects and methods from external scripts (called *Script-Fu*)

(Continued...)

Was the Gimp installed? Starting the Gimp

Whether the Gimp was installed depends on the selections you made during installation of Red Hat Linux 6 from this book's CD. In addition, a menu item for the Gimp may—or may not—have been added to the Graphics menu fly-out of your Gnome main menu.

♦ If a menu item for the Gimp was created, choose that item to start the Gimp. You will be walked through a few final installation screens before the Gimp opens.

♦ If there is no menu item for the Gimp, use the File Manager to check whether a file named gimp is present in your /usr/bin directory. If it is, double-click it. This will complete the Gimp's installation and add a menu item for the Gimp to the Graphics menu for you to use the next time you want to start the Gimp.

♦ If there is no menu item for the Gimp and the gimp file is not present in /usr/bin, then the Gimp has probably not been installed. You can check this by running GnoRPM and seeing whether the Gimp package is present. It should be listed with the Multimedia packages in the Applications hierarchy. (For more information on GnoRPM, see Chapters 2 and 3.)

♦ If the Gimp is not listed in GnoRPM, then you will have to install it from the Red Hat Linux 6 CD as explained in Chapters 2 and 3.

♦ If all else falls, you can download the most recent version of the Gimp from `http://www.gimp.org`

◆ Multiple levels of Undo and Redo (limited only by available disk space)

◆ The ability to have a virtually unlimited number of images open at one time

◆ An extremely powerful gradient editor and Blend tool

◆ The ability to load and save animations in a convenient frame-as-layer format

◆ Transformation tools, including Rotate, Scale, Shear, and Flip tools

◆ Many supported file formats, including .gif, .jpg, .png, .xpm, .tiff, .tga, .mpeg, .ps, .pdf, .pcx, and .bmp

◆ The ability to load, display, convert, and save using many file formats

◆ Selection tools, including Rectangle, Ellipse, Free, Fuzzy, Bezier, and Intelligent Selection tools

◆ Numerous filter effects

◆ Many plug-ins, which enable easy addition of new file formats and new effect filters

◆ Support for custom brushes and patterns

I'll show you how to use a few of the Gimp's features here, to give you a taste of how the Gimp works.

To start the Gimp:

With the Gnome desktop running, select the Gimp from the Graphics menu fly-out on the Gnome main menu. The Gimp toolbox will open (**Figure 7.33**).

✔ Tips

■ If there is no menu item for the Gimp on the Graphics menu, see the previous sidebar "Was the Gimp Installed? Starting the Gimp" for instructions.

■ Most of the Gimp's functionality can be accessed by right-clicking and using fly-out menus with an image open in the Gimp.

Figure 7.33 The Gimp's functionality can be accessed from its toolbox, which is what opens when you first start the Gimp, or by right-clicking an open image and using the fly-out menus.

Figure 7.34 You can use the Screen Shot dialog box to capture an image of a specific window or your entire desktop.

Figure 7.35 The window grabbed by the Screen Shot utility appears, ready for editing, in a Gimp window.

Acquiring an image

Before you can really start working with the Gimp, you need an image to work on. There are many ways to obtain an image. You can start a new, empty file and use the Gimp's tools to add distinctiveness, or you can open an existing graphic file.

An interesting possibility is to start with a *screen capture*, or portion of your computer desktop.

To grab a screen capture:

1. Make sure that the image you want to capture is open on your desktop; for example, in a Web browser.

2. Choose Screen Tool from the Xtns menu in the Gimp toolbox.

   (Xtns is short for Extensions.) The Screen Shot dialog box will open (**Figure 7.34**).

3. Make sure that Grab a Single Window is selected.

4. Click OK.

   The Screen Shot dialog box will disappear from view, and a cross-hair cursor will appear.

5. Click with the cross-hair cursor in the window you want to capture.

   Your selection will open, ready for editing, in a Gimp window (**Figure 7.35**).

✔ Tip

■ If you want to capture menus or rearrange the appearance of things before the capture takes effect, set the Screen Shot dialog box to Grab the Whole Screen with a Time Delay. Once the entire screen has been grabbed, you can crop to select the portion you want (see the next section).

WORKING WITH THE GIMP

To crop an image:

1. With an image open in a Gimp window, right-click anywhere in the image.

   The Gimp menu will open.

2. Select Crop from the Tools menu fly-out (**Figure 7.36**).

   A cross-hair cursor will appear on the image.

3. Drag the cross-hair cursor to form the box that you want to crop out of the image.

   The perimeter of the area that you are selecting will be indicated with black box handles.

4. Release the mouse.

   The Crop Information dialog box will appear (**Figure 7.37**).

5. Click Crop.

   The old (larger) image is replaced with the new, cropped image.

To apply a filter to an image:

1. With an image open in a Gimp window, right-click anywhere in the image.

   The Gimp menu will open.

2. Select Filters.

   The Filters fly-out menu will appear (**Figure 7.38**).

3. Choose the filter effect you want

   The filter you selected will be applied to the image. **Figure 7.39** shows the Glass Lens filter effect.

✔ Tip

■ To undo a filter effect (or other effect), hold down the Control key and type **z**, or select Undo from the Edit fly-out menu.

Figure 7.36 To crop an image in a Gimp window, select Crop from the Tools menu fly-out.

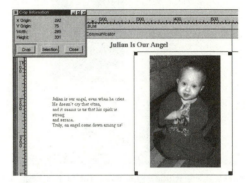

Figure 7.37 The area you are selecting to crop is indicated with perimeter handles; once you release the mouse, the Crop Information dialog box appears.

Figure 7.38 The filter you select will be applied to the image in the Gimp window.

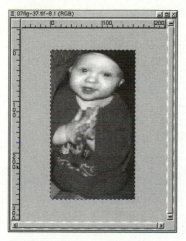

Figure 7.39 You can choose from many filter effects, including the Glass Lens, which is shown.

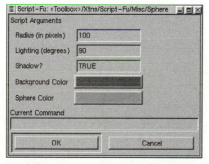

Figure 7.40 The Script-Fu Arguments dialog box is used to provide input parameters for a script.

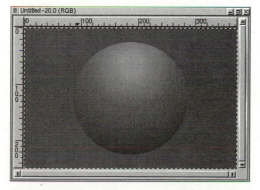

Figure 7.41 A sphere will open in a Gimp window that is based on your entries.

To use Script-Fu to create a sphere:

1. Select the Script-Fu fly-out menu from the Gimp Xtns menu.

2. Select Sphere from the Misc fly-out menu.

   The Sphere Script-Fu Arguments dialog box will open (**Figure 7.40**).

3. Enter the sphere's radius (in pixels), enter the lighting (in degrees), and select background and foreground color by clicking the appropriate buttons.

4. Click OK.

   A sphere that matches the specifications you entered will open in a Gimp window (**Figure 7.41**).

Working with the xPDF Viewer

xPDF is used is to view (and print) portable document files (.pdf files). These files can be created from documents that include text, graphics, or both using Adobe's Acrobat distiller.

To open the xPDF viewer:

With the Gnome desktop running, select xPDF from the Applications menu fly-out on the Gnome main menu. The xPDF viewer will open.

To open a .pdf file:

1. With the xPDF viewer open, right-click the viewer window.

2. Select Open from the xPDF menu.
   A file selection dialog box will open.

3. Enter the name of the .pdf file you want to view, either by typing it or by selecting it using the Browse button.

   The .pdf file will be displayed in the viewer window (**Figure 7.42**).

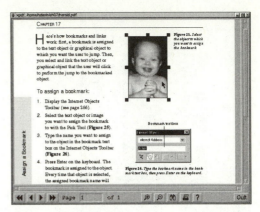

Figure 7.42 You can use xPDF to view Acrobat files containing text and graphics.

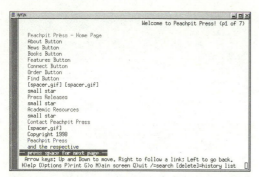

Figure 7.43 Text-only versions of sites are displayed in Lynx.

Working with Lynx

Lynx is a text-based Web browser—meaning that it does not display images. It does handle frames, tables, and most other HTML tags.

The great advantage of Lynx is, in a word, speed. Lynx opens and closes Web pages with lightning speed. Also, Lynx is great if you're tired of all those fancy images and "just want the facts." A final virtue: Lynx will not accept cookies without your explicit permission. (Cookies are small files of information about your Web browsing activities that some Web sites store on your hard drive.)

For more information on Lynx and useful Lynx links, visit **http://lynx.browser.org**.

To open Lynx:

1. Open a terminal window.

2. At the prompt, type **xterm -e lynx &**. Lynx will open.

✔ Tips

■ You can add a menu item for Lynx following the instructions in Chapter 3. The command for the item should be, as just shown, **xterm -e lynx &**.

■ In the default Red Hat installation, Lynx loads with the Red Hat documentation page (as does Navigator). For information on changing the default Lynx start page, see the following paragraphs.

To open a location:

1. With Lynx open, type **G** (for Go). You will be prompted for a URL to open.

2. Type a URL: for example,
www.peachpit.com

3. Accept—or decline to accept—cookies offered by the site.
The site will open in Lynx (**Figure 7.43**).

✔ Tip

■ Unless the site has a special text-only version, you may be confused at first by the text-only appearance of Web sites, even those with which you are familiar.

To change Lynx's default starting page:

1. Edit the file lynx.cfg by placing a pound sign (#) in front of the current STARTFILE line to comment it out (**Figure 7.44**).

2. Add a new start page: for example, enter

   `STARTFILE:http://www.bearhome.com/cub/1999/`

3. Save the lynx.cfg file.

   The next time you start Lynx, the new location will open (**Figure 7.45**).

✔ Tips

■ By default, the Red Hat installation places lynx.cfg in the /etc directory.

■ The lynx.cfg file may be set to read-only mode. To change this, you may have to be logged on as root. Then, in the terminal window, in the /etc directory, enter the command `chmod a+w lynx.cfg`. For more information on changing the attributes of files, see Chapter 11.

■ You have many options for text editing files. For more information, see Chapter 10.

Figure 7.44 By changing the STARTFILE line in lynx.cfg, you can change Lynx's default start page.

Figure 7.45 The next time you start Lynx, a new start page will open.

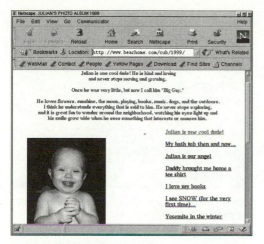

Figure 7.46 Netscape Communicator for Linux is the same powerful suite you may have used under other operating systems.

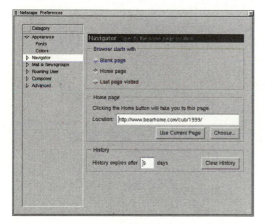

Figure 7.47 To change your Navigator and Communicator start page, open the Navigator Preferences dialog box.

Working with Netscape Communicator

The Netscape Communicator 4.51 Suite that ships with Red Hat Linux 6 is about as far from Lynx as two browsers could possibly be! The Communicator suite of applications includes a number of well-known programs. You have probably used them with other operating systems. The important thing to realize is that they are just as powerful in Linux as in Windows or any other operating system. In addition, you should understand that they operate identically across platforms. From the viewpoint of Netscape, when you've seen one operating system, you've seen them all!

To open Netscape Communicator:

Click the Netscape button on the Gnome control panel *or* select Netscape Communicator from the Internet fly-out on the Gnome main menu. Netscape Communicator will open with a Navigator window (**Figure 7.46**).

To change the default start page for Communicator (and Navigator):

1. With a Navigator window open, select Preferences from the Edit menu.

    The Netscape Preferences dialog box will open.

2. Click Navigator in the left pane.

    The Navigator Preferences dialog box will open on the right (**Figure 7.47**).

3. Type your new home page in the Location box.

4. Click OK.

    The next time you open Communicator (or a new Navigator window), it will start at the page you entered.

✔ Tip

■   The Home button will also take you to the page you entered.

The Communicator menu

Communicator serves as the command center for the extensive list of applications in the suite (as well as being a browser window itself). Communicator's Communicator menu is used to open the various applications. From the Communicator menu, you can open the following applications:

◆ Navigator, which opens a new Navigator window.

◆ Messenger, which opens the Netscape mail manager (**Figure 7.48**). For more information on configuring Netscape Messenger to send and receive email, see Chapter 4.

◆ Composer, which can be used to create and edit HTML.

◆ Newsgroups, which can be used as a newsgroup reader.

◆ Address Book, which is a sophisticated contact management tool that can by used in conjunction with Messenger.

The point here is not to provide a detailed list of all of Netscape's features—that would be impossible! It is to point out that they are all available to you when you install Red Hat Linux 6.

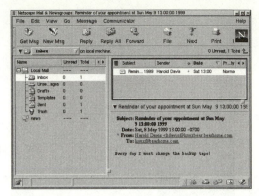

Figure 7.48 Netscape Messenger is a powerful email management program.

Summary

In this chapter, you learned how to:

◆ Use the Gnome Calendar.

◆ Work with the GnomeCard contact manager.

◆ Use Gnotepad+, a middleweight word processing contender.

◆ Work with the Gnumeric spreadsheet.

◆ Keep track of your time with the Gnu time-tracking tool, GTimeTracker.

◆ Work with the Gimp, a world-class photo-manipulation program.

◆ View acrobat files in the xPDF viewer.

◆ Use Lynx for text-based browsing of the Web.

◆ Access the power of Netscape's Communicator suite in Linux.

SUMMARY

WORDPERFECT FOR LINUX 8

Back in the days before Corel Corporation owned WordPerfect—in fact, before Novell owned WordPerfect, if you can remember that far back—WordPerfect was known as the best, most full-featured word processing program available.

WordPerfect, of course, is still giving Microsoft Word a run for its money in the Windows world. Some WordPerfect features—such as its table-handling abilities—are greatly superior to Word's capabilities in the same area. However, under Windows, which word processor you think is better is ultimately a matter of individual opinion.

The good news is that a world-class word processing program, Corel WordPerfect 8, is available for use with Red Hat Linux 6. Once you install WordPerfect, you'll have every word processing feature that you'll conceivably need. You'll find WordPerfect on the Linux platform incredibly easy to use. For one thing, you can open and save documents in Microsoft Word format—as well as documents created in most common word processors. (For more information, see the sidebar "Importing and Exporting Documents.")

In this chapter, you'll learn how to obtain and install Corel WordPerfect. In addition, I'll show you how to use some of WordPerfect's advanced features.

You should understand that—unlike Linux, Gnome, or KDE—Corel WordPerfect is neither open source nor available under the GNU General Public License. Rather, Corel has decided to make a "personal" edition of WordPerfect available free of charge, provided you register it with WordPerfect. In this chapter, I'll show you how to do so. You should note that the personal edition of WordPerfect for Linux lacks some of the features of the commercial edition, primarily a large font library and the ability to access online help.

Note that Corel WordPerfect for Linux will run just as happily under KDE as under Gnome.

Installing WordPerfect

Corel WordPerfect is available from a number of sources, including:

◆ From the Corel Web site, as a free download

◆ From the Red Hat Web site

◆ On the supplemental CD if you purchase the commercial version of Red Hat Linux 6 from Red Hat Software

◆ On a commercial CD that you can order from Corel Corporation and its distributors

In this chapter, I'll guide you through the installation of the free download from Corel. (After all, why spend money if you don't have to—and why not go to the source?)

To download Corel WordPerfect 8 for Linux:

1. In your browser, go to
   `http://linux.corel.com`
   Corel's Linux site will open (**Figure 8.1**).

2. Click the Free Download link on the right side of the page.

   The Download Now page will open. This page provides links with installation instructions and a way to purchase Word-Perfect if you prefer not to spend time downloading it. In addition, there are buttons for several download sites that you can use.

3. Click the CNet Downloads button to proceed to Download.com.

   The CNet Download.com page will open in a new browser window with the Corel WordPerfect for Linux page open.

4. Click Download Now.

   A new window with the Corel WordPerfect for Linux User Agreement will open.

5. Click Yes, I Accept in the lower-left corner.

   A new window showing full and segmented downloads will open (**Figure 8.2**).

Figure 8.1 Corel's Linux Web site is located at `http://linux.corel.com`.

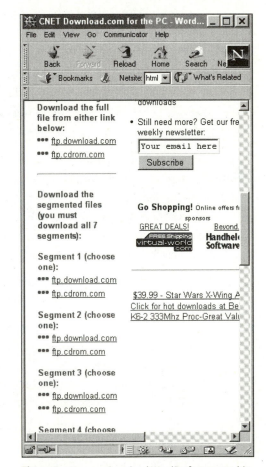

Figure 8.2 You can download WordPerfect as one big file or in segments.

6. Click to download the entire file in one download, or click in a series to download each of seven segments one after the other.

✔ Tips

■ Download the entire file, which is about 24MB, all at once only if you have a broadband connection. Otherwise, if you are using a dial-up modem, you should download the seven segments, each of which is less than 4MB.

■ A full WordPerfect installation requires about 70MB of free hard-drive space.

To install WordPerfect:

1. Using Linux File Manager or a terminal window, create a new directory.

    This directory will be used as a temporary directory for expanding the downloaded WordPerfect files.

2. Copy the file (or files) that you downloaded to your new temporary directory.

    If you downloaded one file, it will be named guilg.gz. If you downloaded the seven segments, they will be named gui00.gz...gui06.gz.

3. For each file you downloaded, in your terminal window in the temporary directory you created, issue a command of the form

    ```
    gunzip gui00.gz ; tar -xvf gui00
    ```
    If you downloaded just the one large file, the command will be
    ```
    gunzip guilg.gz ; tar -xvf guilg
    ```

4. At the prompt, type `./Runme` to start the installation program.

    You will be asked to provide an installation location, and when, the program starts, a registration number (see the following sections).

To start WordPerfect:

1. In a terminal window, change to the wpbin subdirectory of the directory in which you installed WordPerfect.

2. Type `xwp`.

✔ Tip

■ You can add a menu item for Word-Perfect using the Menu Editor, which was explained in Chapter 3. The command for the WordPerfect item should be *path*/`wpbin`/`xwp`, where *path* is the location where you installed WordPerfect.

Every time you open WordPerfect, you will be prompted for a license number. If you don't supply one within 90 days, your copy of WordPerfect will stop working, and you will have to download a new one and reinstall it.

There is no charge for obtaining a license number, but you do have to register your copy.

To register WordPerfect:

1. Open the Corel Linux Web page, at
   `http://linux.corel.com`

2. Click the Free Download link on the right of the page.
   The Corel Download Now page will open (**Figure 8.3**)

3. Scroll down until you see the Register Now link on the right.

4. Click the Register Now link.

5. Fill out the form.

6. Click Submit.
   Your license number will appear on the next page.

7. Write down your license number.

8. The next time you open Corel Word-Perfect, enter the license number in the initial box that opens.

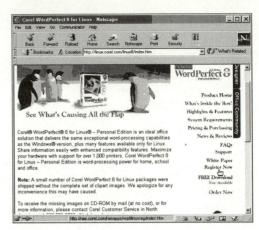

Figure 8.3 Click the Register Now link to obtain a Corel Linux license number.

Figure 8.4 The WordPerfect Control window opens when you start WordPerfect.

New Window	Ctrl+N
Open Window...	
Remote Window...	
Save All	Shift+Ctrl+S
File Manager...	
Printer Control...	
Exit	Shift+Ctrl+F4

Figure 8.5 To open a blank document, select New Window from the WordPerfect Control window's Program menu.

The WordPerfect Control Window

The WordPerfect Control window (**Figure 8.4**) is a separate window that opens when you start WordPerfect. It is used for opening document windows, manipulating files, setting preferences, and performing similar, related tasks.

To open a new blank document:

With the WordPerfect Control window open, select New Window from the Program menu (**Figure 8.5**). A WordPerfect document window with a blank document will open (**Figure 8.6**).

Importing and exporting files

You can import and export WordPerfect files in a variety of formats including:

◆ AmiPro (various versions)

◆ FrameMaker (various versions)

◆ Interleaf (various versions)

◆ Microsoft Word 2.0

◆ Microsoft Word 6.0/7.0

◆ Postscript

◆ Rich Text Format (RTF)

To export a file in one of the available formats, select the File Format type from the Save Options frame in the Save As dialog.

You don't have to do anything special to import a file in a format that WordPerfect recognizes. When you open the file, it will be converted automatically.

WordPerfect is also very Internet savvy. You can format a WordPerfect document in HTML by choosing Internet Publisher on the File menu and then clicking Format as Web Document.

To use WordPerfect's File Manager to create a directory:

1. With the WordPerfect Control window open, select File Manager from the Program menu.

   The WordPerfect File Manager will open (**Figure 8.7**).

2. Use the directory list to position your new directory.

3. Choose Create Directory from the File menu.

   You will be prompted for a name for the directory (**Figure 8.8**).

4. Enter a name for your new directory.

5. Click OK.

   The new directory will appear in the directory list in File Manager (**Figure 8.9**).

To save a file:

1. With a document window open, choose Save or Save As from the File menu.

   The Save As dialog will open (**Figure 8.10**).

2. Use the directory list to choose a location for the file.

3. Enter a name for the file in the Filename/Current Selection box.

4. Click OK.

To change your WordPerfect preferences:

1. With the WordPerfect Control window open, select Preferences from the menu bar.

   The Preferences Navigator will open (**Figure 8.11**).

2. Click a button that corresponds to the preference area that you want to change. For example, change your WordPerfect user name by clicking Environment.

   The Environment Preferences dialog box will open (**Figure 8.12**).

3. Enter your new user name as you want WordPerfect to display it.

4. Click OK.

Figure 8.6 A new WordPerfect window displays a blank document.

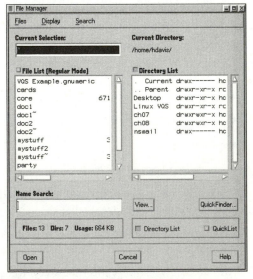

Figure 8.7 The WordPerfect File Manager can be used to copy, move, and save files.

Figure 8.8 You can use WordPerfect File Manager to create a directory with the name you specify, in the location you specify.

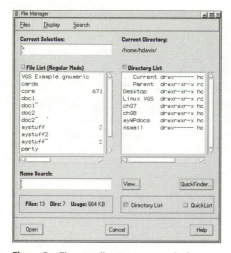

Figure 8.9 The new directory appears in the WordPerfect File Manager's directory list.

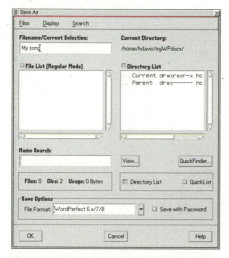

Figure 8.10 The File Save As dialog box works in the same fashion as WordPerfect's File Manager.

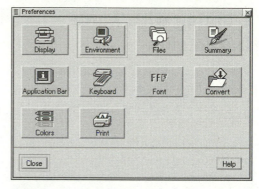

Figure 8.11 You can use the Preferences Navigator to choose a preference area.

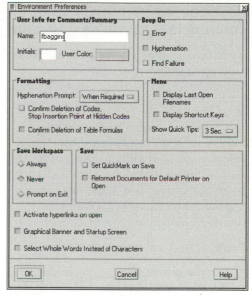

Figure 8.12 Many aspects of WordPerfect's functionality can be customized using the Environment Preferences dialog box.

THE WORDPERFECT CONTROL WINDOW

Working with WordPerfect Documents

WordPerfect has many useful and powerful features. If you are not familiar with the program, you can easily learn about these features as you use it.

Of course, all of WordPerfect's features cannot be covered in a book on Red Hat Linux. If you haven't used WordPerfect before—or even if you have—hopefully you'll come away from this chapter with the realization that word processing on the Linux platform has come of age.

Entering text anywhere on a page

Have you ever wanted to start a Word document somewhere in the middle of a page without having to use the Enter and Tab keys to reach the location?

Using the WordPerfect *shadow cursor*—a rectilinear cursor that follows the mouse pointer—you can easily do so. (If you've used Microsoft Word, you'll know that you cannot do this in Word. The cursor can only be placed in an area that has been first accessed using the keyboard.)

To enter text anywhere on the page:

1. Open a new WordPerfect document.

   You'll see the insertion point is at the upper left of the document. When you move the pointer using the mouse, you'll also see the shadow cursor, a blue line with arrows on either side (**Figure 8.13**).

2. Using the mouse, move the shadow cursor to where you want to enter text.

3. Click and then start typing.

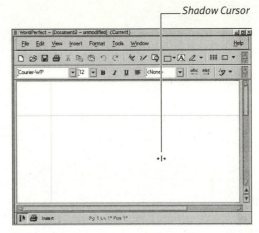

Shadow Cursor

Figure 8.13 You can use the shadow cursor to start typing anywhere in a document.

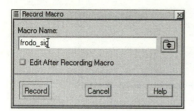

Figure 8.14 Give the macro you are recording a name that will remind you what it does.

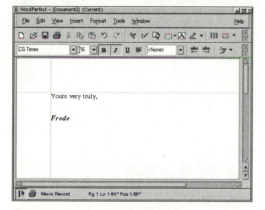

Figure 8.15 If you are in Macro Recording mode, the status bar will display the message "Macro Record."

Macros

Macros are used to automate repetitive tasks. You can *record* a macro, create a macro using WordPerfect's macro language, or first record a macro and then edit it.

A common simple macro is one that creates the standard closure you like to use in a letter.

To record a macro that closes a letter:

1. With a WordPerfect document open, choose Record from the Macro fly-out menu on the Tools menu.

   The Record Macro dialog box will open (**Figure 8.14**).

2. Enter a name for the macro in the Macro Name box. You can also specify a location (that is, a path) to store the macro file.

3. If you think you will want to edit the macro code after it has finished recording, make sure that Edit after Recording Macro is checked.

4. Click Record to start recording.

   The Record Macro dialog box will disappear, and you will be back in your open WordPerfect document.

5. Check status bar at the lower left to make sure that it says Macro Record (**Figure 8.15**).

   Type the keystrokes you want recorded. For example, type this:

   ```
   Yours very truly,
   Frodo Baggins
   ```

6. Stop the recording by again choosing Record from the Macro fly-out.

7. To try out your macro, open a blank new document.

(Continued...)

8. Choose Play from the Macro fly-out menu.
The Play Macro dialog box will open
(**Figure 8.16**).

9. Enter a macro name (and a path, if
appropriate).

10. Click Play.
The keystrokes generated by the macro
you recorded will be added to the blank
document (**Figure 8.17**).

✔ Tip

■ For each macro you record, WordPerfect
adds a menu item to the Macros fly-out
menu. You can use this item to start the
macro directly without having to go
through the Play Macro dialog box.

Watermarks

A *watermark* is a gray background character
or word that is added to a document to create distinctiveness or make a point: for
example, "Confidential." It's easy to create
and add watermarks in WordPerfect.

To insert a watermark:

1. Create a document to which you want to
add a watermark.

2. Choose Watermark from the Insert
menu.
The Watermark dialog box will open.

3. Click Create.
A watermark design window, where you
can create the watermark, will open
(**Figure 8.18**).

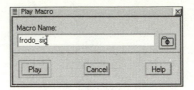

Figure 8.16 To play a macro, enter its
name in the Play Macro box.

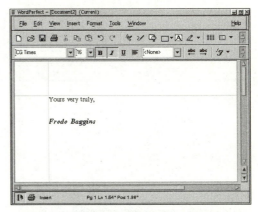

Figure 8.17 The text and keystrokes you recorded are
added to the current document when you play a macro.

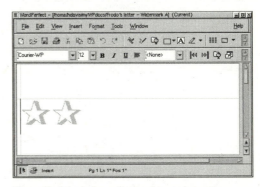

Figure 8.18 A window will open for you to create a
watermark.

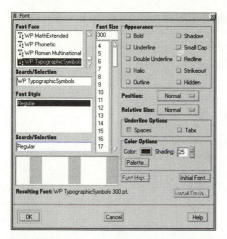

Figure 8.19 You can use the Font dialog box to get your watermark effect exactly the way you want it.

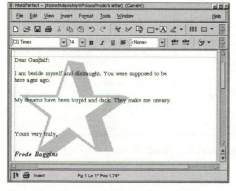

Figure 8.20 The watermark you created will appear in the background of your document.

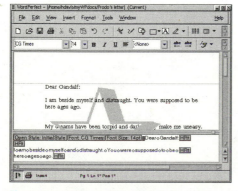

Figure 8.21 Hidden codes control the formatting and appearance of a WordPerfect document.

4. Use the tools provided to create your watermark.

If you like, you can use typographic symbols, and you can use the Font dialog box to make the symbols you choose become large (**Figure 8.19**).

5. Close the watermark design window.

The watermark will be added to your document (**Figure 8.20**).

Hidden codes

Hidden codes are the behind-the-scenes tags that determine WordPerfect's formatting and the appearance of WordPerfect documents. If you want to become a power WordPerfect user, you will need to learn about hidden codes and how to work with them.

To reveal hidden codes:

Choose Reveal Codes from the View menu. The hidden codes will appear in a new pane at the bottom of your WordPerfect document (**Figure 8.21**).

To close the Hidden Codes pane:

Choose Reveal Codes from the View menu again. The Hidden Codes pane will close.

Tables

WordPerfect's table formatting facilities are quite extraordinary. You can easily create fancy tables and format individual cells.

To create a table:

1. With a WordPerfect document open, choose Table from the Insert menu.

    The Create Table dialog box will open (**Figure 8.22**).

2. Enter the number of rows and columns for your table.

3. To preformat the table, click SpeedFormat. The Table SpeedFormat dialog box will open (**Figure 8.23**).

4. Select a style from the list on the left. A preview of the style appears on the right.

5. Click Apply.

    Your new table will be created.

Figure 8.22 Use the Create Table dialog box to insert a table.

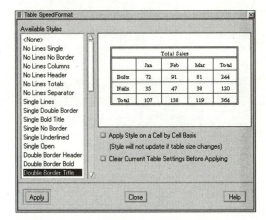

Figure 8.23 The Table SpeedFormat dialog box is used to preformat a table in the way you specify.

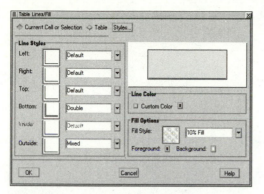

Figure 8.24 You can use the Table Lines/Fill dialog box to format individual table cells.

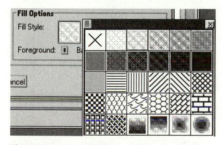

Figure 8.25 From the Texture fly-out, select a texture to use as a cell fill.

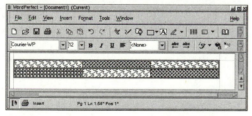

Figure 8.26 Each cell in a table can be formatted differently.

Individually editing cells

WordPerfect cells can be individually edited. This gives you tremendous flexibility in creating tables.

To add a fill to a table cell:

1. Right-click a table cell.

2. Choose Borders/Fill from the fly-out menu.

   The Table Lines/Fill dialog box will open (**Figure 8.24**).

3. Click the texture illustrated to the right of Fill Style in the Fill Options frame.

   A Textures fly-out window will open (**Figure 8.25**).

4. Choose the texture you want to use.

5. In the Table Lines/Fill dialog box, click OK.

6. Select another cell and repeat the process until all the cells in your table are formatted to your satisfaction (**Figure 8.26**).

WORKING WITH WORDPERFECT DOCUMENTS

Summary

In this chapter, you learned how to:

- Download Corel WordPerfect 8 for Linux.

- Install WordPerfect.

- Register WordPerfect for personal use.

- Open a new WordPerfect document.

- Use the WordPerfect Control window.

- Use the WordPerfect File Manager.

- Save a document.

- Change your user preferences.

- Enter text anywhere on a page with the shadow cursor.

- Record a macro.

- Play back a macro.

- Create a watermark.

- Insert a watermark in a document.

- View hidden codes.

- Format a table and cells.

SUMMARY

DOING THE DATABASE THING

9

Databases are the meat-and-potatoes—or perhaps the stomach—of any application. They are by no means sexy or glamorous, but they are essential.

Everything and anything that is organized at all uses some form of a database: for example, files and directories in a file system.

Even the most mundane chores—tracking users and their preferences at a Web site, for instance—require the use of a database. (For information on using Linux and the Apache Web server, see Chapter 14.)

When you think about a database on a server operating system like Linux, you should understand that the database is, itself, a client and server affair. For the database to work, the two pieces must be communicating. This leads to some interesting issues.

First, the database server pretty much feels like an operating system: It needs to control users, access, and processes, and it typically provides a prompt of its own.

Next, you need to consider the interaction between your clients and the server. Generally, a database server provides a client program for administrative purposes or to permit ad-hoc queries against databases. The client program connects to an instance of the database server and allows you to list the tables it contains. More important, it allows you to issue the SQL statements that create and populate relational databases and to run ad-hoc queries against the data they contain. The PostgreSQL Interactive SQL Monitor (explained later in this chapter) is an example of this kind of utility, as is Informix's DB-Access.

But outside users—for example, those running queries against the database via a program activated by submitting a Web form—will need a custom interface created using a programming language spoken by the database server. This is a job for an experienced programmer. The language the programmer employs depends on a variety of factors, but the database server must be able to supply a client connection in that language. Common choices include C, C++, and in the Web space, Perl and Java.

SQL, or Structured Query Language, is the common lingua franca of relational databases.

While on the topic of languages, what language does a database server—also called a DBMS—speak? SQL, or Structured Query Language, is the common lingua franca of relational databases. Although there are slight variations in this language from DBMS to DBMS, most standard SQL statements will work with any database that bills itself as SQL compliant.

SQL itself is divided conceptually into three components:

◆ Data Definition Language—DDL—which is responsible for creating tables and relationships

◆ Data Manipulation Language—DML—which performs operations on the data contained in the database entities

◆ Data Control Language—DCL—which is responsible for transactions and for controlling users and privileges

The Red Hat Linux 6 VQS CD includes a powerful database server, PostgreSQL, that runs well on Linux. PostgreSQL was probably installed on your system when you installed Red Hat Linux and Gnome. It is free for you to use (although not under the Gnu license, as I'll explain later).

This chapter explains how to configure and run PostgreSQL.

I'll also provide an overview of how to download and install Informix Dynamic Server (IDS), Linux Edition. IDS is commercial software with a 30-day free trial. If you need the very best in an enterprise database server for Linux, Informix Dynamic Server may be for you.

PostgreSQL

PostgreSQL is a descendant of Postgres, which was written under the leadership of Michael Stonebraker at the University of California at Berkeley.

Most likely, PostgreSQL version 6.4.2 was installed on your system when you installed Red Hat Linux 6 (see the next section).

As I mentioned earlier, PostgreSQL is not public domain software. The Regents of the University of California own the copyright to PostgreSQL. They have granted general permission to "use, copy, modify, and distribute" PostgreSQL and its documentation at no cost provided their copyright notice and two specific paragraphs of legalese appear in all copies. For more information on the PostgreSQL license, and for information on PostgreSQL in general, visit

`http://www.postgresql.org/`

It's important to understand that there are many different programming languages that can initiate client access with a PostgreSQL server. This kind of access is called an *interface*. You can think of it as a programming "hook." If you need a program to talk to a database server, then you should make sure that the database has an interface for the language in which the program is written. Available PostgreSQL interfaces include:

- C
- C++
- Java
- Perl
- ODBC
- Python
- Tcl

POSTGRESQL

For more information on using the programming languages that ship with Red Hat Linux 6, see Chapter 12.

To check that PostgreSQL has been installed:

1. Choose GnoRPM from the System fly-out of the Gnome main menu.

   Gnome RPM will open.

2. In the Packages list, click the plus sign to the right of Applications.

   The Applications category list will expand.

3. Select Databases.

   In the Packages pane, you should see two packages: postgresql and postgresql-client (**Figure 9.1**).

4. In turn, right-click each package and select Query from the pop-up menu.

   You will see information about PostgreSQL (**Figure 9.2**) and the PostgreSQL client (**Figure 9.3**) package and a list of the files that were installed.

✔ Tips

■ Depending on your choices during installation, PostgreSQL may not have been installed. If the PostgreSQL packages are not present in Gnome RPM on your system, you can use Gnome RPM to add them from the Red Hat Linux 6 VQS CD following the steps explained in Chapter 3.

■ Alternatively, you can download PostgreSQL from

   `http://www.postgresql.org`

   If you do, be sure to follow the installation procedures detailed in Chapter 4 of the *PostgreSQL Administrator's Guide*, also available at the PostgreSQL Web site.

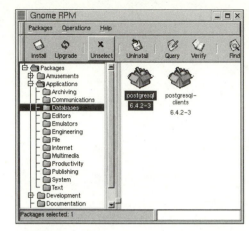

Figure 9.1 If PostgreSQL has been installed, Gnome RPM will have packages for the PostgreSQL server and clients.

Figure 9.2 The Package Info window displays information about PostgreSQL and the files that were installed.

Figure 9.3 To use PostgreSQL, you will also need to have the client package installed.

POSTGRESQL

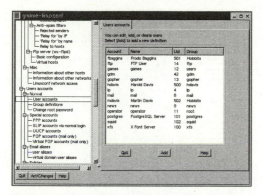

Figure 9.4 In the Linux Configuration utility, choose User Accounts from the Normal category under Users Accounts.

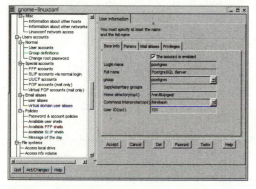

Figure 9.5 The user postgres—known as the PostgreSQL superuser—must be configured to run the PostgreSQL server.

The postgres user

The PostgreSQL server must be run by a user named postgres. It is extremely important for security reasons that this user *not* be given root privileges. (If you grant the postgres user root privileges, the security of your entire server is completely compromised.) The postgres user is sometimes referred to as the *postgres superuser*. In other words, postgres is to PostgreSQL as root is to your Linux system.

The postgres user may have been already added by the Red Hat installation process—in which case, you still need to have a look to make sure, and to change the user's password.

If there is no postgres user, you should add one using the settings that appear in **Figure 9.5**.

For information on adding and editing users in Gnome, see Chapter 6.

To configure the postgres user:

1. While logged on as root, open the control panel's Linux Configuration utility.

2. Scroll down the list on the left until you see User Accounts.

3. Expand Users Accounts.

4. Expand the Normal category below Users Accounts.

5. Click User Accounts.

   A list of user accounts will open in the right pane (**Figure 9.4**).

6. Scroll down in the list until you see postgres.

7. Double-click postgres.

8. The User Information dialog box will open (**Figure 9.5**).

9. Make a note of the postgres user's home directory, /var/lib/pgsql.

(Continued...)

POSTGRESQL

10. Click Passwd.

The Changing Password tab will open (**Figure 9.6**).

11. In the New Unix Password box, enter a new password for postgres: for example, `postgres`. (Although *postgres* is an easy password to remember when you are testing this software, in a production situation you should, of course, use a password that is not so easy to guess.).

12. Make a note of the password you have selected.

13. Enter the password again to confirm it; then accept the changes.

14. Close the Configuration tool.

15. Select File Manager from the Gnome main menu to open the Gnome File Manager.

16. Locate the directory containing the file local1_template1.bki.source. This will probably be /usr/lib/pgsql.

17. Use File Manager to copy the contents of the directory you found to the postgres user's home directory, /var/lib/pgsql.

18. Choose Preferences on File Manager's Edit menu.

The File Manager Preferences dialog box will open (**Figure 9.7**).

19. Place a check mark next to Show Hidden Files.

20. Click OK.

21. View the contents of the postgres user's home directory, /var/lib/pgsql (**Figure 9.8**).

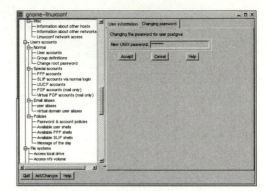

Figure 9.6 You must change the postgres user's password so that you know what it is.

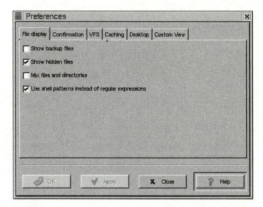

Figure 9.7 To see if the postgres user already has a profile file, make sure you can view hidden files.

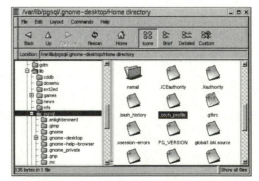

Figure 9.8 If the file .bash_profile is present, you will need to edit it; if it is not present, you will need to create it.

POSTGRESQL

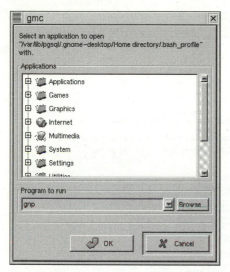

Figure 9.9 You can edit the profile by opening it in Gnotepad+ (gnp).

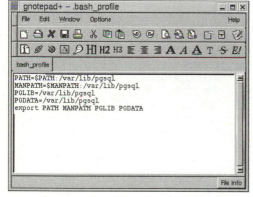

Figure 9.10 PostgreSQL's environment variables should be added to the postgres user's profile.

22. Check to see if a file named .bash_profile is present.

This file is the profile for the postgres user under the Bash shell, meaning that it is loaded to set environment variables when postgres logs on. (For more information on Bash and profiles, see Chapter 10.) The period at the beginning of the file name means that it is a system file and is hidden.

23. If .bash_profile already exists, right-click the file and select Open With from the pop-up menu.

The gmc window will open (**Figure 9.9**).

24. If .bash_profile is not present, then open Gnotepad+ and create it with the information in the next few steps.

   A. Type **gnp** in the Program to Run box.

   B. Click OK to open Gnotepad+ (**Figure 9.10**).

   C. Type the following lines:

```
PATH=$PATH:/var/lib/pgsql
MANPATH=$MANPATH:/var/lib/pgsql
PGLIB=/var/lib/pgsql
PGDATA=/var/lib/pgsql
export PATH MANPATH PGLIB _
    PGDATA
```

   D. Click Save on the File menu.

25. Close any open applications and log off.

26. Log back on as postgres. Use the password you created.

27. Open a terminal window by clicking the terminal icon on the Gnome desktop.

28. Type **env** to check that the environment variables you entered in the postgres user's profile are correctly displayed.

If they are there, you are ready to fire up your database server.

POSTGRESQL

✔ Tips

- The nuances of individual configurations may vary greatly depending on many variables.

- You can change file locations, for example, the postgres user's home location, to suit yourself, provided appropriate permissions are in place.

- The /usr/bin directory must be on your path. You can check this by typing **env** or by typing **$PATH**.

- The best source for further configuration information is the *PostgreSQL Administrator's Guide*, available at

  http://www.postgresql.org/

To initialize your database server:

1. With the terminal window open, type **initdb** at the prompt.

2. Press Enter.

The Postmaster daemon

The Postmaster daemon is the back-end process that must be running for clients to be able to connect to the database server.

To start Postmaster:

1. With the terminal window open, type **postmaster -I** at the prompt.

2. Press Enter.

   So long as Postmaster is running, the terminal window will not return to the prompt (**Figure 9.11**).

✔ Tip

- In a production situation, you will probably want to have the Postmaster daemon started automatically (which must be done by the postgres user). For a variety of ways to do this, see Chapter 4 of the *PostgreSQL Administrator's Guide*.

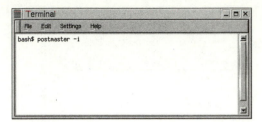

Figure 9.11 The Postmaster daemon must be running for clients to connect with the server.

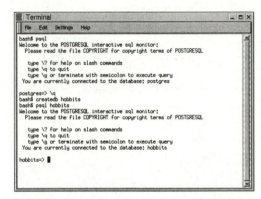

Figure 9.12 The PostgreSQL Interactive SQL Monitor provides a way to directly enter SQL commands that are processed by the server.

POSTGRESQL

Figure 9.13 You can list the commands available in the Interactive SQL Monitor by typing \ ? at the prompt.

Figure 9.14 You can issue a simple SQL statement to make sure that your client server connection is working.

To test a connection:

1. With the Postmaster daemon running in a terminal window, open a new terminal window.

2. Create a new database named *hobbits* by typing `createdb hobbits` at the prompt.

3. Press Enter.

4. Connect to the new database by typing `psql hobbits` at the prompt.

   The PostgreSQL Interactive SQL Monitor will open (**Figure 9.12**).

5. At the Interactive SQL Monitor's prompt—which appears with the name of the database to which you are connected—type \ ? to see a list of available commands (**Figure 9.13**).

6. Quit the menu screen by typing \ q.

7. At the Monitor prompt, enter a SQL query that does not depend on any table data:

   `SELECT datetime 'now';`

8. Press Enter.

   The current date and time will be displayed (**Figure 9.14**).

✔ Tips

- It's conventional, but not required, to type SQL keywords in all uppercase. SQL statements are not case sensitive.

- Each SQL statement entered in the Monitor must conclude with a semicolon.

To delete a database:

In a terminal window, at the shell prompt, type
`destroydb databasename`

For example, enter
`bash$ destroydb hobbits`
to delete the hobbits database.

POSTGRESQL

Creating a table

Tables, consisting of columns—also called *fields*—and rows, are the basic building blocks of relational databases.

To create a table:

1. With the Interactive SQL Monitor connected to a database, for example, to myfundb, create a table named hobbits by typing the following:

   ```
   CREATE TABLE hobbits(
       fname varchar (20)
       lname varchar (20)
       ssn int);
   ```

2. Press Enter.

3. To verify that your table was created, type \dt at the Monitor prompt.

   Your table will appear in the display (**Figure 9.15**).

✔ Tip

- For information on SQL syntax, types, and reserved words, consult a book on SQL and database design.

To populate a table:

1. With the Interactive SQL Monitor still connected to the myfundb database, populate the hobbits table by typing the following:

   ```
   INSERT INTO hobbits VALUES
   ('Frodo', 'Baggins', 12345678);
   ```

2. Press Enter.

3. Repeat steps 1 and 2 for each row you want to insert in the database.

4. To see all the rows entered in the database, at the monitor prompt type:

   ```
   SELECT * FROM hobbits;
   ```

5. Press Enter.

   All rows and columns will be displayed (**Figure 9.16**).

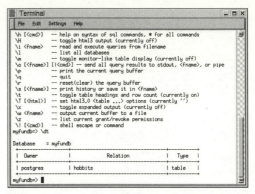

Figure 9.15 You can use standard SQL to create a table, and then verify that it has been created by using the PostgreSQL Interactive SQL Monitor's \dt option.

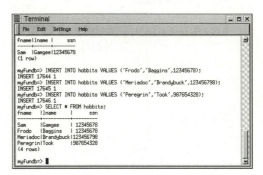

Figure 9.16 You can display all table rows and columns with SELECT *.

✔ Tip

- If you have a lot of data to insert in a table, the normal procedure is to insert it based on a selection from another table or to load it from a delimited ASCII file. An insertion statement for each row would not be feasible in a situation with a lot of data.

To query a table:

1. With the Interactive SQL Monitor still connected to the myfundb database, query the hobbits table by typing the following:

   ```
   SELECT lname FROM hobbits
   WHERE ssn < 100000000;
   ```

2. Press Enter.

   The results that match the criteria will appear (**Figure 9.17**).

To update a table:

1. With the Interactive SQL Monitor still connected to the myfundb database, type the following to update the hobbits table by changing the first name of Sam Gamgee to Samwise Gamgee:

   ```
   UPDATE hobbits SET fname =
   'Samwise' WHERE lname =
   'Gamgee';
   ```

2. Press Enter.

3. To verify the change, display the table contents by typing the following:

   ```
   SELECT * FROM hobbits;
   ```

4. Press Enter.

   The field has been updated (**Figure 9.18**).

```
myfundb=> SELECT lname FROM hobbits where ssn < 100000000;
lname
-------
Gamgee
Baggins
(2 rows)
```

Figure 9.17 When you use SELECT with a FROM clause and a WHERE clause, only the data that matches the criteria is returned.

```
myfundb=> select * from hobbits
myfundb-> ;
fname    |lname      |      ssn
---------+-----------+---------
Frodo    |Baggins    | 12345678
Meriadoc |Brandybuck |123456798
Peregrin |Took       |987654328
Samwise  |Gamgee     | 12345678
(4 rows)
```

Figure 9.18 You can update individual fields using the criteria that you want.

Table inheritance

It is possible to create a table that *inherits* all columns (fields) from another table. The new table might have additional columns besides the ones inherited from the original table.

PostgreSQL calls table relationships used in this way *classes*, which makes sense when one is talking about inheritance.

To create a new table that inherits from an existing table:

1. With the Interactive SQL Monitor still connected to the myfundb database, create a new table, hobbitsplus, that inherits from the hobbits table, by typing the following:

   ```
   CREATE TABLE hobbitsplus
   (alias varchar(20)) INHERITS
   hobbit;
   ```

2. Press Enter.

✔ Tip

■ The new table, hobbitsplus, has a new column, alias, that wasn't present in the hobbits table.

To insert the hobbit rows into hobbitsplus:

1. With the Interactive SQL Monitor still connected to the myfundb database, type the following:

   ```
   INSERT INTO hobbitsplus
   SELECT * FROM hobbits;
   ```

2. Press Enter.

   If you run a SELECT * query on hobbitsplus, you will see that the rows from hobbits have been inserted (**Figure 9.19**).

```
myfundb=> INSERT INTO hobbitsplus SELECT * FROM HOBBITS;
INSERT 0 4
myfundb=> SELECT * FROM hobbitsplus;
fname    |lname      |      ssn|alias
---------+-----------+---------+-----
Frodo    |Baggins    | 12345678|
Meriadoc |Brandybuck |123456798|
Peregrin |Took       |987654328|
Samwise  |Gamgee     | 12345678|
(4 rows)
```

Figure 9.19 Using table inheritance, you can move fields and rows from one table to another.

To populate a new field:

You can populate the new field by typing a SQL command along these lines:

```
UPDATE hobbitsplus SET alias =
'Underhill' WHERE lname =
'Baggins';
```

If you then compare the contents of hobbits and hobbitsplus, you will see that the new table has data in the new field (**Figure 9.20**).

Adding users

If users need to access the PostgreSQL server, they must do so as the postgres superuser, or as a new user that you create. Creation in this sense has nothing to do with Linux access privileges; it gives a user rights to access the database server.

To add a new user:

1. In a terminal window, at the shell prompt, type **createuser** followed by the user name: for example, **createuser hdavis**

2. When prompted, supply an ID number and specify the user's PostgreSQL privileges (**Figure 9.21**).

   After the questions have been answered, your user will be created.

✔ Tip

■ The default ID number for an existing Linux user will be that user's Linux ID.

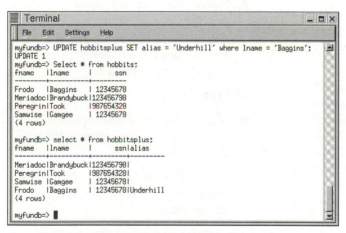

Figure 9.20 You can then insert data into the new table's fields.

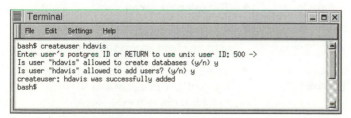

Figure 9.21 Createuser is used to add PostgreSQL users who can connect with the database server.

POSTGRESQL

Informix Dynamic Server, Linux Edition

Informix Software, a leading database vendor, was one of the first enterprise software companies to make a port of their industrial-strength software available on Linux. The version of Informix Dynamic Server (IDS) that runs on Linux differs from the flagship version that runs on commercial Unix operating systems such as Solaris only in some arcane areas.

Be forewarned however: Informix Dynamic Server is no lightweight to install or maintain. Nor is it inexpensive. This is commercial software in all its costly glory. You can download a 30-day free trial version. (If you prefer, you can order a CD with the trial version directly from Informix.)

After that, IDS is normally licensed on a per-user basis, with a fee of $99 per user, though in a practical production setting you would need to contact Informix to negotiate a license.

Many of the concepts involved in installing and running Informix Dynamic Server are comparable to those discussed earlier in this chapter in the section on PostgreSQL. However, unlike PostgreSQL, Informix Dynamic Server is a commercially supported product. If configured correctly, it has world-class performance characteristics. If this is what you need, IDS may be for you.

This section provides an overview of the steps required to install IDS, Linux Edition. For more, read the *Installation Guide*, available in PDF format at

```
http://www.informix.com/informix
/products/linux/5274.pdf
```

Downloading of the "try and buy" version is handled by Intraware, at

```
http://www.intraware.com
```

To download IDS:

1. Open the Intraware "try and buy" page for IDS, Linux Edition, at

```
http://www.intraware.com/
membership/index.html?source=83
```

2. Complete the form on the page.

3. Click Submit Membership Info.
   An Intraware logon ID and password will be emailed to you.

4. Proceed to the download page, `http://member.intraware.com/shop/trybuy/images.html?PLNE=000200`, using your logon ID and password for access.

5. Click Submit to accept the license terms.

6. Select a file download method (for example, FTP).
   You will be provided with detailed instructions for your download, as well as a serial number and key.

✔ Tips

- Make sure to write down the serial number and key. You will need these to install IDS.

- The compressed installation file is about 19MB. You can download it in one file or in segments.

The installation package contains three products:

- The Informix server

- Informix-Connect, which is used to achieve client access to the server

- The Informix Client Software Developer's Kit (SDK), which contains the programming interfaces for the server

You do not need to install the Client SDK unless you are planning to create programming interfaces for your databases. By the way, the interface most commonly used with Informix is ESQL/C, a special C library that can be compiled with programs written in Gnu C.

To create an informix user:

1. Log on as root.

2. Use the procedures outlined earlier in this chapter to create an Informix superuser named `informix` (see "To configure the Postgres user").

3. Make sure that the user informix belongs to a group you create named `informix`.

To create an installation directory:

Using `mkdir` at the command line or in the Gnome File Manager, create a top-level location for the Informix products you will install. By default, this is /opt/informix, although you can change the location if you'd like.

To set environment variables:

Add settings for the PATH and INFORMIXDIR environment variables to the .bash_profile files of the informix user and any other user that will be connecting to the database server. You should add these lines:

```
INFORMIXDIR=/opt/informix

export INFORMIXDIR

PATH=$PATH:$INFORMIXDIR/bin

export PATH
```

To install the Informix software:

The Informix software is delivered in Red Hat's RPM package format. Running as root, use Gnome RPM to install the packages, as described in Chapter 3.

To run the Informix installation scripts:

1. Log on as root.

2. Verify that an informix user and an informix group both exist.

3. Verify that INFORMIXDIR is set to the installation directory by typing `$INFORMIXDIR` at the prompt.

4. Run a script to install the client connection and Informix Dynamic Server modules by typing

    `./installconn -o`

5. Press Enter.

6. When prompted, enter the serial number and key that you recorded at the Intraware site.

7. Press Enter.
   A series of installation messages will appear on the screen. If no error messages appear, the installation was successful.

Initializing IDS

After Informix Dynamic Server has been installed, there are a number of steps that must be taken to initialize Informix Dynamic Server for use. These are briefly outlined in the following section. For more detailed information, read the *Informix Dynamic Server 7.3 Administrator's Guide*, available in PDF format at

`http://www.informix.com/answers/`

To initialize IDS (general steps):

1. Set the required environmental variables (in addition to INFORMIXDIR and PATH, these include ONCONFIG and INFORMIXSERVER). These are generally placed in users' profile files.

2. Create a sqlhosts file, which specifies database server names, connection types, and service names.

3. Edit the onconfig file in the INFORMIXDIR/etc directory to set the parameters for the database engine.

4. Start the database engine by typing

   ```
   oninit -i
   ```

You should now be able to use client access tools, such as DB-Access, to connect to the database server, create tables, and run queries.

Oracle for Linux

Oracle is the leading vendor of enterprise database software. Several versions of Oracle products now run well on Red Hat Linux. Free trial versions are generally available. For more information, go to

```
http://platforms.oracle.com/linux/
```

Oracle 8i is a database product intended specifically for Web development. It has now been ported to the Linux platform. Advanced features include:

◆ An integrated Enterprise Resources Planning (ERP) suite: Oracle Applications for Linux

◆ A wizard-based development environment for building, deploying, and managing Web database applications and content-driven Web sites: Oracle WebDB on Linux

◆ Tools for building and deploying Internet database applications: Oracle Developer and Oracle Developer Server on Linux

Summary

In this chapter, you learned how to:

◆ Check that PostgreSQL was installed.

◆ Configure the postgres user.

◆ Create a user profile file in the Bash shell.

◆ Start the Postmaster service.

◆ Test the database connection.

◆ Create a database.

◆ Use the Interactive SQL Monitor.

◆ Remove a database.

◆ Create a table.

◆ Populate a table.

◆ Query a table.

◆ Use table inheritance.

◆ Add a database user.

◆ Download Informix Dynamic Server for Linux.

◆ Install Informix Dynamic Server for Linux.

SUMMARY

Part 3
Working with Linux on the Command Line

If you use Red Hat Linux 6 to enjoy the Gnome productivity suites and Corel WordPerfect, it's quite possible that you may never need to use Linux at the command line. But if you are a power user, or if you just want to know what is going on "beneath the hood," this part is for you.

Chapter 10: The Bash Shell explains the concept of Linux shells, and provides information about working with the bash shell.

Chapter 11: Files, Processes, and Permissions covers working with files. After you read the chapter, you will understand the concepts of ownership and permissions.

Chapter 12: Shell Scripting and Programming explains how to get started writing bash shell scripts. You'll also learn about some of the other great development tools that ship with Red Hat Linux 6.

Part 3
Working with
Linux on the
Command Line

THE BASH SHELL

This chapter, along with Chapter 11, tells you most of what you always wanted to know—but were afraid to ask—about working with Linux at the command line. When you interact with Linux at the command line, you are interacting with a Linux *shell*, just as you interact with Command.com, a DOS shell, when you work with a DOS prompt. Chapters 11 and 12 primarily cover the bash shell, which is Linux's default.

If you are new to Linux, you can comfortably perform such tasks as sending email, browsing the Web, and writing letters using Gnome and applications like Netscape and WordPerfect without ever even seeing a command line. But there comes a time when even the casual user wants to delve deeper.

You might find that there are some things that *have* to be done at the command line. Then again, there are some things that are simply easier to do at the command line.

In addition, some people simply do not like graphical user interfaces and prefer working at the command line.

Finally, it is simply interesting to understand the way a Linux command shell works!

Topics covered in this chapter include the following:

- ◆ How to access the command line
- ◆ Available shells
- ◆ The bash shell
- ◆ Profiles, paths, and environment variables
- ◆ How to get your bearings: session history, location, and identity
- ◆ How to edit text files and send email

Getting to the Prompt

Before you can interact directly with a command-line shell, you must get to the command-line (or *prompt*). You can access the command line in a number of ways:

◆ If Gnome (or another desktop environment) is running, you can open a terminal window.

◆ You can access your Linux server remotely, using a telnet application.

◆ You can start in Failsafe mode at the Red Hat logon screen. (This is somewhat like using Windows 95/98's Safe mode.)

◆ You can set your system to boot directly to the command prompt.

In the bash shell, the interactive prompt is indicated with a dollar sign (**$**). In other words, at **$**, you type your command and press enter: for example,

```
$ logout
```

To reach a command prompt in a Terminal window:

Choose the Terminal icon on the Gnome panel (it looks like a monitor, just to the left of the Netscape icons) *or* select GNOME terminal from the Utilities fly-out on the Gnome main menu. A terminal window will open (**Figure 10.1**).

✔ Tips

■ You can have multiple terminal windows open at the same time. In fact, it is quite often useful and desirable to do so. For example, you might be logged on as a normal user in one window and working as root in another. Or—to borrow an example from Chapter 9—you could start a database server engine in one terminal window and interact with it as a client in another.

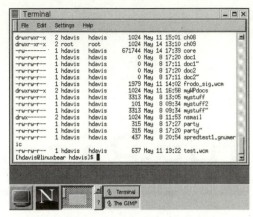

Figure 10.1 To open a terminal window, choose the Terminal icon on the Gnome panel.

■ If you are logged on as root, the interactive prompt is indicated with a **#** rather than a **$**.

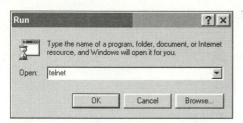

Figure 10.2 To open a Windows telnet client, type **telnet** in the Windows Run Program dialog box.

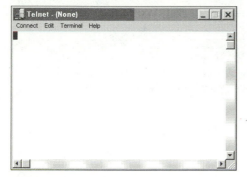

Figure 10.3 A telnet session that is not connected specifies None in its title bar.

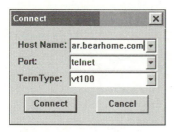

Figure 10.4 The Connect dialog box is used to specify a remote computer connection.

Figure 10.5 When you connect with a telnet session, you will be asked to log on.

To telnet from Microsoft Windows:

1. Choose Run from the Windows Start menu. The Run Program dialog box will open (**Figure 10.2**).

2. Type **telnet** in the Open box.

3. Click OK.

   An empty Telnet window—referred to as a *telnet session*— will open (**Figure 10.3**).

4. Choose Remote System from the Connect menu.

   The Connect dialog box will open (**Figure 10.4**).

5. In the Host Name box, type the IP address or fully qualified host name for the remote computer you want to telnet to.

6. Click Connect.

   You will be connected to the logon screen at the remote system (**Figure 10.5**).

7. Type your logon ID and password. The command prompt will appear.

✔ Tips

- You can enter the remote host name as part of the command that invokes the Telnet window in the Run Program dialog box, for example:

  ```
  telnet linuxbear.bearhome.com
  ```

- As with terminal windows, you can (and often will) have multiple telnet sessions open. Of course, you can also mix and match Telnet and terminal windows—and have several of each open simultaneously.

- There are many Windows telnet applications available as shareware or commercial software in addition to the utility that ships with Microsoft Windows.

- For more information on connecting remotely to your Linux server from Microsoft Windows, see Chapter 13.

To start Failsafe mode:

1. At the Red Hat logon screen, click the Options button.

2. Choose Failsafe from the Sessions fly-out menu.

✔ Tip

■ For more information on the Red Hat logon Sessions options, see Chapter 6.

To default to the command prompt:

1. Log on as root.

2. Open the Linux Configuration applet.

3. Set Initial System Services to Run Level 3 (**Figure 10.6**).

4. Click Accept.

✔ Tip

■ For more information on how to default to the command prompt, the meanings of the various run levels, and the procedure for reversing this process, see Chapter 3.

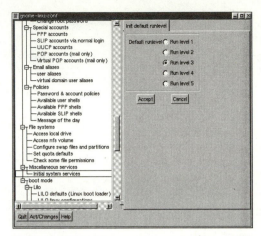

Figure 10.6 If you set your system run level to 3, it will boot to the command line.

Shells

In brief, you cannot interact with the core functionality of Linux—called its *kernel*—without a *shell*. As I mentioned earlier in this chapter, a shell is to the Linux kernel as Command.com is to DOS—except that with Linux, you have the choice of more than one shell.

A Linux shell is a program that provides a command-line interface between a user and the kernel. The kernel contains all the routines needed for input and output, file management, and other core functionality. A shell enables the user to access these routines from the command-line prompt that it provides.

In addition, a shell includes a language used for programming, which—in the context of shells—is called shell scripting. (For more information on shell scripting, see Chapter 12.)

Generally, shells are used in three ways:

- Interactively, when the user types commands

- For customizing a Linux session

- For shell programming (for more information on shell programming, see Chapter 12)

To determine what shell you are using:

1. At a command prompt, type
   `echo $SHELL`

2. Press Enter.
   Most likely, the response `/bin/bash` will come back, which means that you are using the bash shell, Linux's default.

✔ Tips

- The content of the SHELL environment variable is the path and name of the shell. If you strip the path away, you will get the name of the shell. In the example above, if you strip away the path, **/bin/**, you get the name of the shell, **bash**.

- You can also find out what shell you or anybody is using with the finger command. For example, **finger hdavis** displays my shell, plus a good bit of other information, including hdavis's home directory and when hdavis last logged on.

- Remember that, unlike with DOS, commands and file names in any Linux shell are case sensitive.

To find out what shells are available:

1. At a command prompt, type
   cat /etc/shells

2. Press Enter.
   A list of available shells will be displayed (**Figure 10.7**).

Table 10.1 lists the more commonly used shells that are available in Red Hat Linux 6.

Changing your shell

I suppose that even turtles and tortoises would like to change their shells from time to time! You can easily change shells.

To use a temporary shell:

At the prompt, type the executable path and program name for the shell you want to use. For example, to temporarily use the C shell, type **/bin/csh**.

✔ Tip

- Think of the temporary shell as a shell within a shell, or a subshell.

Figure 10.7 You can use the cat command to display the shells included in the /etc/shells file.

Table 10.1

Common Shells		
PROGRAM NAME	**SHELL**	**COMMENTS**
/bin/sh	Bourne Shell	This is the granddaddy of Unix shells, but it lacks a great deal of functionality
/bin/bash	Bourne Again Shell	This is the default shell in Linux
/bin/csh	C Shell	The syntax and constructs of this shell resemble those of the C programming language
/bin/tcsh	Enhanced C Shell	This is an enhanced version of the C shell
/bin/ksh	Korn Shell	This is one of the most popular Unix shells, but it generally is not the default in Linux

Figure 10.8 Administrators can change a user's shell by editing the /etc/passwd file.

To return to the original shell:

At the prompt, type **exit**.

To change the shell "permanently":

1. At the command prompt, type **chsh**.

2. Enter your password when you are prompted.

3. At the new shell prompt, enter the path to the new shell you want to use: for example, **/bin/tcsh**.

4. To activate the new shell, log off and then log on again.

Alternatively, if you have root access, you can change each user's default shell by editing each user's entry in the /etc/passwd file. Information in /etc/passwd is contained in a line for each user.

To edit the /etc/passwd file:

1. Log on as root.

2. Open the /etc/passwd file in a text editor (**Figure 10.8**).

3. The last entry on each user line is the user's shell. Edit the users as you want to reflect the new shell choices.

4. Save the file.

   The next time the user logs on, the new shell that you set will be activated.

The Bash Shell

Bash is short for Bourne Again Shell. This shell is available as free software under the GNU license. The name reflects the bash shell's origins as an enhanced version of the Bourne shell. It also is typical of the sly sense of humor—some might say silliness—sometimes used in naming Linux free software programs.

Bash is the default Red Hat Linux shell. It is generally an easy shell to work with. According to the Free Software Foundation, "bash is an sh-compatible shell that incorporates useful features from the Korn shell ksh and the C shell csh."

Unless you are already used to another shell, you probably should stick with the bash shell.

Working with environment variables

An *environment variable* is used to expose information to the shell and to programs invoked at the shell's prompt. In other words, the information contained in an environment variable is used to determine interactions among the user, the shell, the system, and programs.

By convention, environment variables are all uppercase. Also, you need to know that $ is used as a special character to mean the content of a variable rather than the literal string that is the variable's name.

It is typical for an environment variable to be used to contain a location. For example, the environment variable HOME is used to store a user's home directory.

Some environment variables are used to tell a particular program the location of files it needs. For example, to invoke the PostgreSQL's Postmaster service, the user postgres—described in Chapter 9—had to

have the environment variable PGLIB set to the location of PostgreSQL's data files.

Many environment variables are set in the overall or default configuration files. (Configuration files are explained later in this chapter.) Until they are changed for a particular user, these environment variables are set the same for all users.

Other environment variables are specific to a particular user, like the postgres user I just mentioned. This occurs when the environment variable is set on the fly interactively, or added only to a user-specific configuration file.

The echo command displays a line of text.

To see the current value of an environment variable:

1. At the command prompt, type **echo** followed by the environment variable. Here are some examples:

echo $HOME	(user's home directory)
echo $LOGNAME	(user's logon ID)
echo $SHELL	(current shell)
echo $PATH	(path)

2. Press Enter.

✔ Tips

■ If the environment variable you attempt to echo doesn't exist, the line echoed back will be empty.

■ If you leave off the $, for example, if you enter **echo HOME** the response will be the literal HOME.

To list all the current environment variables:

1. At the command prompt, type **set**.

2. Press Enter.

   The environment variables will be displayed (**Figure 10.9**).

Figure 10.9 To display the environment variables, type **set**.

Figure 10.10 To view a directory listing one screen at a time, use the ls command piped to the more command.

Piping to more

When you displayed your environment variables using the set command, they may have filled more than one terminal or telnet screen, so you couldn't view the variables at the beginning.

The more Linux command displays file contents one screen at a time. When you've finished viewing each screen, you press the spacebar to move on to the next screen.

To *pipe* a command means to send the output of one Linux command to another. The symbol that indicates piping is |.

To view environment variables one screen at a time:

1. At the command prompt, type

   set | more

2. Press Enter.

✔ Tip

■ The Pipe symbol (|) is usually found above the backslash key on the keyboard. It is often represented with two dotted vertical lines rather than a solid vertical line.

"Piping to more" is very useful and can be used to view directory listings.

To view a directory listing one screen at a time:

1. At the command prompt, type

   ls -a -l | more

2. Press Enter.

   The directory listing will appear, one screen at a time (**Figure 10.10**).

The more command can also be used to read the contents of files.

To use more to view the contents of a file:

1. At the command prompt, type `more` followed by the file name: for example, `more .bash_profile`.

2. Press Enter.

   The contents of the file will be displayed one screen at a time.

Setting environment variables

You can set environment variables interactively at the command line. This is true for environment variables that you make up on the spot, those that programs require, and those that come preconfigured—although you should probably be a bit circumspect about editing variables that the shell sets automatically.

Keep in mind that an environment variable set on the fly exists only as long as the session in which it was created. This is sometimes useful in debugging configuration issues, but if you want the environment variable to have its value the next time you log on, you will need to set it in a configuration file. I'll explain how to do this later in this chapter.

Setting an environment variable involves two steps:

◆ Assigning the variable

◆ Exporting it so that it is available to all programs and scripts running in the current session

To set an environment variable on the fly:

1. At the command prompt, type the name of the environment variable followed by the value you want assigned to it.

This value is often a file name or location, but it can also be a text string or number: for example, `MYENV ah-goo!` assigns the text string `ah-goo!` to the environment variable MYENV.

2. Press Enter.

3. At the prompt, export the environment variable: for example, `export MYENV`.

4. Press Enter.

5. Verify that the value has been assigned by typing `echo $MYENV` at the prompt.

   The value of the variable will be displayed on the next line (**Figure 10.11**).

Figure 10.11 Environment variables must be exported before they are available in scripts and programs.

✔ Tip

■ The two steps—assigning and exporting—can be combined into one: for example, `export NEXTENV=42`.

Setting the PATH environment variable

A very important environment variable, PATH is used to store the value of the path—the directories where the shell can look for files that have been invoked without a fully qualified path being required.

THE BASH SHELL

For example, if myprogram is in the /harold/ bin directory, I can run myprogram simply by typing **myprogram** if /harold/bin is on the path—that is, if /harold/bin is included in the PATH environment variable.

On the other hand, if /harold/bin is not on the path, to invoke myprogram I would have to include its location:

`/harold/bin/myprogram`

Within the PATH variable, the various directories that are on the path—that is, that are available without full qualification—are separated by colons (**:**), like this:

`/bin:/usr/bin:/usr/X11R6/bin:/harold:/harold/bin`

If you were adding a new directory to your path, one thing you would not want to do would be to delete the current contents of the PATH variable. If you did so, a number of things quite possibly wouldn't work right.

Fortunately, the **$** operator can be used to reference the contents of the current PATH variable. New additions to the PATH variable can then be concatenated with the existing value.

To add a directory to the PATH variable:

At the command prompt, type

`export PATH=$PATH:`*`new directory`*

For example, type

`export PATH=$PATH:/harold/bin`

✔ Tip

■ If the PATH string contains any spaces, you should use quotation marks. For example,

`export PATH="$PATH:/harold/my wpdocs"`

Editing the configuration files

Editing or adding environment variables at the command prompt is all very well and good, but your changes do not *persist*, meaning that the next time you log on, they will be gone.

If you want to create environment variables (or change existing ones) and have your work persist between sessions, you need to edit a configuration file.

If you are using Red Hat Linux 6 and the bash shell, there are four relevant configuration files, listed in **Table 10.2**.

When you look at **Table 10.2**, you'll see a special character being used: the tilde (~). This character indicates the user's home directory.

To go to your home directory:

1. At the command prompt, type the following:

   cd ~

2. Press Enter.

If you look at **Table 10.2**, you'll see that the files in the user's home directory start with a period: for example, .bash_profile. The period means that they are *hidden* files.

If you open the Gnome File Manager with its default settings, hidden files will not be displayed.

Table 10.2

Typical Red Hat Linux 6 \bash Configuration Files		
LOCATION AND FILE	PROCESSING ORDER	CONTENTS
/etc/profile	First	System-wide environment variables and startup programs
/etc/bashrc	Second	In theory, system-wide functions and aliases; in practice often only the prompt configuration
~/.bash_profile (in user's home directory)	If it exists, third	User-specific environment variables and startup programs
~/.bashrc (in user's home directory)	If it exists, last; this file	User-specific functions and aliases is invoked by .bash_profile

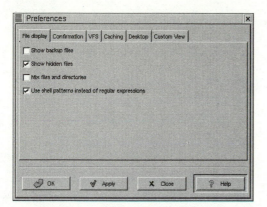

Figure 10.12 To view hidden files in Gnome File Manager, check Show Hidden Files in the Preferences dialog box.

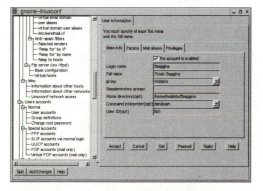

Figure 10.13 Users assigned a home directory below /home have the template configuration files located in etc/skel automatically copied to their home directories.

To view hidden files in Gnome File Manager:

1. Open Gnome File Manager.

2. Choose Preferences from the Edit menu. The File display tab of the Preferences dialog box will open (**Figure 10.12**).

3. Select Show Hidden Files to place a check mark next to it.

4. Click OK.

✔ Tip

- For information on how to display hidden files using the command line, see Chapter 11.

From a system administrator's viewpoint, if you create a user with the Gnome/Linux Configuration tool (see **Figure 10.13**), and if the home directory you set is under the /home directory, then the configuration files stored in /etc/skel are automatically copied to the user's new home directory.

In this case, *skel* is shorthand for skeleton, meaning a template. As an administrator, if you want to change all of the configuration files for new users, you would simply edit the files in etc/skel.

Of course, it would be the administrator's option to manually tweak a specific user's configuration files—or to add a user with no configuration files at all, for that matter.

For more information on using the Gnome/Linux Configuration tool to add users and groups, see Chapter 6. For information on administering users at the command line, see Chapter 11.

THE BASH SHELL

To add an environment variable for a user:

1. On the Gnome\Linux desktop, open Gnome File Manager.

2. Find the .bash_profile file located in the user's home directory (**Figure 10.14**).

3. Right-click .bash_profile and choose Open With from the fly-out menu.

   The gmc dialog box will open (**Figure 10.15**).

4. Type **gnp** in the Program to Run box.

5. Click OK.

   The .bash_profile file will open in Gnotepad+ (**Figure 10.16**).

6. Using the techniques described earlier in this chapter in "To set an environment variable on the fly," add and export an environment variable: for example,

   ```
   MYENV="Lions, and tigers, _
       and bears,  Oh my!"
   export MYENV
   ```

7. Choose Save from the Gnotepad+ File menu and close Gnotepad+.

8. Log on as the user whose configuration file was changed.

9. At the prompt, type **echo $MYENV**.

   The new environment variable will be displayed (**Figure 10.17**).

✔ Tips

- You can edit configuration files using the text editors available at the command line rather than Gnotepad+. Some of the more popular command-line text editing tools are described later in this chapter.

- To add an environment variable globally rather than for a single user, edit the etc/profile file rather than the user's .bash_profile file.

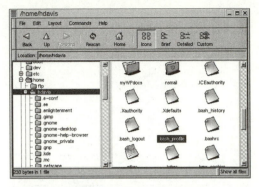

Figure 10.14 You can use Gnome File Manager to locate a user's .bash_profile file.

Figure 10.15 To edit a file in Gnotepad+, type **gnp** in the Program to Run box.

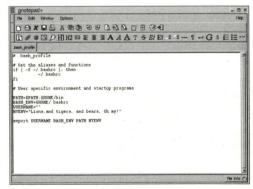

Figure 10.16 It's easy to edit a text file, such as a user's .bash_profile configuration file, in Gnotepad+.

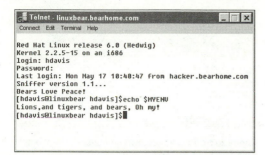

Figure 10.17 Changes made in a user's configuration file are available the next time the user logs on.

Figure 10.18 By editing the etc/profile file, you can make changes to everyone's path.

Figure 10.19 Changes made to the path will be available the next time you log on.

To add to the path globally

1. Use the techniques described in "To add an environment variable for a user" to open the file etc/profile in Gnotepad+ (**Figure 10.18**).

2. Using the techniques described in "To add a directory to the PATH variable," add a directory to the path. For example, enter:

   ```
   PATH="$PATH:/home/hdavis/ _
       linuxvqs"
   ```

3. Make sure the PATH variable is exported.

4. Save the file.

5. To verify the addition, log on.

6. At the prompt, type `echo $PATH`.

7. Press Enter.

   The new directory will be displayed on the path (**Figure 10.19**).

✔ Tips

- If you delete any directories from the path without knowing what they do, it is quite possible that some things will not work any more.

- To change a user's path, rather than the global, edit that user's .bash_profile file rather than etc/profile.

Changing the bash prompt

You can easily configure the command-line prompt to include various useful pieces of information. To change the system-wide prompt, edit /etc/bashrc. To change a single user prompt, edit the .bashrc file in that user's home directory.

In either case, you will need to edit the line beginning **PS1**, which is often the only line that is not a comment in these files. The various kinds of information that you can include go between the square brackets and are represented by code letters (see **Table 10.3**). You can also include literal text if you wish.

To add full directory, date, and time information to the prompt:

1. Open /etc/bashrc in a text editor (Gnotepad+ is shown in **Figure 10.20**).

2. Place a hash symbol (#) in front of the current prompt line (it begins with **PS1**).

   This will comment out the line, disabling it but leaving it in place in case you want to go back to it.

3. Add a new PS1 line. For example, enter:
   ```
   PS1="[\u working in \w Date: _
       \d Time:    \t]\\$ "
   ```

4. Save the file.

5. To verify the results, log on.

   The new prompt should appear (**Figure 10.21**).

✔ Tip

■ Consider testing a proposed prompt interactively to see how you like it by changing the PS1 environment variable before making a global change.

Figure 10.20 To change the appearance of the prompt, edit the PS1 line in /etc/bashrc.

Figure 10.21 You can include various kinds of information in the prompt.

Table 10.3

Prompt Codes

CODE	MEANING
\u	Displays the user ID of the current user
\w	Shows the current path and directory; the user's home directory is represented with a ~ character
\W	Shows the current directory without the path
\t	Shows the current time
\d	Shows the current date
\n	Forces a new line within the prompt, making the prompt split between two lines
\h	Shows the host name of the Linux server

Figure 10.22 You can enter p w d to find out where you are.

Figure 10.23 To list the files in the current directory, enter l s.

Figure 10.24 To list files—including those that are hidden—in the current directory, enter l s −a.

More Bash Features

The bash shell includes a great many more features that make it easy—or possible—for you to perform your tasks.

Location, location, location

For starters, if you don't know where you are already because you added information to your prompt, you can find out!

To find out where you are:

1. At the command prompt, type p w d.

2. Press Enter.

   Your current location is displayed (**Figure 10.22**).

To list the files in the current directory:

1. At the command prompt, type l s.

2. Press Enter.

   The files in your current directory that are not hidden are listed (**Figure 10.23**).

To list the files—including hidden files—in the current directory:

1. At the command prompt, type l s −a.

2. Press Enter.

   All the files are listed, including hidden ones (**Figure 10.24**).

Using command completion

Command completion in the bash shell means that after you enter just part of a command, the rest will be filled in automatically when you press the Tab key.

Of course, command completion works only if there is a valid way to complete the command you started.

Command completion can be used to complete shell commands, file and directory names, and more.

MORE BASH FEATURES

To use command completion:

1. At the command prompt, enter a partial command. For example, as a start on the command more test, to view the contents of the file test, enter `more te`.

2. Press the Tab key. Bash will complete your command, so that it now reads `more test`.

3. Press Enter to see the contents of the more command displayed (**Figure 10.25**).

Figure 10.25 If you use the Tab key with an incomplete command, bash will do its best to read your mind.

Using session history

In the bash shell, the Up arrow key lets you scroll through the list of previous commands entered during your session. The Down arrow will bring you back to the current command.

To access a command you previously used:

Press the up arrow key until you reach the command.

To see a numbered list of your session commands:

1. At the command prompt, type `history`.

2. Press Enter.

   A numbered list of your session command will be displayed (**Figure 10.26**).

Figure 10.26 Use the history command to display a numbered list of your session commands.

✔ Tip

■ If you follow `history` with a number, *n*, the command will display the last *n* commands. For example, `history 12` will display the last 12 commands you entered.

To reuse a numbered session command:

1. At the command prompt, type `!` followed by the command number. For example, type `!144`.

2. Press Enter.
   The referenced command will be executed.

Text Editors and Email

Up to this point in this book, I've made the assumption that text editing and emailing would take place in Gnome windows.

Under Gnome, to edit text you can use one of the GUI desktop environment editors, such as Gnotepad+. Netscape Messenger is available for email.

However, what if Windows-like desktop environments don't make you feel all warm and gui inside? That's okay. If you like to edit your text using a nonwindowing application, there are many good choices available.

In this section, I'll give you a brief high-level look at two of the more popular text editors available, vi and Pico, and briefly mention emacs. Which, if any, you choose to use is, of course, up to you.

One reason you might want to use text-based utilities is that you are connecting remotely and cannot use programs that require an X11 server (such as those on the Gnome desktop).

Using vi

The vi text editor is very powerful, but it's complicated to learn. If you're a vi power user, then you know already what it can do and have the ability to make it do it. Anyone else might think twice about taking the time to get up to speed with vi. Perhaps the best reason for learning vi is that the vi editor is almost certain to be present on any flavor of Unix, so if you learn vi, you can expect to be able to edit text almost anywhere.

The version of vi that ships with Red Hat Linux 6 is vim—vi *improved*—which is freely distributable and was primarily written by Bram Moolenaar.

You'll find some of the commonly used vi commands in Appendix A.

To start vim:

1. At the command prompt, type **vi**.

2. Press Enter.

   The vim editor will open (**Figure 10.27**).

✔ Tips

■ You can open vi with a file already loaded by including the file name in the command: for example, **vi test**.

■ You can open a number of files using a wildcard specification: for example, **vi *.html**. You can then move through the files that you opened by pressing the Escape key followed by **:n** (for next).

To add text to a vi file:

1. With vim open, type **i**.

   You will now be in Insert mode.

2. Type some text. To see the text you are typing, you may have to scroll to the top of the terminal or telnet window, if you are using one (**Figure 10.28**).

3. When you are through entering text, press Escape to move into Command mode.

4. Type **a**, to add the text after the cursor.

To save a vi file:

1. Press Escape to enter Command mode.

2. Type **:w** (for write) followed by the file name: for example, **:w vitest**.

✔ Tip

■ To save a file that has already been named, you can just enter **:w**, without a file name.

To exit vi without saving:

1. Press Escape to enter Command mode.

2. Type **:q!**

Figure 10.27 To use vim, type **vi** at the command prompt.

Figure 10.28 Insert mode is used to add text in vi.

Figure 10.29 Pico features an intuitive interface.

Using Pico

Pico is much more user friendly than vi because Pico is menu driven. You do not have to remember arcane keystroke commands or keep track of the mode you are in.

To start Pico:

1. At the command prompt, type `pico`.

2. Press Enter.
   Pico will open.

To enter text in a Pico window:

Start typing. Your text will appear in the Pico window (**Figure 10.29**).

✔ Tip

■ If you are editing configuration files, start Pico with word wrapping disabled using the –w flag: `pico -w filename`.

To save a Pico file:

1. Hold down the Control key.

2. Press **0** (for write out).

To exit Pico:

1. Hold down the Control key.

2. Press **X**.

The emacs text editor

Another popular choice is emacs. Red Hat Linux 6 ships with a version of this powerful program: GNU Emacs.

The emacs editor is tremendously customizable and has so many features that it could, itself, be the subject of a Visual QuickPro Guide. Notably, emacs is a good programming editor. Arguably just as powerful, emacs is a great improvement over vi. For one thing, it doesn't have vi's different modes to keep track of.

TEXT EDITORS AND EMAIL

To send an email message using Linux mail:

1. At the bash command line, type the word `mail` followed by the addressee. For example, type

   `mail harold@bearhome.com`

2. Press Enter.

3. At the subject line, type a subject.

4. Type the text of your message.

5. To end the message, type a period by itself on a line (**Figure 10.30**).

6. Press Enter.

7. You will be prompted for CC addressees. If there are none, press Enter.

✔ Tip

■ As an alternative to sending your email with a period on a line by itself, holding down the Control key and typing **D** will also send email.

Figure 10.30 A Unix mail message can be concluded and sent by typing a period by itself on the message's final line.

Pine email

Several text-based email programs ship with Red Hat Linux 6. Pine is particularly notable. This menu-driven program is intuitive and powerful.

Pine was written at the University of Washington.

Full documentation is available on-line.

To start pine, type **pine** at the command prompt.

Summary

In this chapter, you learned how to:

◆ Find a prompt.

◆ Tell what shell you are in.

◆ Determine what shells are available.

◆ Use a temporary shell.

◆ Change your shell.

◆ View the contents of environment variables.

◆ List all environment variables.

◆ Pipe to more.

◆ Use the more command to view a file.

◆ Set environment variables on the fly.

◆ Add a directory to the PATH variable.

◆ Go to your home directory.

◆ View hidden files.

◆ Add an environment variable for a user.

◆ Add to the global path.

◆ Change the bash prompt.

◆ Find where you are.

◆ Use command completion.

◆ Use session history.

◆ Open and save files in vi and Pico.

◆ Send email with Linux email.

FILES, PROCESSES, AND PERMISSIONS

Chapter 11 picks up where Chapter 10, "The Bash Shell," left off. In other words, this is—for the most part—a chapter that takes place at the command line.

The exceptions to the command-line focus are the discussions of how to mount devices and create default permissions for a group. These tasks can be done at the command line or using the Gnome interface. This chapter describes how to mount devices both ways and how to create default permissions with Gnome.

This chapter addresses these questions: How do you find out about a system? How do you find out about disk space and directories? How do you find files and text within files?

This chapter also shows you how to view and monitor processes. If the time has come for a process to die, you will learn how to kill it.

Finally, file ownership and permissions are explained. What does it mean to own a file? How can a file have more than one owner? What are permissions, and how are they changed?

Topics covered in this chapter include the following:

- ◆ Getting information about your system
- ◆ Processes
- ◆ The file system
- ◆ Permissions and ownership

Learning About Your System

Since knowledge is power, it is logical to want to know more about your system—or at least to know what tools are available at a given point in time.

If there are issues of software compatibility, it may be helpful to know the exact kernel build that you are running on.

To view information about the machine and operating system:

1. At the command prompt, type
   `uname -a`.

2. Press Enter.
   The computer will respond with text along these lines:
   ```
   Linux linuxbear 2.2.5-15 #1
   Mon Apr 19 23:00:46 EDT 1999
   i686 unknown
   ```
   The response to the uname -a command provides the following information:
   `Linux`: Name of the operating system (-s)
   `linuxbear`: Host name (-n)
   `2.2.5-15 #1`: Release number of the kernel (-r)
   `Mon Apr 19 23:00:46 EDT 1999`: Build information about the kernel (-v)
   `i686`: Machine (-m)
   `unknown`: Processor (-p)

✔ Tip

■ You can issue the uname command with a specific flag, as indicated in the list above, rather than returning all the information with -a.

Determining free disk space

In Linux, the file system is an artificial construct made up of an overall tree structure beginning with the root directory (represented by /). The location of a directory on this artificial tree does not imply that the directory is physically on a particular hard drive.

A file system that is *mounted* is in use in the system. The directory that represents the nexus between a mounted file system and the overall tree structure is called a *mount point*.

You can see which file systems are mounted, how much space they have, and their mount points with the df command.

To determine free disk space:

1. At the command prompt, type **d f**.

2. Press Enter.
   You will see a response along the lines of the following code, displaying each mounted file system, its used and available space, and its mount point. You can use the df command to find out where file systems are mounted and how much space they have available. (See **Table 11.1** below).

Table 11.1

Determining Free Disk Space					
Filesystem	1k-blocks	Used	Available	Use%	Mounted on
/dev/hda2	2208347	1182338	911853	56%	/
/dev/hdc	556054	556054	0	100%	/mnt

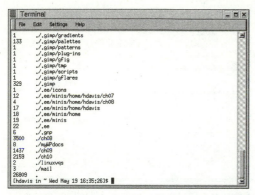

Figure 11.1 You can use the du command to list disk usage in the current directory.

To determine disk use in a directory:

1. At the command prompt, type **du**.

2. Press Enter.

    Information will be displayed about disk use in the current directory and subdirectories, in kilobytes (**Figure 11.1**).

✔ Tips

- If you name a path with the du command, for example,

    du /home/hdavis/linuxvqs

    the disk use in that directory and its subdirectories will be displayed.

- You can pipe the output of du to more, by typing **du | more**, to make the output readable if it fills multiple screens.

Determining the file type

In Windows, you can usually make a guess about the type of a file from its extension. In Linux, files are often not named with an extension, and you have no way of knowing the file type based on the file name.

To find out the file type:

1. At the command prompt, type **file** followed by the path and name of the file. For example, type

    file /home/hdavis/wpdocs/testwp

2. Press Enter.

    The system will respond with a message about the file, like this:

    /home/hdavis/wpdocs/testwp: WordPerfect document

✔ Tip

- The file command will not provide help-ful results for all files. This command first checks the file for the kind of data it con-tains. It next reads a file correspondence table from the so-called magic file (this is usually /etc/magic if you want to exam-ine it). For example, a WordPerfect file is recognized because the WordPerfect installation program added information to the magic file.

Determining the system users

To find out who is logged onto your system and all kinds of other information about these users, you can use the finger command.

To find out who is logged in:

1. At the command prompt, type `finger`.

2. Press Enter.

   A list of users who are logged on and their home directories will be displayed (**Figure 11.2**).

✔ Tips

- Fingering a particular user, for example, by entering `finger hdavis`, will pro-duce some additional information about that user, including the user's shell, elapsed time since logon, and idle time since logon.

- Needing to know who you are may seem unlikely if you already know yourself—or more the subject for an existential French movie than an issue in Linux system administration. But if you're logged onto your system with multiple identifications and haven't customized your prompt to display IDs, things can get confusing. In that case, the whoami command will tell you the user ID you have used to log on.

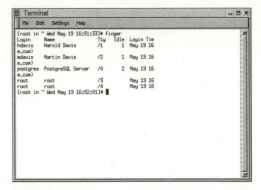

Figure 11.2 The finger command will tell you who is logged on.

It's My Process, and I'll Do What I Want To

Perhaps you've had the experience in Microsoft Windows of a rogue program that will not stop running, or a window that is plastered in an open position on the screen and will not close. The only way to close the program or window is to press Ctrl+Alt+Del. (This is sometimes called a three-fingered salute.)

Ctrl+Alt+Del opens the Close Program dialog box in Microsoft Windows. The Close Program dialog box probably reports that the errant program as not responding. To stop it, you select the program and click End Task. (True: There is one other way, too—turning off the power.)

As a Linux administrator or developer, you may need to perform an analogous job. In Linux, this job is not known as ending a task but, rather, as killing a process.

In Linux, *process* is shorthand for an abstraction that manages the memory, CPU, and input and output resources necessary to run a program. Although Linux gives the impression that many things are happening simultaneously, in fact, only one process can be executing on one CPU at any given instant. The illusion of simultaneous execution of processes is achieved through *time slicing*, in which the operating system changes the process that is active at regular, very short intervals.

To view all processes associated with a terminal:

1. Log on as root.

2. At the command prompt, type **ps -a**.

3. Press Enter.

   A table will appear (**Figure 11.3**), showing the process ID (PID), the terminal that originated the process (TTY), the CPU time that the process has consumed (TIME), and the command that started the process (COMMAND).

To monitor all processes:

1. Log on as root.

2. At the command prompt, type
   ps -aux | more

3. Press Enter.

   A screen-by-screen display will appear (**Figure 11.4**). For an explanation of the columns, see **Table 11.2**.

4. Use the spacebar to scroll through the screens.

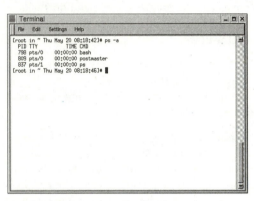

Figure 11.3 To view all running processes that are associated with a terminal, enter **ps -a**.

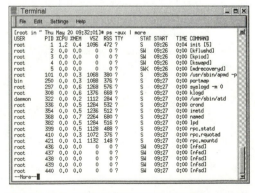

Figure 11.4 To monitor all processes, pipe **ps -aux** to more.

Table 11.2

ps -aux Columns	
FIELD	**MEANING**
USER	User name of the process owner
PID	Process ID
%CPU	Percentage of the CPU this process is using
%MEM	Percentage of memory this process is using
VSZ	Virtual size of the process, in kilobytes
RSS	Amount of physical memory used by the process
TTY	Associated terminal.
STAT	Status of the process; some values are:
	R (Runnable)
	D (In disk wait state)
	I (Sleeping for less than 20 seconds)
	S (Sleeping for more than 20 seconds)
	T (Stopped)
	Z (Zombie, an orphaned process that should have previously been killed by another process)
	W (Process that is swapped out)
	N (Nice value, which influences the execution priority of the process)
START	Time the process was started
TIME	CPU time the process has consumed
COMMAND	Command name (and its arguments) that started the process

IT'S MY PROCESS, AND I'LL DO WHAT I WANT TO

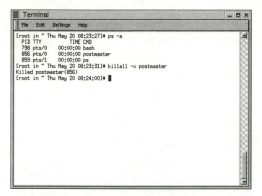

Figure 11.5 Enter `killall  -v` to kill a process by name and receive confirmation.

To kill a process:

1. Log on as root (or as the owner of the process).

2. At the command prompt, type `kill` followed by the process ID (PID). For example, type `kill 856`.

3. Press Enter.

✔ Tips

■ Only root—or the owner of a process— can kill a process.

■ Process IDs vary from session to session for the same program. Be careful about what you kill!

To kill a process by name, with confirmation:

1. Log on as root (or as the process owner).

2. At the prompt, type
`killall -v processname`
For example, type
`killall -v postmaster`

3. Press Enter.

The system will respond with a message reporting that the process has been killed (**Figure 11.5**).

IT'S MY PROCESS, AND I'LL DO WHAT I WANT TO

199

The File System

The Linux file system can be thought of as a single abstract "tree." When you add files on a removable device—such as a floppy drive or CD-ROM—or a remote system, these subsidiary file systems are "grafted" onto the original file system at a mount point.

Mount points are usually empty directories.

A mount point—and, indeed, the entire abstract tree—has no relationship with physical reality. This behavior is different than in Microsoft Windows, where the files and directories on drive E are all on the logical or physical drive E.

Actually, the term *file system* has two meanings:

◆ The entire Linux abstract file system

◆ A subsection, or "branch," of the file system tree: in other words, a directory, possibly with subdirectories

Generally, it is apparent from the context which usage is meant.

There's no requirement that a Linux file system be organized in a particular way, but over time a kind of organizational convention has grown up. The root file system includes the root directory, the Linux kernel, /dev for device files, /etc for critical system files, and /bin for important utilities. Other standard directories and their contents are listed in **Table 11.3**.

It's also important to understand that every Linux file has a *mode*. The mode of a file controls who can read, write, and execute the contents of a file; it is also called the file's *permissions*. Generally only the owner of a file or the root superuser can change a file's permissions.

Mounting devices

File systems are extended by mounting devices, such as a CD-ROM, floppy drive, or removable hard drive.

To mount and dismount a file system:

The general syntax for mounting is

`mount special-device directory`

The *special-device* argument indicates the device driver file: for example, /dev/fd0 for the first floppy disk drive, or /dev/cdrom for a CD-ROM drive. The *directory* argument can refer to any directory, which you can create if you want, but by convention, it is often a subdirectory of /mnt.

The general syntax for unmounting is

`umount name` where *name* is either the special-device file or its mount point.

Table 11.3

Standard Linux Directories and Their Contents	
PATH NAME	**CONTENTS**
/	The root directory
/bin, /sbin	Important utilities necessary for minimum system operability
/dev	Device files for terminals, disks, modems, and so on
/etc	Critical system files
/tmp	Temporary files that disappear between reboots
/usr/bin	Executable files
/usr/lib	Support files for standard Linux programs
/usr/man	Man pages
/usr/src	Source code
/var/log	Log files
/var/spool	Spooling directories for printers, mail, and so on
/var/tmp	Temporary space (files that don't disappear between reboots)

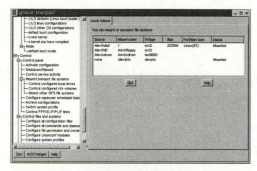

Figure 11.6 You can mount and unmount file systems using the Gnome control panel.

Figure 11.7 You will be asked to confirm a mount or unmount.

To mount a CD-ROM:

1. At the prompt, type

`mount /dev/cdrom /mnt/cdrom`

2. Press Enter.

To unmount a CD-ROM:

1. At the prompt, type

`umount /dev/cdrom`

or

`umount /mnt/cdrom`

2. Press Enter.

To mount a floppy drive:

1. At the prompt, type

`mount /dev/fd0 /mnt/floppy`

2. Press Enter.

To unmount a floppy drive:

1. At the prompt, type

`umount /dev/fd0`

or

`umount /mnt/floppy`

2. Press Enter.

To mount a device using Gnome:

1. Log on as root.

2. On the Gnome desktop, open the Linux Configuration applet on the control panel.

3. Scroll down until you see Mount/Unmount File Systems in the list on the left (**Figure 11.6**).

4. Select a device to mount it: for example, /dev/cdrom.

5. Respond as appropriate when asked to confirm the mount (**Figure 11.7**).

✔ Tip

■ You can use the control panel to unmount devices as well.

THE FILE SYSTEM

Creating directories

Directories are the containers for other Linux directories and files. Most likely, every time you start a new project or want to group related files together, you will create a directory.

To create a new directory:

1. Move to the location in the directory tree where you want to create the new directory.

2. At the command prompt, type

   `mkdir mynewdir`

3. Press Enter.

4. Type `ls -l` to list the current directories. You will see mynewdir listed with a "d" in the leftmost column, indicating that it is a directory (**Figure 11.8**).

✔ Tips

- If you try to create a directory using a name that already exists within the container directory, you will receive a message stating that a file of that name already exists, proving once again that directories *are* files in Linux.

- The following are illegal characters in Linux file and directory names: <> {} [] () "" " * ? | /\ ^ ! # $ & ~

- In addition to the illegal characters, avoid using spaces and dashes (-). Some Linux programs cannot handle them.

To delete a directory:

1. Using the cd command, navigate to the parent of the directory you want to delete.

2. At the prompt, use the rmdir command to remove the directory: for example, type `rmdir mynewdir`.

3. Press Enter.

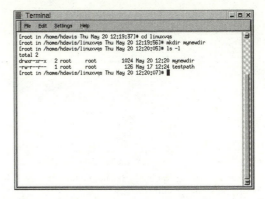

Figure 11.8 Directories are indicated with a "d" in the leftmost column when you list the contents of the current directory.

THE FILE SYSTEM

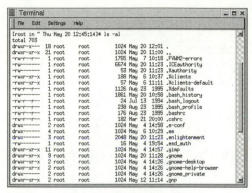

Figure 11.9 The command for listing files is **l s**.

Creating files

If directories are the filing system, then files are the contents.

To list all files in a directory:

1. At the prompt, type **ls -al**.

2. Press Enter.

    The files in the current directory will be displayed (**Figure 11.9**).

✔ Tip

■ The -l flag displays full information about the files; the -a flag displays all files, including hidden files. For more information on ls flags, see Appendix A.

To create a file:

1. At the prompt, type **touch** followed by the new file name. For example, type

    touch happy.file

2. Press Enter.

✔ Tip

■ There are many ways to create files. One approach is to use a text editor such as vi.

To copy a file (or directory):

To copy a file (or directory), use the cp command. For example, enter

cp myfileordir yourfileordir

To move a file (or directory):

To move a file or directory, use the mv command. For example, enter

mv thefileordir /newloc/thefileordir

To delete a file:

1. At the prompt, type **r m** followed by the name of the file. For example, type

    rm this.file.is.history

2. Press Enter.

THE FILE SYSTEM

✔ Tip

■ The rm command, depending on the flags you use, and whether you are logged on as root, can be extremely dangerous. For example, the -f flag removes write-protected files without prompting, and the -r flag deletes files and directories recursively. This means that if root issues the command **rm -rf**, the entire file system could be removed. *Don't try this at home!*

To find a file:

The find command is an extremely flexible means of finding files. (For more information on the find command, see Appendix A.)

For example, to find all the files in the /home/hdavis/ch11 directory that contain the word *fig* in the name, use the following syntax:

```
find /home/hdavis/ch11 -name _
  '*fig*' -print
```

This displays all the files that match the condition (**Figure 11.10**).

To find text within a file (or files):

Use the grep command to search one or more files for specific text, or for text that matches a *regular expression*.

For example, the following grep command (See **Figure 11.11**) would search all the files in the current directory for the string *elephant*, printing three lines on either side of the occurrence of *elephant* and providing line numbers (because of the -n flag):

```
grep -n -3 elephant *
```

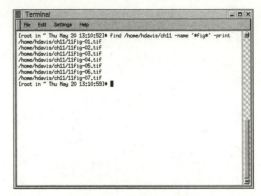

Figure 11.10 You can use the find command to display files whose name matches the supplied criteria.

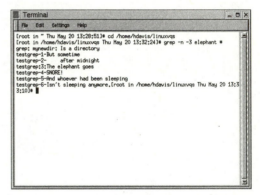

Figure 11.11 The grep command is used to find text that matches expressions within a file.

To view the beginning of a file:

1. Type `head myfile`.

2. Press Enter.

   The first 10 lines of the file will be displayed.

✔ Tips

- You can use the head command to view as many files as you want: for example, **`head -42 myfile`** displays the first 42 lines of myfile.

- You can view the beginnings of multiple files by piping them to more: for example, **`head -5 my* | more`**

To view the end of a file:

1. Type `tail myfile`.

2. Press Enter.

   The last 10 lines of the file will be displayed.

✔ Tips

- As with the head command, you can determine the number of lines that are displayed and display multiple files in a single tail command.

- The tail command is useful for keeping track of the most recent changes to log files when you are tracking or debugging the operation of a program—such as a database engine—that writes to a log file as it progresses.

Ownership and Permissions

Every Linux file (and directory) is *owned* and has a set of associated permissions—which specify who can do what with it—collectively referred to as a *mode*.

There are three kinds of owners:

- **User**, a single user ID indicating the user who is primarily responsible for the file. You automatically own, as user, any files you create.

- **Group**, the group of the user who owns the file. (For information on associated users and groups using the Gnome desktop control panel, see Chapter 6.) All users within a group have the same permissions in relation to a file.

- **Other**, meaning any user who is not a user-owner or member of the group that owns a file.

It's worth noting again that a Linux owner need not be a human being. Programs—such as PostgreSQL, discussed in Chapter 9—often run as a particular user. If these programs create files, then the files "belong" to the program's user.

Permissions are of three types:

- **Read**, meaning that users can view a file but cannot change it. In an ls -l listing, this permission is represented with an "r."

- **Write**, meaning that users can edit (or delete) a file. In an ls -l listing, this permission is represented with a "w."

- **Execute**, meaning that users can run the file (if it is a program or script) and view directories. In an ls -l listing, this permission is represented with an "x."

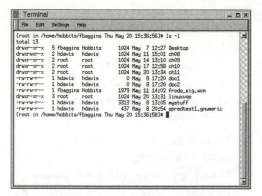

Figure 11.12 You can determine file ownership and permissions by entering l s - l.

To determine ownership and permissions:

1. At the command prompt, type l **s** - l.

2. Press Enter.

   The files and directories within the current directory will be displayed (**Figure 11.12**).

It's necessary to decode the columns in **Figure 11.12** to determine ownership and permissions.

- ◆ The column on the left, made up of 10 single-spaced letters, tells you the permissions for the various kinds of owners.

- ◆ A dash (-) means that the user does not have that level of permission.

- ◆ The first letter is "d" if the object is a directory; otherwise, it is -.

- ◆ The next three letters indicate read, write, and execute permissions for the user.

- ◆ The next three letters indicate read, write, and execute permissions for the group.

- ◆ The final three letters indicate read, write, and execute permissions for other users and groups.

   For example, - r w - r w - r indicates a file whose user and group have read and write permissions; everyone else has read permission only.

- ◆ The user and group names appear in the middle of each row. For example, in **Figure 11.12**, user fbaggins is a member of the Hobbits group.

To change the ownership of a file or directory:

1. At the command prompt, type `chown` followed by the new owner and the file name. For example, type

   `chown fbaggins ring.o.power`

2. Press Enter.

✔ Tip

■ You can use the -R flag with chown, for example, `chown -R`, to recursively change owners in all subdirectories.

To change the group associated with a file:

1. At the command prompt, type `chgrp` followed by the new group name and the file name. For example, type

   `chgrp hobbits ring.o.power`

2. Press Enter.

To change permissions for a file or directory:

At the command prompt, type `chmod` followed by three sets of permissions separated by commas and then the file name.

For example, `chmod u=rw,g=rx,o=r rin*` assigns read and write permissions to the user, read and execute permissions to the group, and read only permission to all others, for all files and directories in the current directory starting with *rin*. The equals sign (=) means that these permissions replace rather than supplement any previous permissions.

✔ Tips

■ There are many possible ways to enter permissions using the chmod command.

■ To apply permissions recursively, use the -R flag.

■ To add a permission to an existing set of permissions, use the plus sign (+). For example,

   `chmod u+x,g+w ring.of.power`

   adds execute permission to the user and write permission to the group for the file ring.of.power.

■ To revoke a permission, use the minus sign (-). For example,

   `chmod go -rwx ring.of.power`

   removes all permissions except those belonging to the user.

You can also set permissions using *numeric equivalents*.

Table 11.4 lists the numeric equivalents for the permissions mnemonics that I've explained.

For example, `chmod 777 ring.o.power` grants read, write, and execute permissions to the file's user and group and to others.

By the way, it has often been noted that 666, called by some the "mark of the beast," represents read and write access across the board.

Unfortunately, the information about numeric equivalents is more than arcane numerology. The numeric equivalent is used to set default permissions for files created by specific groups.

Table 11.4

Numeric Equivalents for Mnemonic Permissions	
MNEMONIC PERMISSION	NUMERIC EQUIVALENT
---	0
--x	1
-w-	2
-wx	3
r--	4
r-x	5
rw-	6
rwx	7

OWNERSHIP AND PERMISSIONS

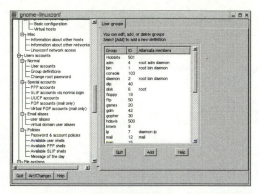

Figure 11.13 Using Gnome, you can edit group defaults.

Figure 11.14 Default permissions for files created by members of a group must be entered using numeric equivalent notation.

To set default create permissions for a group using Gnome:

1. Log on as root.

2. On the Gnome desktop, open the Linux Configuration applet on the control panel.

3. Scroll down the list and click Group Definitions.

   The User Groups tab will open (**Figure 11.13**).

4. Select the group you want to edit: for example, Hobbits.

   The Group Specification dialog box will open.

5. Click the Directories tab (**Figure 11.14**).

6. In the Creation Permissions box, enter the numeric equivalent for the default permissions you want to apply to files created by the members of this group.

7. Click Accept.

✔ Tip

■ For safety reasons, Linux will not allow you to establish execute permissions as a default. Execute permissions need to be set manually for all files. Thus, if you enter a setting that calls for default execute permissions—for example, **742**—the 7 will be treated as a 6.

Summary

In this chapter, you learned how to:

◆ View information about your machine and operating system.

◆ Determine the amount of free disk space.

◆ Determine disk use in a directory.

◆ Find a file's type.

◆ Find out who is logged on.

◆ View and monitor processes.

◆ Kill a process.

◆ Mount and unmount drives at the command line and in Gnome.

◆ Create and delete directories.

◆ Create, copy, move, and delete files.

◆ Use the find command to locate a file.

◆ Use the grep command to find text in a file.

◆ Use the head and tail commands to view the beginning and end of a file.

◆ Determine file and directory ownerships and permissions.

◆ Change ownerships.

◆ Change permissions.

◆ Set default permissions for a group in Gnome.

SUMMARY

SHELL SCRIPTING AND PROGRAMMING

12

Chapters 10 and 11 explained how to interact with Linux at the command prompt. This interaction took place one command at a time, with commands processed as soon as you pressed the Enter key.

This chapter shows you the next step: how to schedule commands for processing in the future and how to batch commands together in scripts for processing. These commands are called *shell scripts* because they use the syntax and language built into Linux's bash shell. The analogy in the Microsoft Windows world is to DOS batch files—but shell scripts are more powerful and easier to write. You can think of shell scripts as comprising an extended macro language that works with the operating system.

In this chapter, I'll explain the basics of how to schedule commands for future processing. Then I'll show you how to create and run simple shell scripts.

If shell scripting doesn't provide the capabilities you need, you can use one of the many development languages bundled with Red Hat 6 Linux. I'll provide overviews of some of the most popular languages: Awk, Perl, Python, and Tcl.

A final bonus for users of Linux is, of course, that the Linux source code is included. I'll show you a fascinating way to idle away those long empty hours: viewing the source code for the Linux kernel!

SHELL SCRIPTING AND PROGRAMMING

211

Scheduling Jobs

Using the at command, you can schedule commands for execution at a specified time. If you need to schedule repeated execution of a command, you can add the command to the cron file for a user.

To send an email with at:

1. At the command prompt, type **at** followed by a time expression (see sidebar). For example, type

    `at teatime + 5 minutes`

2. Yes, Virginia, **teatime** is a valid time expression for use with **at** (it means 4:00 P.M.), so **teatime + 5 minutes** means 4:05 P.M.

3. Press Enter.

    On the new line, the shell prompt will be replaced with an at prompt, **at>** (**Figure 12.1**). Each valid command you type at the at> prompt will be executed at the specified time.

4. Give your email a subject and addressee: for example,

    `at> mail -s "Lemon cake!" _`
    `   harold@bearhome.com`

5. Press Enter.

    The **at>** prompt for the next line will appear.

6. Type the text of your email on as many lines as you need.

Time expressions in the at command

Time can be entered in a variety of ways. By default, a 24-hour clock is assumed. Minutes are optional. If the designation *am* or *pm* is used, then the clock is a 12-hour clock. If the keyword *zulu* is used, then the time is Greenwich Mean Time, rather than local time. In addition, the following keywords can be used in the place of a numeric time: *midnight, noon, teatime, now*.

The *teatime* keyword translates to 4:00 P.M.; the *now* keyword must be followed by an increment.

Besides numeric time, months can be used (specified as numbers 1 through 12 or with the first three letters of the month name). Years are specified with four digits. Days of the week can be spelled out or abbreviated using their first three letters. The keywords *today* and *tomorrow* can be used in place of the current day.

Increments are used to specify time in relation to the current time. A plus sign is used, followed by a number, followed by **minute**, **hour**, **day**, **week**, or **year**. (The plural form of these keywords can be used.) The keyword *next* means the same thing as **+ 1**.

Here are some examples of at command time expressions (the first two are the same):

```
at 1412 January 9

at 2:12pm Jan 9

at 1 am Sat

at now + 5 minutes

at teatime next day
```

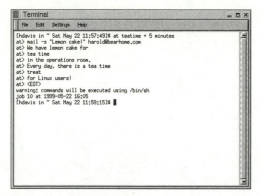

Figure 12.1 Commands entered at the at> prompt will be executed at the time you specify.

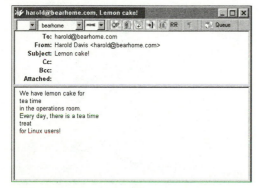

Figure 12.2 You can enter *a t* to send email or execute sequential commands.

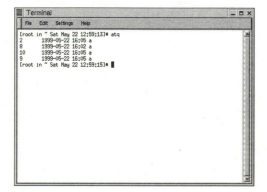

Figure 12.3 To display the queue of jobs, enter *a t q*.

7. After you've entered your final line of text, press Enter to start a new line at the **at>** prompt.

8. Hold down the Ctrl key and press D to complete the at command.

   The email that was specified in the at job will be sent at 4:05 P.M. (**Figure 12.2**).

✔ Tips

■ The email example shows the use of a single command. However, there is nothing to stop you from using the at command to schedule multiple jobs, each entered at the **at>** prompt. All the commands you enter will be executed at the time you specify.

■ You can email the contents of a file using this syntax:

```
mail harold@bearhome.com _
   < ~/filename
```

To remove a job that has been scheduled with at:

1. List all the current jobs by typing *a t q* at the prompt.

2. Press Enter.

   The user's current jobs in the queue will be displayed (**Figure 12.3**). If the user is root, all jobs will be displayed. The first column in the display is the job number; the second column indicates when the job is supposed to execute.

3. To eliminate a job, enter *a t r m* followed by the job number: for example, *a t r m 2*.

4. Press Enter.

5. To verify that the job has been deleted, enter *a t q* again (**Figure 12.4**).

SCHEDULING JOBS

Using cron files

The purpose of a user's cron file is to launch commands that are executed periodically. For example, the file can be used send an email once a day to remind the administrator to back up the system, or it can be used to run the weekly accounting program, well, once a week.

It makes sense to script commands and then call the script from the cron file, rather than individually calling a lot of separate commands from the cron file.

The superuser, root, can use the crontab command to access each user's cron file, as I'll explain in a little while. Including crontab, root has three means of adding or editing cron settings:

◆ Using the Linux Configuration applet in the control panel

◆ Editing the cron file directly

◆ Using the crontab –e command

I'll explain each of these options in the following paragraphs. Bear in mind that in a multiuser environment, security precautions may be in place to prevent individual users from modifying their cron files. If you need to modify your cron file, and you are not the system administrator, well then—contact your system administrator.

To set a cron command for root using the Linux control panel:

1. Log on as root.

2. Open the Linux configuration applet.

3. Scroll down the list on the left until you see Configure Superuser Scheduled Tasks (**Figure 12.5**).

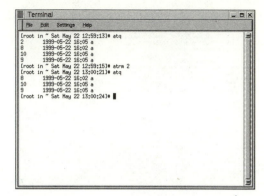

Figure 12.4 Jobs can be removed from the queue by entering **a t r m**.

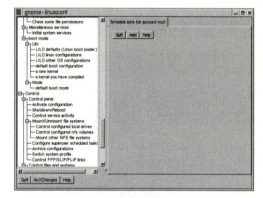

Figure 12.5 You can use the Linux control panel to add a scheduled command for the root user.

SCHEDULING JOBS

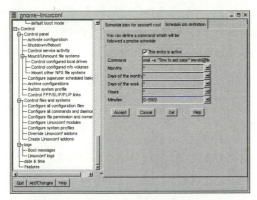

Figure 12.6 The Schedule Jobs Definition tab lets you add jobs to the cron file without editing it directly.

Figure 12.7 Cron files, which are stored in the /var/spool/cron directory, can be edited directly.

You're on cron time now...

In a cron file, numbers are supplied before each command to specify the execution time. Numbers appear in five fields, separated by commas, with a hyphen indicating the range and an asterisk indicating all values. (If the Day of Month field is set to *, that means the command is executed every day.) Here are the five fields and their range of values:

Minute	0–59
Hour	0–23
Day of Month	1–12
Month	1–12
Day of Week	0–6, 0=Sunday

---

4. On the Schedule Jobs for Account Root tab, click Add.

The Schedule Job Definition dialog box will open (**Figure 12.6**).

5. Check This Entry Is Active.

6. In the Command box, enter the command you want executed.

The command shown in **Figure 12.6** sends an email:

```
mail -s "It's time to eat _
    cake!" harold@bearhome.com
```

7. In the Time boxes, enter your scheduling parameters (see the sidebar for help deciphering cron time).

The setting shown in **Figure 12.6**, 0-59/2 Minutes, with an asterisk for all other times, starts the command twice a minute.

8. Click Accept.

✔ Tip

■ Writing cron jobs that send email is something that can easily be abused. Think before you do whether the email function really needs to be scheduled.

To edit a cron file directly:

Each user's cron file is located in the user's /var/spool/cron directory. You can open that file directly and add, edit, or delete cron commands using your favorite text editor (**Figure 12.7**). (The cron file for root shown open in **Figure 12.7** was created using the Linux control panel.) You can add a cron file if one doesn't already exist for a particular user by giving it that user's logon ID as a name and placing it in the /var/spool/cron directory.

SCHEDULING JOBS

To add a cron command using crontab:

1. At the command prompt, type

   `crontab -e`

   The cron file that corresponds to your logon ID will open in the default text editor (**Figure 12.8**). The vi editor is shown.

2. Use the commands of the text editor to add, edit, or delete cron commands (for more information on command-line text editors, see Chapter 10).

✔ Tips

- If a cron file doesn't already exist, entering `crontab -e` will create one.

- Root can use crontab –e –u to edit the cron file of any user: for example,

  `crontab -e -u hdavis`

- Those emails do mount up (**Figure 12.9**).

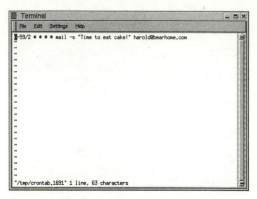

Figure 12.8 Entering `crontab -e` opens a user's cron file in the default text editor.

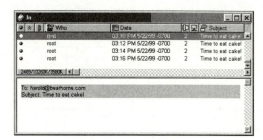

Figure 12.9 My name is not Marie Antoinette! Stop, I've had enough cake!

Figure 12.10 Shell scripts can be created in any text editor (Gnotepad+ is shown).

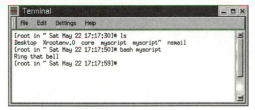

Figure 12.11 A script can be run as an argument to the shell command.

Creating Shell Scripts: the Basics

Creating a shell script is a matter of writing a text file containing valid commands and saving the text file. The script can then be run as an argument to the shell command or as a standalone executable file. Generally, you'll want to make scripts executable on their own.

To create a shell script:

1. Open a text editor, such as Gnotepad+ (**Figure 12.10**).

2. For the script's first line, type the following:

   `#! /bin/bash`

   This is the complete path to the shell that should run the script.

3. For the script's next line, on general principles, type a pound sign (indicating a comment line) followed by a description of the script:

   `# A baby script`

4. Type the line that does the business of the script (it echoes text to the screen and rings the computer's bell):

   `echo -e "Ring that bell! \a"`

5. Save the file as `myscript`.

To run a script using the shell:

At the command prompt, type the name of the shell followed by the name of the script:

`bash myscript`

The text is echoed to the screen, and the bell rings (**Figure 12.11**).

To make a script executable:

1. Change the permissions on the script file to make it executable using chmod as explained in Chapter 11: for example,

   `chmod u+x myscript`

2. Check to make sure that the location of the script is on the path by comparing the output of the `pwd` and `echo $PATH` commands. If the script is not on the path, add it using the techniques explained in Chapter 10.

3. At the prompt, type the name of the script, `myscript`.

   The text will echo to the screen, and the bell will ring.

✔ Tips

- You can use the contents of the history file, explained in Chapter 10, to turn your recent commands into a shell script by redirecting the last *n* lines of the history file to a script file, using a command like this: `history 10 > myscript`. This command functions pretty much as a macro recorder.

- If your script isn't on the path, provided execute permissions have been set, you can start the script by using the dot operator: for example, `. myscript`.

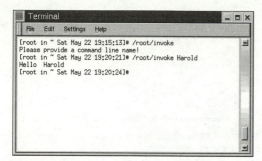

Figure 12.12 Positional parameters can be used within a shell program.

Scripting Syntax

Shell variables are not typed, meaning that you do not specify whether a variable is a string or a number (or whatever).

Variables are declared and assigned in one statement using the equal sign: for example,

```
counter = 0
custname = "Harold Davis"
```

If a string has no embedded spaces, you do not need to use quotation marks.

A $ is used to assign the contents of one variable to another: for example,

```
counter = $myvar
```

Using command-line parameters

You can pass a shell script command-line parameters and retrieve them from inside the script. The first command-line parameter is referenced as $1, the second as $2, and so on.

The following script illustrates how this works:

```
# Display that command line _
  parameter

if [ $# -eq 0 ]

then

  echo "Please provide a _
    command line name!"

else

  echo "Hello " $1

fi
```

If you save this script as invoke and run it with no command-line parameters, the shell script asks, "Please provide a command line name!" Otherwise, the name you entered on the command line is echoed back (**Figure 12.12**).

By the way, **f i** is not a typo—it is *if* spelled backward, and it represents the end of an if statement. In a similar fashion, case statements are ended with **esac**.

In the script, **$ #** is a built-in variable containing the number of command-line variables (see **Table 12.1**). The entry **– eq** is used to compare **$ #** with **0** (see **Table 12.2**). The entry **$ 1** represents the first command-line variable.

To accept interactive user input:

1. Open a text editor.

2. Type the following script:
   ```
   #! /bin/bash
   # Interactive user input

   echo "Enter your name:"
   read yrname
   echo "Is it time for tea, $yrname?"
   ```

3. Save the file as **yrname**.

4. At the command line, change the file to make it executable:
   ```
   chmod +x yrname
   ```

5. Run the script by typing **yrname**.

   The script will prompt for a name and then echo it (**Figure 12.13**).

✔ Tips

- By placing read statements within infinite loops, you can create menus and menu-driven applications.

- You are better off programming anything other than very simple tasks in a language such as Perl than as a shell script. Longer scripts are very hard to read and debug.

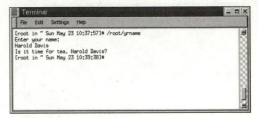

Figure 12.13 To accept interactive user input in a script, use the read command.

Table 12.1

REPRESENTATION	MEANING
Built-in Variables	
$#	Number of command-line arguments passed to the shell
$o	The name of the shell program
$*	A single string made up of all the command-line arguments

Table 12.2

OPERATOR	MEANING
Comparison Operators	
=	String equality
!=	String inequality
-eq	Arithmetic equality
-ge	Arithmetic greater than or equal to
-le	Arithmetic less than or equal to
-ne	Arithmetic not equal to
-gt	Arithmetic greater than
-lt	Arithmetic less than

Iterative and Conditional Syntax

Iterative and conditional statements include the following:

- for...do...done statements
- while...do...done statements
- until...do...done statements
- select item in itemlist...do...done statements
- if...elif...else...fi statements
- case statements

For the syntax of these commands, have a look at the online bash2 documentation (see "To open command documentation").

Here's a bash script that uses interactive user input and an infinite while loop to sum as many integers as the user wants:

```
#! /bin/bash
# Interactive user input
sum=0
while :
do
    echo -n "Add another number (y/n): "
    read onward
    if [ $onward = n ] ; then
        break
    fi
    if [ $onward != y ] ; then
        echo '"y" or "n" please!';
    continue
    fi
    echo -n "Enter a number to add to the sum: "
```

(Continued...)

```
    read newnum

    sum=$(($sum + $newnum))

    echo "Sum so far is $sum"

done

echo -e "Your sum is $sum"

echo "Bye"
```

To run the integer sum script:

1. Save the script in a file named **sum**.

2. Give execute permissions to sum:
    `chmod +x sum`

3. Type **sum** at the prompt.

4. Press Enter.

    The script will start interactive prompting for numbers (**Figure 12.14**).

✔ Tips

- The colon after while in the command `while :` provides while with an argument that is always true, meaning that the script will loop forever. This infinite loop is broken in the if statement when the user types **n**.

- The script does not provide error checking for the user input. If anything besides an integer is entered, the script will end with a syntax error.

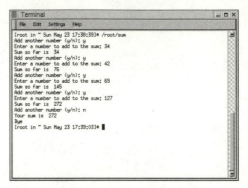

Figure 12.14 You can build shell applications by enclosing interactive statements in loops.

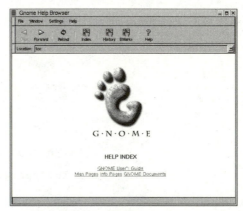

Figure 12.15 The Gnome Help Index is a starting point for finding syntax documentation.

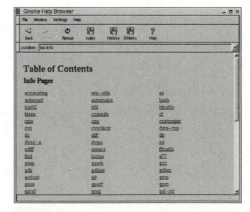

Figure 12.16 The Info Pages Table of Contents helps to organize Linux and Gnome documentation.

ITERATIVE AND CONDITIONAL SYNTAX

Figure 12.17 Bash-specific documentation is accessed through the bash2 link.

Figure 12.18 Use the links in the bash2 Contents to learn about bash shell programming.

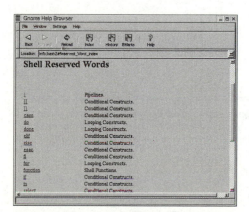

Figure 12.19 You can use the list of reserved shell words to determine the syntax for a particular command.

To open command documentation:

1. Click the Question Mark icon on the control panel.

   The Gnome Help Browser will open to its index page (**Figure 12.15**).

2. Click the Info Pages link.

   The Info Pages Table of Contents will open (**Figure 12.16**).

3. Click the bash2 link to open bash-specific documentation.

   The Bash Features page will open (**Figure 12.17**).

4. Scroll down the page until you reach the Contents (**Figure 12.18**).

5. Click the Reserved Word Index link.

   A list of reserved shell words will open (**Figure 12.19**).

6. Click the link for a particular command— such as the if command (**Figure 12.20**)—to determine its syntax.

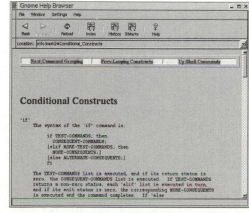

Figure 12.20 Each command is listed, along with related constructs.

ITERATIVE AND CONDITIONAL SYNTAX

Using Awk

GNU awk—or gawk—is a version of the text processing and patterning language originally developed by Alfred V. Aho, Peter J. Weinberger, and Brian W. Kernighan (the name *awk* comes from the first letters of their last names).

Awk is best used for processing text files because it "thinks" in fields and records, typically words and lines. Therefore, it's not very good at handling binary files. A typical awk application is one that translates data into a formatted approach.

You'll find a great deal of information about programming with gawk in your /usr/doc/gawk-3.0.3 directory.

Gawk can be used from the command interactively, in which case the gawk commands need to be enclosed in single quotation marks to tell the shell not to process them. Gawk programs longer than a command or two should be written in a file.

In Gawk, NF is a predefined variable holding the number of fields in each record (words in a line), $0 contains the record (line), $1 contains the first field in the line (first word), $2 contains the second field in the line (second word), and so on.

To display a listing with the number of words in each line in a text file:

1. Create a text file (**Figure 12.21**).

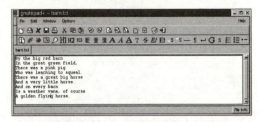

Figure 12.21 Gawk is best used for manipulating structured text files.

2. Save the file as **barn.txt**.

3. At the command prompt, type

```
cat barn.txt | gawk '{print NF ": " $0}'
```

This line uses the cat command to pipe the text file to the gawk command.

4. Press Enter.

The number of words in each line of the file will be displayed, along with the full text of each line (**Figure 12.22**).

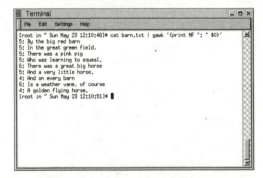

Figure 12.22 You can use gawk interactively or run gawk commands in a file. Here, here gawk is used to display the number of words in each line of a file.

✔ Tip

■ The full text of this gawk script is

```
{print NF ": " $0}
```

Using Perl

Perl is a high-level programming language that derives from C, scripting languages such as awk, and shell scripting. Although Perl compilers are available, Perl usually is compiled on the fly at run time. Perl is highly portable. Perl code can be run without major changes on almost every operating system.

Perl is good at handling processes, files, and text. It is commonly used to process the common gateway interface (CGI) results of user input to Web forms. Because of its popularity on the Web, Perl is a very good language to get to know.

In addition, Perl is often used for automating administrative functions because it has access to the shell.

Perl variables are not typed, but the language does have several different kinds of variables:

◆ **Scalar variables** are numbers or strings, depending on the context.

◆ **Arrays** can be accessed by index.

◆ **Associative arrays** can be accessed by key.

For more information on Perl, check out *Perl and CGI: Visual QuickStart Guide*, published by Peachpit Press. And visit

`http://www.perl.com`

the Web site for the Perl community.

To display the user's ID number using Perl:

1. In a text file, type

```
#!/usr/bin/perl
print "Hello, your user ID _
  is $< \n";
print "Have a nice day! \n";
```

2. Save the file as **testperl** (**Figure 12.23**).

3. At the command prompt, make the file executable:

```
chmod +x testperl
```

4. Run the file by typing

   testperl

   Your numerical user ID will be shown (0 is the numerical ID for root, shown in **Figure 12.24**).

✔ Tip

■ A large collection of built-in variables are available in Perl, including **$ <** (the user ID) and **$ $** (the process ID).

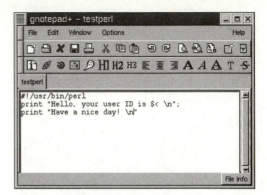

Figure 12.23 Entering `#!/usr/bin/perl` tells the shell to use Perl to process the code file.

Figure 12.24 Perl includes many built-in variables, such as $<, which stores the user's ID number.

Python and Tcl

Many other development languages, systems, and libraries are included with Red Hat Linux 6.

Two of the more interesting are Python and Tcl.

Python is an object-oriented language that can be run interactively or by interpreting code module files. Python is in the public domain. It was created by Guido van Rossum and named after the Monty Python performers. Features in Python include modules, classes, exception and dynamic data typing. You can write programs in Python that can be displayed in X11: for example, on the Gnome desktop. You'll find the Python documentation at /usr/docs/ python – docs –1.5.1.

Tcl—short for *tool control language*—is a simple scripting language designed to be embedded in other languages. In other words, Tcl, originally created by John Osterhout, is intended to be the glue that combines more powerful languages and libraries. Tk is the companion widget set that allows Tcl to be used in a windowing fashion. You will find full Tcl documentation at `http://www.scriptics.com`

Figure 12.25 You can view the make file used to compile the Linux kernel.

Figure 12.26 Kernel code modules such as sched.c are well commented and fun to read.

Exploring the Linux Source Code

If you want to study what makes the Linux operating system tick, the pleasure can be yours!

The source code for Linux is in the subdirectories of /usr/src/linux-2.2.5. You'll find the source code for the Linux kernel in /usr/src/linux-2.2.5/kernel.

A *make file* is used to set compilation options and tell the compiler what modules and libraries should be compiled together.

To view the Linux kernel make file:

Using a text editor, open the file makefile in the /usr/src/linux-2.2.5/kernel directory (**Figure 12.25**).

✔ Tip

- By viewing the make file, you can determine the code modules that do the work of the kernel.

The main kernel file is sched.c. If you open it in a text editor, you'll see that it starts with Linus Torvalds' copyright notice and continues with a list of people who have modified the file (**Figure 12.26**).

As you browse through the code in sched.c, you'll see that it concerns the scheduling and queuing of tasks. The code is well commented and makes a good read.

Summary

In this chapter, you learned how to:

- Schedule a job with the at command.

- Send email with the at command.

- Remove a scheduled job.

- Set a cron command for root in the Linux control panel.

- Add a cron command using crontab.

- Create a shell script.

- Run a shell script.

- Make a shell script executable.

- Accept interactive user input in a shell script.

- Find bash shell command documentation.

- Write a simple awk script.

- Write a simple Perl script.

- Find Python and Tcl resources.

- View the source code for the Linux kernel.

Part IV
Networking
and the Web

Linux is a true workhorse of the network server world. Red Hat Linux 6 includes many network server features that would literally cost thousands of dollars to duplicate in the commercial operating system world.

This part explains how to work with many of the more important server features built into Red Hat Linux 6. With Red Hat Linux 6, these features can largely be configured visually on the desktop, rather than by editing configuration files. Where there is a visual tool that allows you to configure a server feature, I will emphasize it as opposed to the command line configuration file method.

If you need a network or Web server, it is hard to imagine a better choice than Red Hat Linux 6.

Chapter 13: The Linux Server explains how to configure a veritable alphabet soup of important server functions, including FTP, NFS, DHCP, and SAMBA.

Chapter 14: Apache Web Server explains how to work with Apache—the world's most widely used Web server—which ships with Red Hat Linux 6.

Part IV
Networking and
the Web

THE LINUX SERVER

For many people, the primary use of Red Hat Linux 6 is as a *server*. There are many different kinds of servers, but a working definition of the term could be: "A server allows multiple remote users to share or make use of the same resources." Following this definition, a server could allow users to share files and a file system. Going somewhat further afield, servers are used to share database engines and "serve" Web pages.

Linux is an excellent server platform and is used as the operating system of choice in many mission-critical situations. As you may know, it is used as the operating system of choice by a great many Internet service providers (ISPs)—companies that provide services such as Internet access and Web hosting. Closer to home, Linux works well as a file and print sharer in small-scale home and office environments.

This chapter covers a variety of topics related to using your Linux system as a server, including the following:

◆ Telnetting to your server

◆ Configuring Linux as an FTP server

◆ Network File System (NFS) servers

◆ Dynamic Host Configuration Protocol (DHCP)

◆ Connecting Microsoft Windows clients to your Linux server using SAMBA

◆ Connecting to Microsoft Windows systems with smbclient

◆ Using Linux as a mail server

◆ Security guidelines

By way of warning, it's important to keep in mind that network configuration is a black art and a science. Furthermore, every network situation is different. The material here should be enough to get you started, but that is all.

Understanding TCP/IP

TCP/IP is the standard *protocol* used for networking in the Linux world. As you probably know, it is also the protocol that most Unix networks use, and the protocol that the Internet is based upon.

A *protocol* is a language machines use to communicate. It has nothing to do with the physical connection between the computers, which is based on a variety of (mostly) Ethernet technologies. In other words, the cabling between the computers could be made up of 10-Base-T wiring with RJ-45 jacks that connect to network cards. Or the connection could be made with high-speed fiber optic cable. From the viewpoint of the protocol used over the wiring, it just doesn't matter. This software abstraction layer—the TCP/IP protocol—makes it easy to consider networking without paying much attention to the underlying hardware, in much the same way that one can think about Java programming without paying attention to the hardware that will be running it.

The TCP/IP protocol

TCP is short for *Transmission Control Protocol*, and IP stands for *Internet Protocol*.

The job of the TCP part of this combined protocol is to encapsulate packages of information, called *packets*. IP acts as the transmission and routing agent for the TCP packets. IP also steers packets composed in UDP—User Datagram Protocol—which is a protocol similar to TCP.

IP knows nothing about the content of the packets it is guiding. Conversely, TCP packets have no idea where they are going or how they are going to get there. Think of this setup as a pilot fish guiding a blind nurse shark—the fish is needed to get the shark to its destination.

Configuring TCP/IP

If you have the task of configuring a TCP/IP network, or configuring a machine connected to a TCP/IP network—called a *node*—you'll need to understand some important TCP/IP concepts. You'll find that understanding the meaning of this terminology and these concepts will make it much easier for you to get networking up and running. These concepts include the following:

◆ IP addresses

◆ Subnetworking and netmasks

◆ Broadcast addresses

◆ Gateway addresses

◆ Name servers

IP addresses and netmasks

An *IP address* (IP for short) is a four-part number that uniquely identifies a computer, called a *host*. Each of the four numbers, referred to as a *tuplet*, is separated by a period. Every host that has direct access to the network must have a unique IP address.

Each of the four numbers that make up an IP address can have a value between 1 and 255, making a total of around 4.2 billion IP addresses available. These four billion addresses are assigned in groups, known as *networks*, to organizations needing IP addresses. There are three kinds of networks:

◆ Class A, identified by the first tuplet in the IP address. There are 16,777,216 possible IP addresses in a Class A network.

◆ Class B, identified by the first two tuplets in the IP address. There are 65,536 possible IP addresses in a Class B network.

◆ Class C, identified by the final tuplet in the IP address. There are 256 possible IP addresses in a Class C network.

For example, the IP address 24.16.108.142 could be host 142 on a Class C network, host 108.142 on a Class B network, or host 16.108.142 on a Class A network. How's a poor machine to know what type of network it is on?

This is where the *subnetmask*—also called a *netmask*, or *subnetwork mask*—comes in. Netmasks use a logical AND between tuplets to determine the network class. **Table 13.1** shows the meaning of netmasks.

Table 13.1

Netmasks and Their Meanings

NETMASK	MEANING
255.0.0.0	Class A network
255.255.0.0	Class B network
255.255.255.0	Class C network

Note that when you apply a logical AND to an IP address such as 24.16.108.142 with the Class C netmask 255.255.255.0, you get a zero in the final tuplet, 24.16.108.0. This address, called the network address, cannot be used for an actual host on the network.

Broadcast addresses

Another special IP address is the *broadcast address*. The broadcast address is used to send information to all hosts on a network. When you use a broadcast address , instead sending a packet to one host, you broadcast it to all hosts.

The broadcast address is the network IP with the host portion replaced by 255. For the Class C network 24.16.108.0, this would be 24.16.108.255.

The broadcast address cannot be used for an actual host. This means that—subtracting the network address and the broadcast address—a Class C network actually has IP addresses for a maximum of 254 hosts.

Gateway addresses

A *gateway address* belongs to a machine that provides a route to the outside world. These machines are often called *gateways*.

Most often, a gateway has two network interfaces: one connected to a local network, and one connected to the outside world, meaning the Internet as a whole.

For a host to connect to the outside world, it needs to know the IP address of at least one gateway.

Name servers

The Domain Name System (DNS) is a distributed database that resides on *name servers* and that translates IP addresses to domain names. If you know the IP address of a host you want to connect to, then you don't need DNS or name servers. Typically though, most applications and networks assume that users prefer to remember domains, such as **www.bearhome.com**, rather than IP equivalents, such as 204.0.134.135.

Each registered domain has at least two DNS servers responsible for answering lookup queries that apply to the domain.

Every host that wants to be able to translate domain names into IP addresses needs the IP address for at least one DNS server that can contact other DNS servers as necessary to get name lookups. Name server information is usually required when you are configuring TCP/IP.

UNDERSTANDING TCP/IP

Using Ping

Ping is a utility available on both Red Hat Linux 6 and Microsoft Windows that tests basic low-level network functionality. If you can ping a host, you know that the basic network communication with that host is functioning (although you don't know much about what higher-level services might be available on the host).

On the other hand, if ping does not show communication with the host, you can be pretty sure you have a basic networking problem.

To ping a host from Linux:

1. At the command prompt, type **ping** followed by the domain or IP address of the host you want to ping. For example, type

   ping www.bearhome.com

2. Press Enter.

   Unless there is a problem, you'll get a response showing the round-trip packet transmission to the host (**Figure 13.1**).

✔ Tip

- The Linux ping utility will keep on pinging forever. To stop it from pinging until the end of time, and to get the summary information shown in **Figure 13.1**, press Ctrl+C.

To ping a Linux host from Microsoft Windows:

1. Click the Windows Start button.

2. On the Programs menu, select MS-DOS Prompt.

   A DOS box will open.

3. At the DOS prompt, type **ping** followed by the domain or IP address of the Linux host you want to ping. For example, type

   ping 204.0.134.135

   Assuming all is well, you'll see round-trip packet information for several packets (**Figure 13.2**).

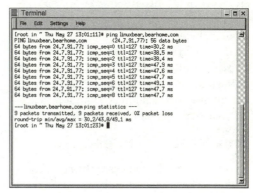

Figure 13.1 If Ping shows round-trip communication of packets with a host, then basic network connection has been established.

Figure 13.2 You can ping a Linux host from a DOS box.

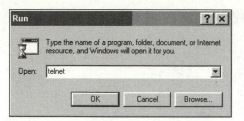

Figure 13.3 To run the Microsoft Windows telnet client, first open the Run dialog box.

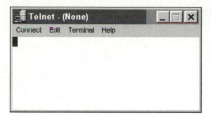

Figure 13.4 If you start the telnet client without specifying a connection, an empty Telnet window will open.

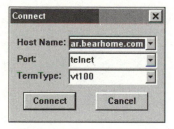

Figure 13.5 The Connect dialog box is used to specify a server connection.

Telnetting to Your Server

Telnet provides one of the most basic and easy ways to use your Linux system as a server, which telnet calls a host. Essentially, this approach reduces your client computer to the status of a dumb terminal. Most people who have worked in large, mixed Unix and NT environments will be familiar with the use of a Windows machine to telnet to a Unix server. Once you get your Linux server running, the procedures, of course, are the same.

To telnet to your server using the Windows telnet client:

1. On the Microsoft Windows Start menu, choose Run.

   The Run dialog box will open (**Figure 13.3**).

2. Type `telnet`.

3. Click OK.

   An empty Telnet window will open (**Figure 13.4**).

4. Choose Remote System from the Telnet window's Connect menu.

   The Connect dialog box will open (**Figure 13.5**).

5. Type the name of the server in the Host Name box.

   This is the Linux server's host name, set as explained in Chapters 3 and 4: for example, type `linuxbear`.

   Depending on the network connection between you and the server, you may be able to type just the name of the server, or you may have to type the name with its fully qualified domain address: for example,

   `linuxbear.bearhome.com`

(Continued...)

In some situations, using a straight IP address works better than using a host name.

6. Click Connect.

You will be prompted for your logon ID (**Figure 13.6**).

7. Type your logon ID.

8. Press Enter.

9. Type your password.

10. Press Enter.

You will be connected to your Linux server, at the shell prompt, in the home directory for your user ID. You can proceed to use the server at the command line using the tools and techniques explained in Chapters 10 through 12.

Figure 13.6 When you connect to a host, you will be prompted for your logon ID and password.

✔ Tips

■ You can enter the host name in the Run dialog box at the same time you start the telnet client: for example, you can enter `telnet linuxbear`. This saves a step.

■ The telnet client keeps a most recently used (MRU) host names list on its Connect menu. You can access one of these hosts without having to retype the information.

■ There are numerous telnet programs available that are a big improvement over the Microsoft Windows telnet client. Many of the programs are shareware or are free. For example, at CNet's site, `http://www.download.com`, if you search for `telnet`, you'll find at least 60 programs available for downloading.

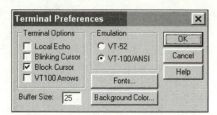

Figure 13.7 You can customize the telnet client by using its Preferences dialog box.

Figure 13.8 When you log off of a telnet session, the connection to the host is lost.

To configure the Windows telnet client:

1. On the Telnet Terminal menu, select Preferences.

   The Preferences dialog box will open (**Figure 13.7**).

2. Make the changes you want.

3. Click OK.

✔ Tip

■ The most common change in the Preferences dialog box is increasing the buffer size (the default size is 25). This has the effect of making more scrolling lines of code from the server available to you.

■ You may also want to change the fonts and colors to improve readability.

To close the connection:

1. At the shell prompt in the Telnet window, type `logout` or `exit`.

2. Press Enter.

   You will receive a message stating that the connection to the host has been lost (**Figure 13.8**).

Using FTP

File Transfer Protocol—or FTP—is one of the most popular (and speediest) means of transferring files between systems. Since FTP client programs are available for every operating system, it's pretty much the closest thing to a universal file transportation mechanism.

Red Hat Linux 6 ships with an FTP server called Wu-ftpd. If you need to provide remote FTP access to your Linux server, Wu-ftpd will allow you to do this.

It is quite likely that Wu-ftpd is already installed on your system, although this depends on the kind of installation you selected and the packages you chose. (Wu-ftpd is part of the default server installation.) If it is not present on your system, use Gnome RPM, as explained in Chapters 2 and 3, to install it from the Red Hat Linux 6 VQS CD.

Assuming that Wu-ftpd is installed on your server, FTP service is automatically invoked whenever anyone connects to the FTP port. (Since you may be prompted for the information by a client FTP program, you should know that this is port 21.)

Generally, there are two sorts of users allowed access to an FTP server:

♦ Those with an account and password

♦ Anonymous, or guest, users

In this context, *account* means a logon ID with a shell account. This means that you must be sure to give every user who needs FTP access a shell account as listed in the /etc/passwd file.

Anonymous FTP is used when you want to give the world access to certain files on your server. Although you can log access to an anonymous FTP server—it is conventional to request an email address—you certainly cannot control who uses it. You therefore

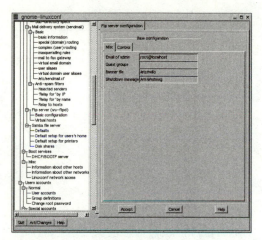

Figure 13.9 You can configure the Wu-ftpd FTP server using the Linux Configuration tool.

Figure 13.10 By default, real users—who have a shell account and logon ID—have most privileges.

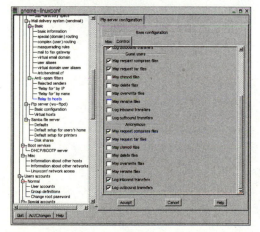

Figure 13.11 By default, guest and anonymous users are not very privileged.

must be careful about what you provide to anonymous FTP users, and you should be aware that any anonymous FTP service introduces some security risks (see "Security" later in this chapter).

To use the Linux Configuration tool to configure Wu-ftpd:

1. Log on as root.

2. Select LinuxConf from the System fly-out of the Gnome Main menu.

   The Linux Configuration tool will open.

3. Scroll down in the pane on the left and select Basic Configuration under FTP Server (wu-ftpd).

   The Misc tab of the FTP Server Configuration dialog box will open on the right (**Figure 13.9**).

4. On the Misc tab, verify your email address.

5. In the Banner File box, enter a file name if you would like a message displayed before a user logs on.

   The text of the message goes in the file you reference. This could be an appropriate place to list available files or to mention security procedures.

6. Similarly, designate a file for a good-bye message in the Shutdown message box.

7. Click the Control tab.

   The control panel lets you set the authority in a number of areas for real users (meaning those with a logon ID and shell account; see **Figure 13.10**) and for guest and anonymous users (**Figure 13.11**).

8. Select the privileges you want each kind of user to have.

9. Click Accept.

USING FTP

✔ Tips

- The access of anonymous and guest FTP users is restricted to the /home/ftp directory and its subdirectories.

- You can control more aspects of Wu-ftpd by working directly with its configuration files:
  - /etc/ftpaccess
  - /etc/ftpconversions
  - /etc/ftphosts

To log on to the FTP server as a real user:

1. Open a Gnome terminal window.

2. At the command prompt, type **ftp** followed by the domain name or the IP address of the FTP host.

3. Press Enter.
   The banner message will be displayed.

4. At the prompt, enter your name (**Figure 13.12**).

5. Press Enter.

6. At the prompt, enter your password.

7. Press Enter.
   You should now see the FTP prompt:
   ftp>

To list FTP commands:

1. At the FTP prompt, type **?**

2. Press Enter.
   The available FTP commands will be displayed.

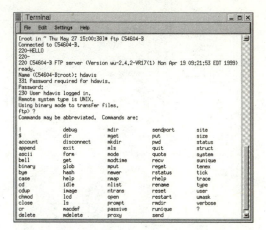

Figure 13.12 When logging on as a real user, you must supply your name and password.

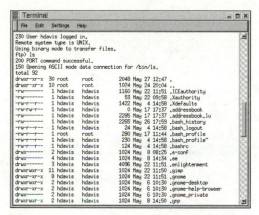

Figure 13.13 To list the files available in the current FTP server directory, type **ls**.

To list files available on an FTP server:

1. At the FTP prompt, type **l s**.

2. Press Enter.

   The files in the current directory will be listed (**Figure 13.13**).

✔ Tip

- The FTP commands available are a subset of the file manipulation commands available in Linux, which are explained in Chapters 10 and 11. For more FTP commands, see Appendix A.

To download a file:

1. At the FTP prompt, enter the **c d** command to go to the directory of the file you want.

2. Enter the **l c d** command to change local directories to go to the location where you want the downloaded file to be saved.

3. Type **b i n a r y** to enable binary file transfer.

4. Press Enter.

5. Type **h a s h** to enable hash mark displays while the file is downloading.

6. Press Enter.

7. Type **get *thefilename***, where *thefilename* is the name of the file you want to download.

8. Press Enter.

To exit the FTP command-line client:

1. At the FTP prompt, type **q u i t**.

2. Press Enter.

USING FTP

To log on anonymously:

1. Type **ftp** followed by the name of the server.

2. Press Enter.

3. When prompted for your name, type **anonymous**

4. Press Enter.

5. When prompted for your password, enter your email address.

Using Gnome FTP

Gnome FTP—gFTP—is a visual FTP client that ships with Red Hat Linux 6 (**Figure 13.14**). Visual FTP clients make the whole business of connecting to FTP servers and transferring files a matter of menu operations and drag-and-drop operations. For many people, this approach is preferable to mastering the arcane aspects of command-line FTP.

To open gFTP:

1. Select File Manager from the Gnome main menu.

2. With the File Manager open, scroll down to the /usr/bin directory.

3. Click /usr/bin to expand the listing of files in the right pane.

4. In the right pane, scroll down until you see the file gftp.

5. Double-click gftp.
   Gnome FTP will open.

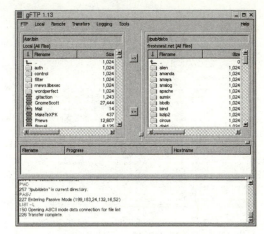

Figure 13.14 Gnome FTP—gFTP—allows you to perform FTP functions without having to know the FTP command syntax.

Figure 13.15 The Windows FTP command-line client works in the same fashion as the Linux utility.

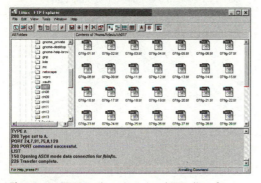

Figure 13.16 FTP Explorer is a visual FTP client for Microsoft Windows.

Using Windows FTP clients

You can connect to your Linux FTP server with great ease using Microsoft Windows FTP clients. The Windows command-line FTP utility accepts the same commands as the Linux version.

To log onto your FTP server using the Windows command-line client:

1. On the Microsoft Windows desktop, click Start.

2. From the Programs menu, choose MS-DOS Prompt.

A DOS box will open.

3. At the DOS prompt, type **ftp** followed by the name or IP address of your FTP server.

4. Press Enter.

After logging on, you will be able to use FTP commands as in the Linux utility (**Figure 13.15**).

✔ Tip

■ There are many good visual FTP clients available for Microsoft Windows. **Figure 13.16** shows FTPx Corporation's FTP Explorer.

USING FTP

Using NFS

NFS—the Network File System—allows you to share files between Linux (and Unix) computers on a TCP/IP network.

In concept, NFS works pretty much the same way as devices such as CD-ROMs or floppy drives added to your file system. In other words, to access a remote NFS file system as a client, it must first be *mounted*. It then becomes part of the file tree structure that you can see, joined at the mount point.

Conversely, for a client to access a file system on an NFS server, the server must make it available for mounting. (By the way, this has obvious security implications, which will be touched on in this section and later in this chapter in the "Security" section.)

When you make your file system available for mounting, you decide what portion can be mounted. If you make everything starting at root available, then your entire file system can be accessed. More typically, you will make only a branch of the file system available for mounting, so that the files on that branch are all that can be accessed.

It's possible to make a NFS mount of your file system available to anyone (at least anyone who can reach your host). It is more usual to make the mount available to a specific host or hosts.

Once an NFS mount that you have exported has been mounted remotely, from the viewpoint of the remote host it becomes part of the remote host's file tree, and it can be used and manipulated in the same fashion as the remote host's local file system.

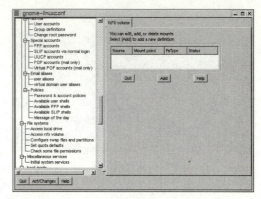

Figure 13.17 The NFS Volume tab is used to add mounts for remote exported NFS file systems.

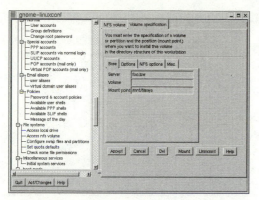

Figure 13.18 The Volume Specification dialog box is used to provide specific information about the remote mount.

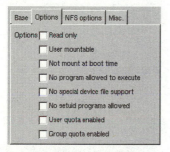

Figure 13.19 You can set options for a remote mount, such as whether files can be executed, and whether the remote file system should be mounted at startup.

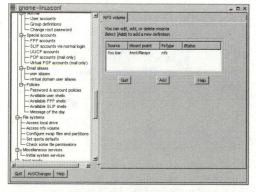

Figure 13.20 Remote file systems that are automatically mounted at startup appear on the NFS Volume tab.

Mounting a remote NFS file system

The mount command can be used to mount a remote NFS file system that has been exported, and the contents of the /etc/fstab file can be edited to start the mount at startup. However, under Red Hat Linux 6 it is easier to use Gnome's visual tools to achieve the same goals.

To mount a remote file system:

1. Log on as root.
2. Open the Linux Configuration applet.
3. Scroll down the left panel to File Systems.
4. Under File Systems, click Access NFS Volume.
   The NFS Volume tab will open (**Figure 13.17**).
5. Click Add.
   The Volume Specification dialog box will open (**Figure 13.18**).
6. Enter the name of the server that is exporting the file system and the local mount point.
7. To set options, click the Options tab (**Figure 13.19**).
   For instance, you might want to not allow file execution. Also, if you check Not Mount at Boot Time, the remote file system will not be automatically mounted at startup.
8. To mount the remote file system, click Mount.
9. To add the file system to the list of remote file systems that are mounted at startup, click Accept.
   The mount will appear on the NFS volume tab (**Figure 13.20**).

The Linux Server

USING NFS

245

Exporting a file system

To export a branch of your file system (or the entire file system, by specifying / as the starting place) the old-fashioned way, you can edit the /etc/exports file. Again, though it's much easier to let the visual configuration tools do the work.

To export a file system:

1. Log on as root.

2. Open the Linux Configuration applet.

3. Scroll down the left panel to Server Tasks.

4. Click Exported File Systems (NFS).
   The Exported File Systems tab will open (**Figure 13.21**).

5. Click Add.
   The One Exported File System tab will open (**Figure 13.22**).

6. Enter the path you want to export: for example,
   `/exports`
   or
   `/home/hdavis`
   Of course, / means root, or your entire file tree.

7. Enter a client name.
   By the way, *client name* means the name of the client host machine. It is not a user's name. If you leave client name blank, then any client host can mount the exported file system.

8. Select the appropriate options (see the following tips).

9. Click Add.
   Your exported file system will now appear in the list of systems accessible through NFS (**Figure 13.23**).

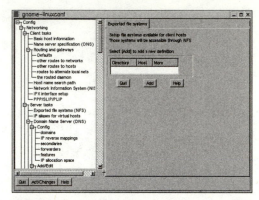

Figure 13.21 The Exported File Systems tab is used to export branches of your file system.

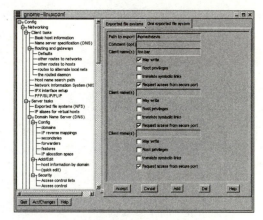

Figure 13.22 Enter export information on the One Exported File System tab.

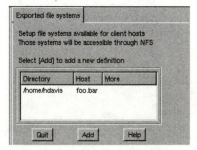

Figure 13.23 Those file systems that are accessible to other client hosts through NFS appear in the Exported File Systems list.

USING NFS

✔ Tips

- Your choices on the One Exported File System tab have substantial security implications.

- Allowing access to your root file structure is a potential danger. Allowing a remote user to have root privileges is giving the keys away—so do so only in a situation in which it is appropriate.

- Allowing write access is also a potential security problem—remote users could delete essential files and attack your file system by overwhelming it.

- Requesting access from a secure port is a prudent precaution.

USING NFS

Using DHCP

DHCP—Dynamic Host Configuration Protocol—enables the automatic assignment of *dynamic* IP addresses to hosts on a network. If you have to administer a Class C—or larger—network, dynamically assigning IP addresses will make your life a great deal easier.

To use DHCP to assign IP address to hosts on your network, you need to have a DHCP server. Your Linux system can be configured to function in this fashion, but you should bear in mind that you cannot just make up the assigned IP pool numbers. The Class C IP addresses you assign dynamically must be yours to assign. Furthermore, this kind of configuration should not be regarded as trivial. The normal configuration advice, "ask your system administrator for the right settings," probably does not apply, because if you are attempting to set up DHCP, you probably *are* the system and network administrator. In this case, you'll have to work with the vendor who supplies you with the Class C network to get the DHCP settings right.

To configure a DHCP server on your Linux system:

1. Log on as root.

2. Open the Linux Configuration applet.

3. Scroll down the panel on the left until you reach Boot Services.

4. Click DHCP/BOOTP server.
   The Dhcp Configuration tab will open (**Figure 13.24**).

5. Click AddNet.
   The One Subnet Definition tab will open (**Figure 13.25**).

6. In the Network Number field, enter the IP address for the network.

7. In the Netmask field, enter the netmask.

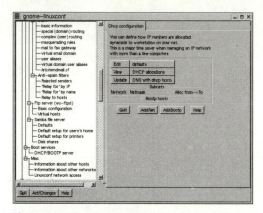

Figure 13.24 The Dhcp Configuration tab is used to dynamically assign IP addresses to hosts on a network.

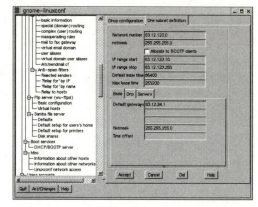

Figure 13.25 Each subnet can be configured to assign a range of addresses.

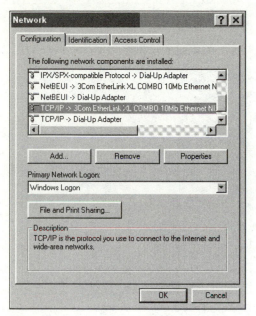

Figure 13.26 Use the Microsoft Windows Network Properties dialog box to configure a Windows client to work with DHCP.

8. In the IP Range Start and IP Range Stop fields, enter the beginning and ending IP addresses that will be assigned.

9. In the Default Lease Time field, enter

`86400`

This number is in seconds, so 86400 means one day. It represents the amount of time a host can hold an IP address before having to renew it with the server.

10. In the Max Lease Time field, enter

`259200`

This is the maximum time that a host can hold onto an IP address.

11. Enter at least one default gateway and a netmask.

12. Click Accept.

✔ Tips

■ You can change the DHCP settings by editing the /etc/dhcpd.conf file.

■ If you choose to manually edit the dhcpd.conf file, you will need to create an empty file named /etc/dhcpd.leases.

■ To start DHCP service manually, use the following command:

`/etc/rc.d/init.d/dhcpd restart`

To configure a Microsoft Windows client to work with DHCP:

1. Right-click the Network Neighborhood icon and select Properties from the fly-out menu.

The Network Properties dialog box will open (**Figure 13.26**).

2. Scroll down the list of installed components until you see the TCP/IP protocol entry pointing to your network card.

3. Select the TCP/IP protocol entry.

(Continued...)

USING DHCP

4. Click Properties.

   The TCP/IP Properties dialog box will open (**Figure 13.27**).

5. On the IP Address Tab, select Obtain an IP Address Automatically.

6. On the WINS Configuration tab, enable Use DHCP for WINS Resolution **(Figure 13.28)**.

7. On the Gateway tab, make sure that no gateways are defined.

8. On the DNS Configuration tab, disable DNS (DNS values are supplied by DHCP).

9. Click OK to return to the Network Properties dialog box.

10. Click OK to accept the new settings.

11. When prompted, click Yes to reboot the client computer.

✔ Tip

■ Depending on the files on the computer, you may need a Windows CD when the computer reboots.

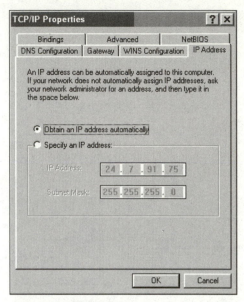

Figure 13.27 Select Obtain an IP Address Automatically.

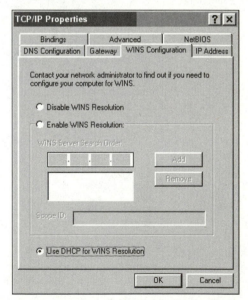

Figure 13.28 Use DHCP for WINS Resolution should be enabled.

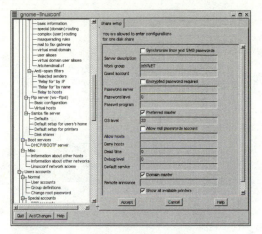

Figure 13.29 Enter the name of the Windows workgroup on the Share Setup tab.

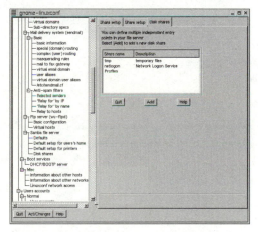

Figure 13.30 You can enter multiple Windows shares using the Disk Shares tab.

Using SAMBA

The networking protocol used by Microsoft Windows is called SMB, or the Server Message Block protocol. Although Microsoft refers to this kind of networking as Windows networking, in fact it is used by many operating systems.

Microsoft Windows clients running an SMB-based network architecture can communicate with your Linux server using a Linux implementation of SMB called SAMBA. You can find more information on SAMBA at `http://www.samba.org`

It's important to understand that SAMBA is not the same as NFS. If you have a mixed network, with Windows clients and Unix clients, you can allow the Unix clients to mount with NFS and the Windows clients to connect to the SAMBA server—but the two must be managed separately.

To configure SAMBA server:

1. Log on as root.

2. Open the Linux Configuration applet.

3. Scroll down the left panel to the SAMBA File Server section.

4. Click Defaults.
   The Share Setup tab will open (**Figure 13.29**).

5. In the Work Group box, enter the name of the Windows Workgroup that your Microsoft Windows clients belong to: for example, `MYNET`.

6. Click Accept.

7. Click Disk Shares.
   The Disk Shares tab will open (**Figure 13.30**).

(Continued...)

8. Click Add to add a new share.

A Share Setup tab will open (**Figure 13.31**).

9. Enter a share name: for example, `tmp`.

10. Enter a directory to export: for example, `/tmp`.

11. Select This Share Is Enabled.

12. Select Browsable.

13. Click Accept.

14. When prompted, activate the changes.

15. Open a terminal window.

16. At the command prompt, type

`/etc/rc.d/init.d/smb restart`

The SAMBA server will start (**Figure 13.32**). Since the server is starting for the first time, it will first "fail to shut down" and then succeed in starting.

✔ Tip

■ You can configure SAMBA at the command line by editing the file /etc/smb .conf. This configuration file is extremely well commented and includes sample entries.

To configure the Windows client:

1. Right-click Network Neighborhood and select Properties from the fly-out menu. The Network dialog box will open.

2. If the SAMBA server is using DHCP, enable dynamic DHCP as explained in "To configure a Microsoft Windows client to work with DHCP."

3. Select Client for Microsoft Networks in the Component Configuration list.

4. Click Properties.

The Client for Microsoft Network Properties dialog box will open (**Figure 13.33**).

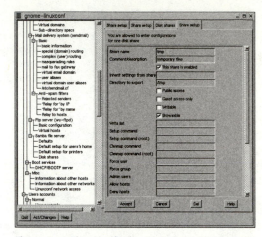

Figure 13.31 The specific directories you want to share are listed using Share Setup.

Figure 13.32 The SAMBA server has started.

USING SAMBA

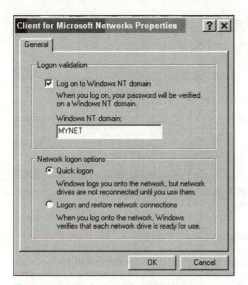

Figure 13.33 Windows NT domain information is set on the Client for Microsoft Network Properties tab.

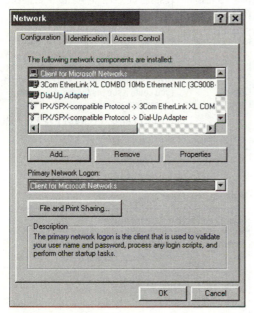

Figure 13.34 Make sure that the primary logon is Client for Microsoft Networks.

5. Select Log On to Windows NT Domain. From the viewpoint of the Windows client, the Linux SAMBA server appears to be a Windows NT machine.

6. Make sure the domain name is the same as the work group entered in the SAMBA configuration: for example, **MYNET**.

7. Click OK.

8. In the Network dialog box, make sure that Primary Network Logon is set to Client for Microsoft Networks (**Figure 13.34**).

9. Click OK.

10. When prompted, click Yes to reboot the client computer.

11. Log on to the Windows computer with a user ID and password that is valid on the Linux server.

✔ Tips

- Depending on the files on the computer, you may need a Windows CD-ROM when the computer reboots.

- For a step-by-step guide to diagnosing problems with a SAMBA server configuration written by Andrew Tridgell, the original author of the Linux SAMBA software, see the file /samba/docs/DIAGNOSIS.html at the SAMBA Web site:

  `http://www.samba.org`

USING SAMBA

Using SMB Client

The SMB Client program—smbclient—is used to connect your Linux machine to networked SMB servers: for example, those running Windows NT.

Smbclient is a command-line program with many options.

To display smbclient syntax:

1. Open a terminal window.

2. At the command prompt, type
   `/usr/bin/smbclient | more`

   The possible commands and flags will be piped to more and displayed one screen at a time (**Figure 13.35**).

To establish a typical connection:

At the command prompt, type
`smbclient \\theserver\tmp psswd`
where *passwd* is the password for the current user, and *tmp* is the resource on **theserver**.

✔ Tips

- **Table 13.2** lists some of the commonly used smbclient command flags.

- Once you are connected to a file resource, there are a number of commands available for manipulating files and directories. These are pretty much like the command-line FTP commands (see "Using FTP" earlier in this chapter). Some of the more common commands available for file operations are listed in **Table 13.3**.

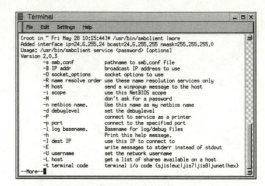

Figure 13.35 Smbclient runs at the command line with many options.

Table 13.2

Common smbclient Command Flags

FLAG	COMMENT
-L host	Displays a list of resources available on the host
-I IP Address	Causes smbclient to use the IP address rather than a host name look up
-N	Used when a password is not required

-U Username	Use the specified user name, rather than the Linux logon ID. Passwords are specified using a percent sign. For example, if you were logged on as root, you could issue the following command to connect as juser:
	
	`smbclient \\theserver\`
	`tmp -U juser%passwd`

-W Workgroup	Specifies the workgroup on the remote SMB server

Table 13.3

File Operation Commands

COMMAND	COMMENT
cd	Changes the directory
del	Deletes a file
dir	Lists a directory
get	Gets a remote file and saves it on the local system
lcd	Changes the local directory
mkdir	Creates (makes) a directory on the remote resource
put	Puts local files on the remote resource
quit	Exits smbclient

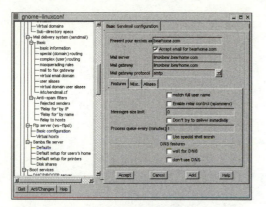

Figure 13.36 A basic sendmail configuration is usually enough to get the mail delivered.

Serving Mail

You are probably used to composing email in a program such as Eudora, Netscape Messenger, or Outlook. These programs are mail clients—for them to work, mail must be served to them by a server program running on the network known generically as a mail transport agent (MTA).

Sendmail is the most widely used Unix MTA. In fact, it is probably the most widely used MTA on any platform. The sendmail program comes bundled with Red Hat Linux 6. If you chose to install the server components when you installed Red Hat Linux 6, it is probably already on your system. Otherwise, you install it from the CD using GnoRPM, as explained in Chapters 2 and 3.

This section shows you how to configure sendmail's basic options (there is not much to it). For information on sendmail's extensive options, refer to

`http://www.sendmail.org`

To create a basic sendmail configuration:

1. Log on as root.

2. Open the Linux Configuration applet.

3. Scroll down the left panel to the Mail Delivery System (Sendmail) section.

4. Click Basic Information.
   The Basic Sendmail Configuration tab will open (**Figure 13.36**).

5. Enter a name for mail presentation.
   All email from your organization will be presented using this name, usually your domain name, no matter what host it originates from.

6. Select Accept Mail for the Domain.

(Continued...)

7. Provide the name of the mail server, which stores email for users and the mail gateway (often the same as the mail server).

8. Set the mail gateway protocol, by default SMTP.

9. Click Accept.

10. When prompted, activate the changes.

✔ Tips

■ The Help file, which you can open from the Basic Sendmail Configuration tab by clicking Help, contains detailed instructions on completing the configuration. (This is in contrast to most of the Linux Configuration Applet Help files, which by and large haven't been written yet.)

■ You may want to activate Relay Control, which prevents spammers from "borrowing" your SMTP server (for example, sendmail) and deluging the world with things like email advertisements for Ponzi schemes and get-rich chain letters.

Security

Generally, it is a truism that Unix—and Linux—systems were not designed with security in mind. In fact, Linux is intended to facilitate easy manipulation of data and files in a networked, multiuser environment. By definition, such a system is vulnerable, particularly with an external Internet connection.

Furthermore:

◆ Linux security is on or off. Either you are the all-powerful superuser, root, or you are not.

◆ Many important administrative functions are performed outside the kernel—for example, by editing configuration files— where they can easily be tampered with.

So, bear in mind that a Linux server is inherently insecure. In addition, the more secure it is made, the less pleasant and convenient it will be to use.

Given these constraints and conditions, what security measures make sense, particularly in the context of a smaller-scale system?

Following some common sense rules is a good starting place:

◆ Don't put files on a system connected to the Internet that are likely to be interesting to hackers or your business competitors. If you must store these files, consider naming them in nonobvious ways and encrypting them.

◆ Become educated about security tools. In particular, use the software freely available at `http://www.cern.org`, such as tripwire, crack, and COPS (see the "Security utilities" sidebar), to set basic traps for intruders.

◆ Investigate any unusual activity.

◆ Make sure that each user has a logon ID, and that logon IDs are not shared.

◆ Require user passwords.

◆ Keep the root password secure and change it regularly.

◆ Make sure that the files /etc/passwd and /etc/group are owned by root and are not world writable.

Security utilities

Tripwire, written by Gene Kim and Gene Spafford, monitors the permissions and checksums of vital system files so that you can easily determine whether important files have been replaced, corrupted, or tampered with.

Crack, written by Alec D. E. Muffett, exposes poorly chosen passwords.

COPS, written by Dan Farmer, monitors various potential security problems and provides email reports with detailed warnings.

Summary

In this chapter, you learned how to:

◆ Define TCP/IP concepts.

◆ Ping a host.

◆ Telnet to a server.

◆ Configure Wu-ftpd.

◆ Use FTP clients.

◆ Mount a remote NFS file system.

◆ Export a NFS file system.

◆ Configure DHCP.

◆ Configure SAMBA.

◆ Use smbclient.

◆ Create a basic sendmail configuration.

APACHE WEB SERVER

Apache is based on the public domain HTTP daemon developed at the National Center for Supercomputing Applications (NCSA) at the University of Illinois. By early 1995, this public-domain software was the most popular server on the Web—but it was badly in need of fixes and updates. A group of volunteer Webmasters released the first version of Apache in April 1995.

The first official release of Apache (version 0.6.2) was based on NCSA httpd 1.3, with numerous bug fixes and enhancements. The name *Apache* refers to the many patches that were applied to the NCSA server: hence, "a patchy server," or Apache.

Apache is developed and maintained by the Apache Project, a collaborative software development effort aimed at creating a robust, commercial-grade, full-featured Web server with freely available source code. The project is jointly managed by a group of volunteers located around the world, using the Internet and the Web to communicate, plan, and develop the server and its related documentation. These volunteers are collectively known as the Apache Group. In addition, hundreds of users have contributed ideas, code, and documentation to the project. The Apache Project can be found on the Web at `http://www.apache.org`.

Today, Apache is the most widely used enterprise-class Web server. It powers myriad Web operations, ranging from "home" Web servers to vast Web "farm" operations. In particular, Apache practically dominates the independent Internet service provider (ISP) market.

No doubt, Apache's price is right. However, even if it were priced comparably to its peers—Netscape's Enterprise Server and Microsoft's Internet Information Server (IIS)—there is little doubt that it would have an important place in the world of Web serving.

Red Hat Linux 6 ships with Apache version 1.3.6. (You can check to see if there is a more recent version and, if so, download it from the Apache Web site.)

Unlike its commercial competitors, Apache does not ship with a visual configuration interface. Until now, configuring Apache has meant editing configuration files. With Red Hat Linux 6, however, most Apache configuration tasks can be accomplished visually using the Linux Configuration applet. Serving Apache Web sites is now truly a straightforward process.

APACHE WEB SERVER

Web Concepts

Undoubtedly, you are familiar with the Web. Having surfed the Web for fun and profit, you have some understanding of what is meant by a Web browser, a Web page, and a Web site.

Nonetheless, before getting started with Apache, it's important to be clear about some key concepts.

URL—uniform resource locator—is an address on the Web, such as

www.apache.org

An *HTML—hypertext markup language—* page is a collection of ASCII content marked with tags. These tags are indicated with brackets: **<I am a tag>**. Concluding tags are identified with a slash:

```
<I am a tag>
I am content
</I am a tag>
```

HTML tags provide formatting directives about the content they accompany. Often, they may include parameters, called *attributes*.

In addition, as Web development has become more complex, tags increasingly are used to delimit scripting content—for example, Java-Script and VBScript—and to house references to executable objects—Java applets and ActiveX controls.

One particularly important HTML tag involves *forms*. Form data, enclosed by **<form> </form>** tags, is used to gather user input and send it to the server for processing.

Well-formed HTML pages begin with an **<html>** tag and end with a **</html>** tag.

A *Web browser* is client software designed to decode HTML pages and display the content according to the formatting directives. Modern Web browsers are also expected to execute embedded script commands and instantiate—meaning create a local copy of—referenced objects.

*HTTP—Hypertext Transfer Protocol—*is a high-level protocol that rides on TCP/IP networks. It is the underlying language that Web clients and servers use to communicate. Essentially, a browser uses HTTP to send a text stream to the server. This text stream takes the form of an HTTP request.

HTTP client requests have three parts:

◆ The first line of a request specifies a *method* and the URL that the client is querying or requesting.

◆ The next part of the request contains header information related to the client and the data that it is sending.

◆ The final part of the request is its body: a stream of text data.

The three most common HTTP methods are the following:

◆ **GET**, which retrieves a specified URL. For example, clicking an HTML link causes an HTTP GET command to be issued for the URL in the link.

◆ **HEAD**, which obtains information about a document on the server without retrieving it.

◆ **POST**, which sends data to the server for server-side processing.

A *Web server* is software that listens on a TCP/IP port (or ports) for an HTTP request and responds by returning an HTML page. The default Web server port is 80.

Common gateway interface (CGI) scripts or programs are used on the server side to process data sent via HTTP from a client browser. This data is usually collected in HTML forms. It is then transmitted most commonly as part of a **POST** command. (When transmitted as part of a **GET** command, it appears as arguments appended to a URL).

From the viewpoint of the program on the server, CGI data takes the form of pairs, where a given name equals a value.

The output of a CGI server program is usually, but not always, an HTML page that can be transmitted back to the browser.

To activate CGI server program processing, the default Apache distribution that ships with Red Hat Linux 6 needs to be recompiled with appropriate modules following the instructions at the Apache site,

`http://www.apache.org`

Server-side includes

A *server-side include* (SSI) is an instruction embedded in an HTML comment that tells the Web server to add something to the HTML page that it is returning to a browser.

Generally, server side includes are used for two purposes:

◆ To eliminate repetitive HTML text entry, by enabling all HTML pages that use a standardized HTML code block to invoke the same SSI

◆ To enable server-side processing before a Web page is shipped back to the browser

For example, to publish the current date at the bottom of all the pages of a site, you could enter a server side include along these lines:

`Date: <!--#config timefmt="%m/%d/%Y"-->`

This would show the date in *dd/xx/yyyy* format.

To get SSI working, you need to recompile Apache with the correct module, mod_include.o. Additionally, either by editing httpd.conf or using the Linux Configuration applet, you need to enable SSI on a domain-by-virtual-domain basis.

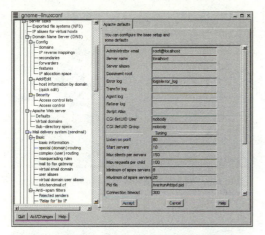

Figure 14.1 If Apache Web server has entries in the Linux Configuration applet, then it has been installed.

Figure 14.2 If httpd.conf was created in /etc/httpd/ conf, then Apache was installed.

Figure 14.3 The Local Volume tab in the Linux Configuration applet is used to mount your Red Hat Linux 6 VQS CD-ROM.

Installing Apache

If you chose the Red Hat Linux 6 Server installation, you probably already have Apache installed. If so, it is patiently waiting for an HTTP request on port 80.

If not, it's easy to install the Apache RPM package provided on the Red Hat Linux 6 VQS CD.

To determine whether Apache is installed:

1. Log on as root.

2. Choose LinuxConf from the System fly-out on the Gnome main menu.

   The Linux Configuration applet will open.

3. Make sure there are entries for Apache Web server (**Figure 14.1**); *or* use Gnome File Manager to check whether an httpd. conf file has been created in /etc/httpd/ conf (**Figure 14.2**); *or* on the Linux server, open **http://localhost/** in Netscape Navigator and make sure the default Apache page appears (see "Displaying the Apache Default Start Page" later in this chapter).

To install Apache:

1. Place the Red Hat Linux 6 VQS CD in your CD-ROM drive.

2. With the Linux Configuration applet open, select Control Configured Local Drives from Mount/Unmount File Systems in the Control Panel section.

   The Local Volume tab will open (**Figure 14.3**).

(Continued...)

INSTALLING APACHE

3. Click /dev/cdrom in the list of file systems. You will be asked whether you want to mount this file system. (**Figure 14.4**).

4. Click Yes.

   You will receive a message stating "Please note mount successful."

5. Click OK. Check that /dev/cdrom appears with a status of Mounted in the File System list.

6. Select GnoRPM from the System flyout on the Gnome main menu.

   Gnome RPM will open (**Figure 14.5**).

7. Click Install on the Gnome RPM toolbar. The Install dialog box will open (**Figure 14.6**).

8. Click Add.

   The Add Packages dialog will open, pre-configured to the Red Hat Linux VQS CD-ROM, /mnt/cdrom/RedHat/RPMS (**Figure 14.7**).

9. Select the package apache-1.3.6-7.i386.rpm from the Files list.

10. Click Add.

11. Click Close.

    The Apache package will now appear in the Install dialog box (**Figure 14.8**).

12. Click Install.

    Apache will be installed.

13. After installation has been completed, to unmount the CD-ROM, select it in the File Systems list in the Linux Configuration applet.

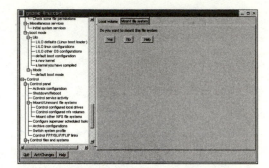

Figure 14.4 You will be asked to confirm a file system mount.

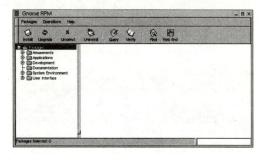

Figure 14.5 Gnome RPM is used to install the Apache package.

Figure 14.6 Open the Install dialog box to add new packages.

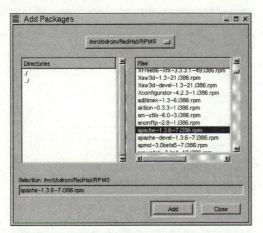

Figure 14.7 The Add dialog box will open preconfigured to the Red Hat Linux 6 VQS CD-ROM.

Figure 14.8 The Apache package has been added and is ready to install.

✔ Tips

■ The Red Hat Linux 6 VQS Apache package is in binary form, meaning it has already been compiled. If you need to install a more recent version of Apache, or to use any Apache modules not included in the Red Hat binary package (see the "Apache modules" sidebar in this chapter), you will probably have to recompile Apache. For instructions on how to do this, go to the Apache Web site, **http://www.apache.org**.

■ Once Apache has been installed, httpd—Apache's HTTP daemon—is probably configured to start automatically with Red Hat Linux 6 in standalone mode.

INSTALLING APACHE

Displaying the Apache Default Start Page

With Apache installed, you can easily test whether it is working properly by checking whether the Apache default start page appears.

To display the Apache default start page:

1. On the local Linux server, open Netscape Navigator.

2. Go to the URL **http://localhost/**. The Apache default start page will open (**Figure 14.9**).

✔ Tips

- You can use the Apache default start page to view Apache's documentation.

- To access the Apache default start page from a browser that is external to the Linux server, use the host IP address or the domain name for the server (provided, of course, that the server and browser are connected).

- You are free to use the Powered by Apache logo that appears on the Apache default start page on any site you create that is powered by Apache.

The Apache default start page is the file /home/httpd/html/index.html. If you want to get going with a quick Apache Web site, you can ignore Apache's configuration for now. Simply replace index.html with your own home page and add HTML pages, graphics, and links as you like. This is the easiest way to get started with Apache!

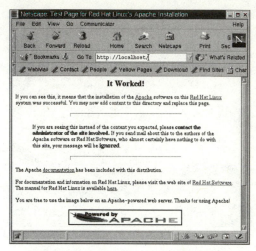

Figure 14.9 If the Apache default start page appears, then all is in good order.

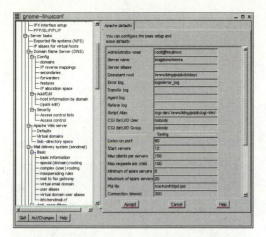

Figure 14.10 Apache can be configured using the Apache Defaults tab in the Linux Configuration applet.

Configuring Apache

It's easiest to configure Apache using Red Hat Linux 6's Linux Configuration applet, as explained in this section. However, they may be times when you need to directly edit the Apache configuration file, /etc/httpd/conf/httpd.conf. For information on directly editing the Apache configuration files, see "Using Apache Configuration Directives" later in this chapter.

To set Apache defaults:

1. Log on as root.

2. Open the Linux Configuration applet.

3. Select Defaults from the Apache Web Server section.

   The Apache Defaults tab will open (**Figure 14.10**).

4. Enter a name for the server.

   The default name is localhost.

5. If you want to change the default Apache document root—the base directory that will be used to store the site's HTML files—enter a new document root.

   If you leave this field blank, the documents in your site will be rooted at the default directory, /home/httpd/html.

6. If you are going to be using CGI scripts, you need to enter a script alias. Scripts should not be run from the same directory as HTML documents, because if they are, they are vulnerable to being read.

(Continued...)

For the Script Alias entry, first indicate what the scripts will be invoked as and then the physical path translation. For example if you enter

`/cgi-bin/ / www/king/public/bin/`

then in the Web site HTML, a script invoked as

`http://www.kingdomofsierras.com/cgi-bin/script.pl`

would physically be located in the /www/king/public/bin/ directory.

Note that the default configuration is set to listen on port 80.

7. Scroll down until the Features check boxes come into view (**Figure 14.11**).

8. Select Host Name Lookups if you want the domain names of site browsers, rather than the corresponding IP addresses, to appear in the Apache logs.

   As the Apache documentation puts it, this is an option that for the sake of the Internet one should have to turn on—which is why by default it is off.

9. If you plan to use server-side includes (SSIs), select Server Side Includes (for more information see the sidebar "Server-side includes" earlier in this chapter).

10. If you plan to run CGI scripts, select May Execute CGI .

11. Click Accept.

12. When prompted, activate the changes.

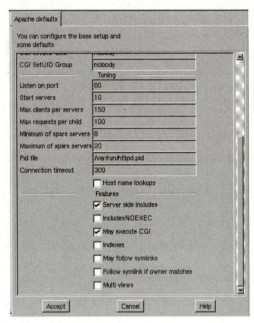

Figure 14.11 Important options can be enabled using the Features check boxes.

CONFIGURING APACHE

✔ Tips

- If a directory is named in an HTTP GET command rather than a specific HTML file, then Apache will open the file named index.html in that directory. For example, the file served in answer to the request

  `http://www.kingdomofsierras.com`

  will be index.html in the document root that applies to

  `www.kingdomofsierras.com`

- If you just want to start playing around with Apache and have no need for it to respond to requests made to a specific named host, you do not need to modify the default configuration. Just start building your site, starting at /home/httpd/html and invoking it as `http://localhost/` or using the IP address.

Using Virtual Hosting

Your Red Hat Linux 6 Apache Web server can easily host multiple sites. The term for this is *virtual hosting*.

Very heavily visited Web sites need dedicated servers. In fact, it is usual to have a "farm" of many Web servers dedicated to the top 100 Web sites. But the run-of-the-mill Web site—however near and dear it may be to its creator's heart—is very different. It rarely generates enough traffic to use substantial resources on even a single Linux server.

This being the case, those responsible for hosting multiple Web sites—for example, many ISPs—tend to rely on virtual hosting.

To add a virtual host:

1. Log on as root.

2. Open the Linux Configuration applet.

3. In the Apache Web Server section, click Virtual Domains.

   The Virtual Domains tab will open (**Figure 14.12**).

4. Click Add.

   The Virtual Host Setup tab will open (**Figure 14.13**).

5. Enter an IP address as the virtual host name.

6. Enter the server name (the domain name for the virtual site).

7. Enter a document root for the virtual site. (A document root is file system location used to store the pages that make up the virtual site.)

   It is important that each virtual site have a separate document root. Otherwise, you are headed for disorganization and confusion.

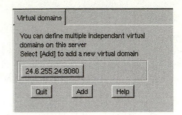

Figure 14.12 Virtual domains can be added, so that your Apache server can host multiple sites.

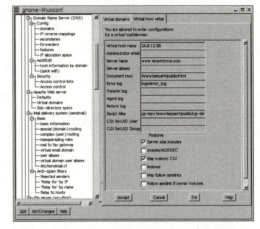

Figure 14.13 The Virtual Host Setup tab is used for configuring virtual domains served by Apache.

8. If the virtual site will include scripts, enter a script alias.

9. Enter other options that you want to use.

10. Click Accept.

11. When prompted, activate the changes.

✔ Tip

- Of course, adding a virtual domain does not give you rights to the domain name. For information on obtaining a domain name and related topics, visit
  `http://www.internic.net`

Using development virtual hosts

Suppose you're in a somewhat different situation. You are not responsible for—and may have no desire to be—hosting multiple sites. But you *do* want to develop multiple site prototypes, each in its own document root. At some future point, each of these Web sites could be transferred to a host: for example by transferring the files to an ISP or to a business client who has commissioned the site.

In any case, provided you have an IP address for your Linux host, you can easily set up this kind of multiple-development environment. The trick is to use different ports for each virtual site.

Suppose your IP address is 24.6.255.24. You can use this IP for your default Apache site (the one that displays the Apache default start page until you change it). This site can be accessed from your host as `http://localhost/` and externally as `http://24.6.255.24/` or by using a qualified domain name if one is available—for example,

`http://linuxbear.bearhome.com`

This site responds to the default port, port 80.

You can then add a virtual site that responds to other ports. For example, one site could respond to port 8080, with a completely distinct document root from the default site. This site would respond to the URL that includes its port: for example,

`http://24.6.255.24:8080/`

or

`http://linuxbear.bearhome.com:8080/`

USING VIRTUAL HOSTING

To add a virtual site that responds to a nondefault port:

1. Log on as root.

2. Open the Linux Configuration applet.

3. In the Apache Web Server section, click Virtual Domains.

   The Virtual Domains tab will open.

4. Click Add.

   The Virtual Host Setup tab will open (**Figure 14.14**).

5. Enter a virtual host IP address followed by a colon followed by the nonstandard port number: for example,

   `24.6.255.24:8080`

6. Enter the server name as the IP address followed by a colon followed by the non-standard port number: for example,

   `24.6.255.24:8080`

7. Enter a document root that is distinct for this particular virtual site: for example,

   `/www/linuxbear`

8. Enter any other options you want.

9. Click Accept.

10. When prompted, activate the changes.

11. In a text editor, open the Apache configuration file /etc/httpd/conf/httpd.conf (**Figure 14.15**).

12. Add a line to the configuration file direct-ing Apache to listen on port 8080:

    `Listen 24.6.255.24:8080`

    This line should go right beneath other Listen directives in the file.

    For more information on the Apache configuration file, see "Using Apache Configuration Directives" later in this chapter.

13. Save the changes to httpd.conf.

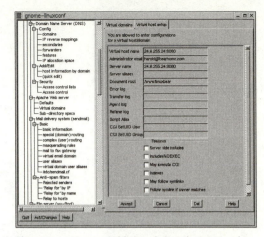

Figure 14.14 You can add virtual sites that respond to nondefault ports to facilitate the development of multiple sites.

Figure 14.15 To add a virtual site using a nonstandard port, you must make sure that Apache is listening on the port.

USING VIRTUAL HOSTING

✔ Tip

- Ports can be any number between 0 and 65535. However, all port numbers below 1024 are already assigned to specific services such as FTP, telnet, and so on. (You can view the list of port-to-service assignments in the /etc/services file.) It is safest to pick a port above 8000 as the nonstandard port.

You are now ready to test the virtual site. First, create a file named index.html containing some basic HTML along these lines:

```
< html>
  <head>
      <title>Kingdom of the Sierras</title>
  </head>
  <body background="harold.gif" link="white">
  <h1>
  <center><font size=7>
            Kingdom of the Sierras</font>
      </center>
  </h1><BR>
  <table cellpadding=80 cellspacing=4>
  <tr>
  <td><font size=5>
  <a href="">Maps of the High Country</a><br>
  <a href="">Lakes like jewels</a><br>
  <a href="">Freedom of the hills!</a><br>
  <a href="">
      Stars like diamonds in the night sky!</a><br>
  <a href="mailto:harold@bearhome.com">
      Contact the Bears
      </a>
      </font>
  </td><td></td>
  <td><br></td>
  </tr>
  </table>
  </body>
</html>
```

To test the virtual site:

1. Copy the file index.html that you just created, along with any graphics files that it
requires, to the virtual host document
root, /www/linuxbear.

2. In a Web browser, enter the URL for the
virtual site, including the port:

   `http://24.6.255.24:8080/`

   The test page that you just created will
   be displayed (**Figure 14.16**).

3. Make sure that the IP address with the
standard port, `http://24.6.255.24/`,
still displays the Apache default start page.

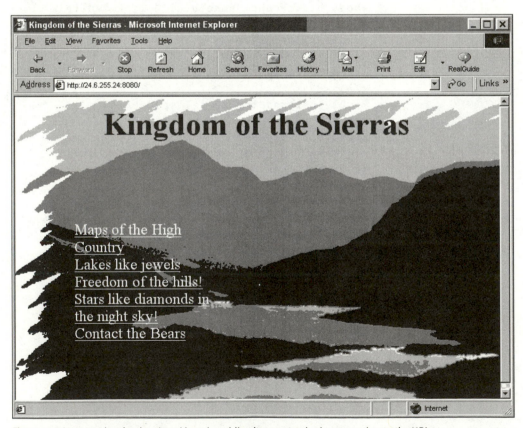

Figure 14.16 You can invoke the virtual host by adding its nonstandard port number to the URL.

Using Apache Configuration Directives

An Apache *directive* is a command in one of Apache's configuration files. Apache's primary configuration file is httpd.conf, located in the /etc/httpd/conf directory.

Using the directives in Apache's configuration files, you can control the behavior of the Apache Web server.

Although you can use the Linux Configuration applet to control basic Apache configuration, most Apache administrators are used to working with directives and httpd.conf rather than a visual administration tool. Fortunately, the file is well commented, so it is pretty easy to understand what each section is supposed to do.

A hash mark (#) at the beginning of a line in the configuration file indicates a comment. Directives that are commented out with a hash mark can be activated by removing the mark.

This section covers some of the more important core Apache directives in httpd.conf in the order that they appear in the file. For more information on editing the file, you should consult the documentation at **http://www.apache.org**. For information on modules, see the sidebar "Apache modules."

Setting the server type

The server type can be set as either stand-alone or inetd. Here are the lines from the configuration file:

```
# ServerType is either inetd, or standalone.
ServerType standalone
```

The default Red Hat Linux 6 Apache setup is standalone—this is also the general Apache default—and it is unlikely that you will want to change this. However, you should know that the setting exists.
In the standalone method, Apache listens to a particular port (or ports) for connection requests. When a Web client makes a request on that port, Apache launches a child Web server process to service it. This is, essentially, a pooled connection setup.

The other method, inetd, is the Internet daemon responsible for listening for connection requests on all ports with numbers less than 1024. In the inetd method, when inetd intercepts a request for a Web server connection, it launches an instance of Apache to handle the request. After the request has been serviced, the instance of the Web server exits.

Setting the port

The Port setting specifies the port that Apache listens on. The default setting is port 80. Two other directives, Listen and BindAddress, can add ports.

```
# Port: The port the standalone listens to. For ports < 1023, you will
# need httpd to be run as root initially.
Port 80
```

Tuning the engine

The next group of directives tune the way Apache works. These settings affect such matters as the number of child instances of Apache that can be created and the maximum number of clients that can be logged on simultaneously. For detailed descriptions, read the comments in httpd.conf.

Here are the directives with the Red Hat Linux 6 defaults:

```
StartServers 10
. . .
MinSpareServers 8
MaxSpareServers 20
. . .
KeepAlive 0
. . .
KeepAliveTimeout 15
. . .
MaxClients 150
. . .
MaxRequestsPerChild 100
```

Setting the server root

The ServerRoot setting establishes the directory where the Apache configuration, error, and log files are stored.

Here is the Red Hat Linux 6 /Apache default:

```
ServerRoot /etc/httpd
```

Setting host name lookups

The Hostname Lookups directive, if set to on, performs a lookup of the IP addresses of the client browser and writes the domain names in the server logs. For example, 204.0.134.135 is translated as

```
www.bearhome.com
```

The default setting is off:

```
HostnameLookups off
```

Setting the server name

The default server name is localhost:

```
ServerName localhost
```

You can set ServerName to any value you want provided the name will resolve to your host.

Using Listen

Listen directs Apache to respond to requests made on particular IP addresses, IP address and port combinations, or just a port by itself: for example,

```
Listen 24.6.255.24:80
```

```
Listen 24.6.255.24:8080
```

Setting virtual host directives

Virtual hosts are specified in httpd.conf using angle brackets and a syntax that resembles HTML. (Directives using this syntax are referred to as *container directives*.)

Here's one example (see "Using development virtual hosts" earlier in this chapter for the Linux Configuration applet settings that produced this virtual host directive):

```
<VirtualHost 24.6.255.24:8080>
    ServerAdmin harold@bearhome.com
    ServerName 24.6.255.24:8080
    DocumentRoot /www/linuxbear
</VirtualHost>
```

Here's another example:

```
< VirtualHost 201.12.34.34>
    ServerName www.snakesrus.com
    DocumentRoot /www/serpents
</VirtualHost>
```

Apache modules

Apache is made up of *modules*, which are code libraries that are compiled together to create the working version of Apache. Modules have their own directives and vary from extremely functional to experimental.

You have a great deal of flexibility as to which modules you include in Apache, but any choice other than the default involves recompiling. Many important modules—such as those that enable server-side includes and CGI execution—are not included in the default Red Hat binary distribution.

You can determine which modules are loaded in Apache by typing

```
/etc/bin/httpd -l
```

at the command prompt.

If you'd like to decide for yourself which modules to include in your compilation, you can download the Apache source code from

```
http://www.apache.org/dist/
```

Figure 14.17 By "tailing" the error log file, you can track errors as they are written to the log.

Using Apache Logs

Proper monitoring of log files is an important part of Web server maintenance.

Apache provides several logs that can be configured and various ways of organizing them. However, Web site log maintenance should be regarded as a black art: There is no single way to do it right. Be aware that decisions you make regarding logs can have unintended consequences. To take one example, Web server logs that are not maintained can swell to fill available disk space.

A useful technique for monitoring log files is to use the tail command with its –f switch to follow the end of the log file as the file grows in a terminal or telnet window. For more information on tail, see Chapter 11.

By default, Red Hat Linux 6 is initialized with only an error log.

To view the Apache error log:

1. Open a terminal or telnet window.

2. At the command line, type the following:

`tail -f /etc/httpd/logs/error_log`

3. Press Enter.

   The error log files will be displayed in the terminal window (**Figure 14.17**), with new lines displayed in the window as they are written to the log.

✔ Tips

- To end the error log display and return to the command prompt, press Ctrl+C.

- If all is well, there will not be much to see in an error log file.

To enable and view the access log:

1. Open the httpd.conf file in a text editor.

2. Uncomment the access log directive by removing the hash symbol from the beginning of the line. It should now read:

   ```
   CustomLog logs/access_log _
       combined
   ```

3. Save the revised httpd.conf file.

4. Open a terminal or telnet window.

5. At the command line, type the following:

   ```
   tail -f /etc/httpd/logs/ _
       access_log
   ```

6. Press Enter.

   The access log files will be displayed in the terminal window (**Figure 14.18**), with new lines displayed in the window as they are written to the log.

✔ Tip

- Unlike error logs, access logs grow quickly if you have a high-traffic site.

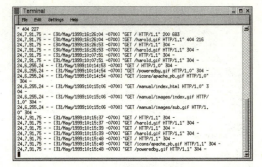

Figure 14.18 You can use the access logs to analyze visitors to your sites and the resources they request.

Summary

In this chapter, you learned how to:

- Describe Apache, the Apache Group, and the Apache Project.

- Define basic Web concepts.

- Install the Red Hat Linux 6 Apache binary package.

- Display the Apache default start page.

- Use the Linux Configuration applet to configure Apache.

- Add virtual Apache hosts.

- Work with Apache configuration directives.

SUMMARY

Appendices

Appendices

USEFUL COMMANDS

This appendix is intended to be used as a quick reference that covers the details of some important commands mentioned in the text of *Red Hat Linux 6 Visual QuickPro*.

The following commands are discussed:

- find
- ftp
- ls
- ps
- vi

If you are going to be doing much work at the Linux command line, I recommend the following two books:

- *Linux in a Nutshell, 2nd Edition*, by Ellen Siever (Sebastopol, CA: O'Reilly & Associates, 1999). This is a bare-bones but comprehensive book in the "Nutshell" style.

- *UNIX: Visual QuickStart Guide*, by Deborah S. Ray and Eric J. Ray (Berkeley, CA: Peachpit Press, 1998). This book does a great job of explaining how to use Unix commands.

find

The find command provides many options for searching for files.

The syntax of the command is

```
find [pathnames] [conditions]
```

Conditions may be grouped between escaped parentheses:

```
/(...conditions...\)
```

They can also be negated with an exclamation point (! - -in Unix-speak, a *bang*) and given as alternatives with - -o. **Table A.1** describes some useful conditions.

Table A.1

Useful find Conditions	
CONDITION	DESCRIPTION
-atime +n | -n | n	Find files that were accessed more than n (+n), less than n (-n), or n days ago
-ctime +n | -n | n	Find files that were changed more than n (+n), less than n (-n), or n days ago
-group *group*	Find files belonging to the specified group name or ID number
-mount	Find files that are mounted on the same file system as `pathnames`
-name *pattern*	Find files whose name matches *pattern*. For example, **find -name 'my*'** returns all files starting with *my*
-print	This is the default condition. It displays matching files and directories, using full path names
-user *user*	Find files belonging to the user (name or ID)

ftp

The ftp utility prompts the user for a command after the user is connected to a host. **Table A.2** lists some useful ftp commands.

Table A.2

Useful ftp Commands

COMMAND	MEANING
ascii	Set the file transfer type to ASCII (use when transferring HTML files between Linux and Windows systems)
binary	Set the file transfer type to binary
bye	End the FTP session and close the ftp utility
cd *remote-directory*	Change the working directory on the remote machine
cdup	Change to the parent directory of the remote directory
delete *remote-file*	Delete a remote file
get *remote-file*	Retrieve a remote file
help *command*	Display help for the command; if no command is used, show help for all commands
lcd *directory*	Change the directory on the local machine
ls *remote-directory*	Display the contents of a remote directory
mget *remote-files*	Get remote files based on a wildcard expression
mkdir *dir-name*	Create (make) a directory on the remote machine
mput *local-files*	Upload local files based on a wildcard specification
open *host*	Open an FTP connection to the specified host
put *local-file*	Upload a file to the remote machine
pwd	Display the current directory on the remote machine
system	Display the operating system running on the remote machine
user *username [password]*	Identify yourself to the remote FTP server if you need to change to a new user ID

FTP

ls

The ls command is used to list the contents of directories. It takes this general form:

```
ls [options] [directory-names]
```

If no directory names are given, it lists the files in the current directory.

Table A.3 shows some of the options that can be used with ls (note that these options are case sensitive).

Table A.3

Some ls Options	
OPTION	MEANING
-a	Lists all files, including hidden files
-d	Reports only on a directory, not its contents
-f	Displays the directory contents in the current order, without attempting to sort
-l	Displays a long-format listing, which includes permissions, owner, size, and modification time
-n	Like -l, but shows group ID numbers and user ID numbers rather than names
-t	Sorts files according to when they were modified (most recent first)
-x	Formats in rows, going across the screen
-B	Ignores backup files (those ending with a ~)
-R	Recursively lists subdirectories, as well as the current directory
-X	Sorts by file extension

LS

ps

The ps command displays information about currently active processes. **Table A.4** shows some common ps options. Note that ps options do not need to be separated by a hyphen (-).

Table A.4

Common ps Options	
OPTION	MEANING
pids	Displays information only on the specified processes, which are presented in a comma-delimited list
a	Lists all processes
l	Produces a verbose listing
r	Excludes processes that are not running
ttty	Displays only processes running on the specified terminal (tty)
u	Includes user name and start time
x	Includes processes without an associated terminal
S	Includes information on child processes

PS

vi

vi is Unix's omnipresent, ubiquitous, cryptic command-line text editor.

There are two vi modes: Command mode and Insert mode. **Table A.5** shows the commands that invoke Insert mode. Once you are in Insert mode, you get back to Command mode by pressing the Escape key.

Table A.5

vi Insert Commands

INSERT COMMAND	MEANING
a	Append after the cursor
A	Append at the end of the line
c	Begin change operation
C	Change to the end of the line
i	Insert before the cursor
I	Insert at the beginning of the line
o	Start a blank line below the current line
O	Start a blank line above the current line
R	Begin overwriting text
s	Substitute a character
S	Substitute entire line

The normal cursor keys are not used to move around in vi. **Table A.6** shows some vi movement commands.

Table A.6

Some vi Movement Commands

MOVEMENT COMMAND	DESCRIPTION
h,j,k,l	Move left, down, up, and right (vi's cursor keys)
Spacebar	Move right
w,W,b,B	Go forward or backward by a word
e,E	Go to the end of the word
)	Go to the beginning of the next sentence
(	Go to the beginning of the current sentence
o	Go to the first position in the current line
$	Go to the end of the current line
/text	Search forward for text
?text	Search backward for text

Table A.7 shows some vi text editing commands.

Table A.7

Some vi Text Editing Commands

COMMAND	MEANING
cw	Change the word
cc	Change the line
C	Change the text from the current position to the end of the line
dd	Delete the current line
D	Delete the remainder of the line
dw	Delete the word
x	Delete the current character
X	Delete the previous character

GNU GENERAL PUBLIC LICENSE

B

Printed below is the GNU General Public License (the GPL or *copyleft*), under which Linux is licensed. It is reproduced here to clear up some of the confusion about Linux's copyright status—Linux is *not* shareware, and it is *not* in the public domain. The bulk of the Linux kernel is copyright ©1993 by Linus Torvalds, and other software and parts of the kernel are copyrighted by their authors. Thus, Linux *is* copyrighted, however, you may redistribute it under the terms of the GPL printed below.

Copyright ©1989, 1991 Free Software Foundation, Inc. 675 Mass Ave, Cambridge, MA 02139, USA Everyone is permitted to copy and distribute verbatim copies of this license document, but changing it is not allowed.

The licenses for most software are designed to take away your freedom to share and change it. By contrast, the GNU General Public License is intended to guarantee your freedom to share and change free software-to make sure the software is free for all its users. This General Public License applies to most of the Free Software Foundation's software and to any other program whose authors commit to using it. (Some other Free Software Foundation software is covered by the GNU Library General Public License instead.) You can apply it to your programs, too.

When we speak of free software, we are referring to freedom, not price. Our General Public Licenses are designed to make sure that you have the freedom to distribute copies of free software (and charge for this service if you wish), that you receive source code or can get it if you want it, that you can change the software or use pieces of it in new free programs; and that you know you can do these things.

To protect your rights, we need to make restrictions that forbid anyone to deny you these rights or to ask you to surrender the rights. These restrictions translate to certain responsibilities for you if you distribute copies of the software, or if you modify it.

For example, if you distribute copies of such a program, whether gratis or for a fee, you must give the recipients all the rights that you have. You must make sure that they, too, receive or can get the source code. And you must show them these terms so they know their rights.

We protect your rights with two steps: (1) copyright the software, and (2) offer you this license which gives you legal permission to copy, distribute and/or modify the software.

Also, for each author's protection and ours, we want to make certain that everyone understands that there is no warranty for this free software. If the software is modified by someone else and passed on, we want its recipients to know that what they have is not the original, so that any problems introduced by others will not reflect on the original authors' reputations.

Finally, any free program is threatened constantly by software patents. We wish to avoid the danger that redistributors of a free program will individually obtain patent licenses, in effect making the program proprietary. To prevent this, we have made it clear that any patent must be licensed for everyone's free use or not licensed at all.

The precise terms and conditions for copying, distribution and modification follow.

0. This License applies to any program or other work which contains a notice placed by the copyright holder saying it may be distributed under the terms of this General Public License. The "Program", below, refers to any such program or work, and a "work based on the Program" means either the Program or any derivative work under copyright law: that is to say, a work containing the Program or a portion of it, either verbatim or with modifications and/or translated into another language. (Hereinafter, translation is included without limitation in the term "modification".) Each licensee is addressed as "you".

Activities other than copying, distribution and modification are not covered by this License; they are outside its scope. The act of running the Program is not restricted, and the output from the Program is covered only if its contents constitute a work based on the Program (independent of having been made by running the Program). Whether that is true depends on what the Program does.

1. You may copy and distribute verbatim copies of the Program's source code as you receive it, in any medium, provided that you conspicuously and appropriately publish on each copy an appropriate copyright notice and disclaimer of warranty; keep intact all the notices that refer to this License and to the absence of any warranty; and give any other recipients of the Program a copy of this License along with the Program.

You may charge a fee for the physical act of transferring a copy, and you may at your option offer warranty protection in exchange for a fee.

2. You may modify your copy or copies of the Program or any portion of it, thus forming a work based on the Program, and copy and distribute such modifications or work under the terms of Section 1 above, provided that you also meet all of these conditions:

   A. You must cause the modified files to carry prominent notices stating that you changed the files and the date of any change.

   B. You must cause any work that you distribute or publish, that in whole or in part contains or is derived from the Program or any part thereof, to be licensed as a whole at no charge to all third parties under the terms of this License.

   C. If the modified program normally reads commands interactively when run, you must cause it, when started running for such interactive use in the most ordinary way, to print or display an announcement including an appropriate copyright notice and a notice that there is no warranty (or else, saying that you provide a warranty) and that users may redistribute the program under these conditions, and telling the user how to view a copy of this License. (Exception: if the Program itself is interactive but does not normally print such an announcement, your work based on the Program is not required to print an announcement.)

These requirements apply to the modified work as a whole. If identifiable sections of that work are not derived from the Program, and can be reasonably considered independent and separate works in themselves, then this License, and its terms, do not apply to those sections when you distribute them as

separate works. But when you distribute the same sections as part of a whole which is a work based on the Program, the distribution of the whole must be on the terms of this License, whose permissions for other licensees extend to the entire whole, and thus to each and every part regardless of who wrote it.

Thus, it is not the intent of this section to claim rights or contest your rights to work written entirely by you; rather, the intent is to exercise the right to control the distribution of derivative or collective works based on the Program.

In addition, mere aggregation of another work not based on the Program with the Program (or with a work based on the Program) on a volume of a storage or distribution medium does not bring the other work under the scope of this License.

3. You may copy and distribute the Program (or a work based on it, under Section 2) in object code or executable form under the terms of Sections 1 and 2 above provided that you also do one of the following:

   A. Accompany it with the complete corresponding machine-readable source code, which must be distributed under the terms of Sections 1 and 2 above on a medium customarily used for software interchange; or,

   B. Accompany it with a written offer, valid for at least three years, to give any third party, for a charge no more than your cost of physically performing source distribution, a complete machine-readable copy of the corresponding source code, to be distributed under the terms of Sections 1 and 2 above on a medium customarily used for software interchange; or,

c. Accompany it with the information you received as to the offer to distribute corresponding source code. (This alternative is allowed only for non-commercial distribution and only if you received the program in object code or executable form with such an offer, in accord with Subsection b above.)

The source code for a work means the preferred form of the work for making modifications to it. For an executable work, complete source code means all the source code for all modules it contains, plus any associated interface definition files, plus the scripts used to control compilation and installation of the executable. However, as a special exception, the source code distributed need not include anything that is normally distributed (in either source or binary form) with the major components (compiler, kernel, and so on) of the operating system on which the executable runs, unless that component itself accompanies the executable.

If distribution of executable or object code is made by offering access to copy from a designated place, then offering equivalent access to copy the source code from the same place counts as distribution of the source code, even though third parties are not compelled to copy the source along with the object code.

4. You may not copy, modify, sublicense, or distribute the Program except as expressly provided under this License. Any attempt otherwise to copy, modify, sublicense or distribute the Program is void, and will automatically terminate your rights under this License. However, parties who have received copies, or rights, from you under this License will not have their licenses terminated so long as such parties remain in full compliance.

5. You are not required to accept this License, since you have not signed it. However, nothing else grants you permission to modify or distribute the Program or its derivative works. These actions are prohibited by law if you do not accept this License. Therefore, by modifying or distributing the Program (or any work based on the Program), you indicate your acceptance of this License to do so, and all its terms and conditions for copying, distributing or modifying the Program or works based on it.

6. Each time you redistribute the Program (or any work based on the Program), the recipient automatically receives a license from the original licensor to copy, distribute or modify the Program subject to these terms and conditions. You may not impose any further restrictions on the recipients' exercise of the rights granted herein. You are not responsible for enforcing compliance by third parties to this License.

7. If, as a consequence of a court judgment or allegation of patent infringement or for any other reason (not limited to patent issues), conditions are imposed on you (whether by court order, agreement or otherwise) that contradict the conditions of this License, they do not excuse you from the conditions of this License. If you cannot distribute so as to satisfy simultaneously your obligations under this License and any other pertinent obligations, then as a consequence you may not distribute the Program at all. For example, if a patent license would not permit royalty-free redistribution of the Program by all those who receive copies directly or indirectly through you, then the only way you could satisfy both it and this License would be to refrain entirely from distribution of the Program.

If any portion of this section is held invalid or unenforceable under any particular circumstance, the balance of the section is intended to apply and the section as a whole is intended to apply in other circumstances.

It is not the purpose of this section to induce you to infringe any patents or other property right claims or to contest validity of any such claims; this section has the sole purpose of protecting the integrity of the free software distribution system, which is implemented by public license practices. Many people have made generous contributions to the wide range of software distributed through that system in reliance on consistent application of that system; it is up to the author/donor to decide if he or she is willing to distribute software through any other system and a licensee cannot impose that choice.

This section is intended to make thoroughly clear what is believed to be a consequence of the rest of this License.

8. If the distribution and/or use of the Program is restricted in certain countries either by patents or by copyrighted interfaces, the original copyright holder who places the Program under this License may add an explicit geographical distribution limitation excluding those countries, so that distribution is permitted only in or among countries not thus excluded. In such case, this License incorporates the limitation as if written in the body of this License.

9. The Free Software Foundation may publish revised and/or new versions of the General Public License from time to time. Such new versions will be similar in spirit to the present version, but may differ in detail to address new problems or concerns.

Each version is given a distinguishing version number. If the Program specifies a version number of this License which applies to it and "any later version", you have the option of following the terms and conditions either of that version or of any later version published by the Free Software Foundation. If the Program does not specify a version number of this License, you may choose any version ever published by the Free Software Foundation.

10. If you wish to incorporate parts of the Program into other free programs whose distribution conditions are different, write to the author to ask for permission. For software which is copyrighted by the Free Software Foundation, write to the Free Software Foundation; we sometimes make exceptions for this. Our decision will be guided by the two goals of preserving the free status of all derivatives of our free software and of promoting the sharing and reuse of software generally.

11. BECAUSE THE PROGRAM IS LICENSED FREE OF CHARGE, THERE IS NO WARRANTY FOR THE PROGRAM, TO THE EXTENT PERMITTED BY APPLICABLE LAW. EXCEPT WHEN OTHERWISE STATED IN WRITING THE COPYRIGHT HOLDERS AND/OR OTHER PARTIES PROVIDE THE PROGRAM "AS IS" WITHOUT WARRANTY OF ANY KIND,

EITHER EXPRESSED OR IMPLIED, INCLUDING, BUT NOT LIMITED TO, THE IMPLIED WARRANTIES OF MERCHANTABILITY AND FITNESS FOR A PARTICULAR PURPOSE. THE ENTIRE RISK AS TO THE QUALITY AND PERFORMANCE OF THE PROGRAM IS WITH YOU. SHOULD THE PROGRAM PROVE DEFECTIVE, YOU ASSUME THE COST OF ALL NECESSARY SERVICING, REPAIR OR CORRECTION.

12. IN NO EVENT UNLESS REQUIRED BY APPLICABLE LAW OR AGREED TO IN WRITING WILL ANY COPYRIGHT HOLDER, OR ANY OTHER PARTY WHO MAY MODIFY AND/OR REDISTRIBUTE THE PROGRAM AS PERMITTED ABOVE, BE LIABLE TO YOU FOR DAMAGES, INCLUDING ANY GENERAL, SPECIAL, INCIDENTAL OR CONSEQUENTIAL DAMAGES ARISING OUT OF THE USE OR INABILITY TO USE THE PROGRAM (INCLUDING BUT NOT LIMITED TO LOSS OF DATA OR DATA BEING RENDERED INACCURATE OR LOSSES SUSTAINED BY YOU OR THIRD PARTIES OR A FAILURE OF THE PROGRAM TO OPERATE WITH ANY OTHER PROGRAMS), EVEN IF SUCH HOLDER OR OTHER PARTY HAS BEEN ADVISED OF THE POSSIBILITY OF SUCH DAMAGES.

If you develop a new program, and you want it to be of the greatest possible use to the public, the best way to achieve this is to make it free software which everyone can redistribute and change under these terms.

To do so, attach the following notices to the program. It is safest to attach them to the start of each source file to most effectively convey the exclusion of warranty; and each file should have at least the "copyright" line and a pointer to where the full notice is found.

> one line to give the program's name and a brief idea of what it does. Copyright ©19yy name of author

This program is free software; you can redistribute it and/or modify it under the terms of the GNU General Public License as published by the Free Software Foundation; either version 2 of the License, or (at your option) any later version.

This program is distributed in the hope that it will be useful, but WITHOUT ANY WARRANTY; without even the implied warranty of MERCHANTABILITY or FITNESS FOR A PARTICULAR PURPOSE. See the GNU General Public License for more details.

You should have received a copy of the GNU General Public License along with this program; if not, write to the Free Software Foundation, Inc., 675 Mass Ave, Cambridge, MA 02139, USA.

Also add information on how to contact you by electronic and paper mail.

If the program is interactive, make it output a short notice like this when it starts in an interactive mode:

The hypothetical commands 'show w' and 'show c' should show the appropriate parts of the General Public License. Of course, the commands you use may be called something other than 'show w' and 'show c'; they could even be mouse-clicks or menu items-whatever suits your program.

You should also get your employer (if you work as a programmer) or your school, if any, to sign a "copyright disclaimer" for the program, if necessary. Here is a sample; alter the names:

> Yoyodyne, Inc., hereby disclaims all copyright interest in the program 'Gnomovision' (which makes passes at compilers) written by James Hacker.
>
> *signature of Ty Coon*, 1 April 1989
> Ty Coon, President of Vice

This General Public License does not permit incorporating your program into proprietary programs. If your program is a subroutine library, you may consider it more useful to permit linking proprietary applications with the library. If this is what you want to do, use the GNU Library General Public License instead of this License.

INDEX

INDEX

INDEX

INDEX

INDEX

red hat.

The Revolution of Choice

Write Down Your Settings

Hardware

(Obtain from Windows Device Manager or hardware documentation.)

Mouse type

Mouse port (if serial): _____

Disk controller type: _____

If SCSI, Make: _____

       Model: _____

CD-ROM

Type: _____

Make: _____

Model: _____

Monitor

Make: _____

Model: _____

Resolution: _____

Horizontal refresh rate: _____

Vertical refresh rate: _____

Video card

Make: _____

Model: _____

Chipset: _____

Video Ram: _____

Network card

Make: _____

Model: _____

Port: _____

Network, Internet and email

(Obtain from your ISP, system administrator, or Windows Network Properties dialog box.)

For direct (or LAN) connection

Host: _____

Domain: _____

I.P. Address: _____

Subnet Mask: _____

Gateway/Router: _____

DNS/Name Server 1: _____

DNS/Name Server 2: _____

For dial-up connection

Phone number: _____

DNS/Name Server 1: _____

DNS/Name Server 2: _____

Login Name: _____

Password: _____

For email

Email address: _____

POP Server: _____

POP login name (may be the same as dial-up login name): _____

POP password: _____

SMTP server: _____

Root

(Very important to write this down)

_____

Important note about the software on the CD-ROM

This book includes a copy of Linux from Red Hat, Inc., which you may use in accordance with the GNU General Public License (see Appendix B).

The Official Red Hat Linux, **which is not the software included in this book** but which you may purchase from Red Hat Software, includes Red Hat's documentation and 90 days of free e-mail technical support regarding installation of Official Red Hat Linux. You also may purchase technical support from Red Hat on issues other than installation. You may purchase Official Red Hat Linux and technical support from Red Hat through the company's Web site (http://www.redhat.com) or its toll-free number 1-888-REDHAT1.

✔ Note

■ This means that the software on this CD-ROM comes with **no free support from either Red Hat or Peachpit Press**. You install this software at your own risk. Neither company shall be held responsible for problems resulting from installing the Red Hat Linux software on your computer. You may purchase support for this software from Red Hat by calling 1-888-REDHAT1.

To install the software on the CD-ROM

1. Use your computer to make a boot floppy from the CD-ROM. (See Chapter 1 for instructions on how to do this.)

2. Power down your computer.

3. Insert the boot floppy in your A: drive and place the CD-ROM in the CD-ROM drive.

4. Turn your computer back on.

5. Follow the instructions on your screen. For a lot more information on installing Red Hat Linux 6, please see Chapters 1 and 2, which explain the installation process in full detail.

✔ Note

■ The installation instructions in this book are the work of the author and Peachpit Press, not Red Hat. For Red Hat documentation, see the Red Hat Web site at http://www.redhat.com